Data Center Storage

Cost-Effective Strategies,
Implementation, and Management

T0330965

Data Center Storage

Cost-Effective Strategies, Implementation, and Management

Hubbert Smith

CRC Press
Taylor & Francis Group
Boca Raton London New York

CRC Press is an imprint of the
Taylor & Francis Group, an **informa** business

AN AUERBACH BOOK

CRC Press
Taylor & Francis Group
6000 Broken Sound Parkway NW, Suite 300
Boca Raton, FL 33487-2742

First issued in paperback 2019

© 2011 by Hubbert Smith
CRC Press is an imprint of Taylor & Francis Group, an Informa business

No claim to original U.S. Government works

ISBN-13: 978-1-4398-3487-9 (hbk)
ISBN-13: 978-0-367-38294-0 (pbk)

This book contains information obtained from authentic and highly regarded sources. Reasonable efforts have been made to publish reliable data and information, but the author and publisher cannot assume responsibility for the validity of all materials or the consequences of their use. The authors and publishers have attempted to trace the copyright holders of all material reproduced in this publication and apologize to copyright holders if permission to publish in this form has not been obtained. If any copyright material has not been acknowledged please write and let us know so we may rectify in any future reprint.

Except as permitted under U.S. Copyright Law, no part of this book may be reprinted, reproduced, transmitted, or utilized in any form by any electronic, mechanical, or other means, now known or hereafter invented, including photocopying, microfilming, and recording, or in any information storage or retrieval system, without written permission from the publishers.

Trademark Notice: Product or corporate names may be trademarks or registered trademarks, and are used only for identification and explanation without intent to infringe.

Visit the Taylor & Francis Web site at
http://www.taylorandfrancis.com

and the CRC Press Web site at
http://www.crcpress.com

Dedicated to my wonderful wife Vicki and to my wonderful children, Thomas, Hannah, Sasha and Leah.
Hope you will vote for them when they run for President.

Contents

About the author

Mr. Smith is an enterprise storage veteran with 25+ years of experience at Kodak, NCR, Intel, WDC, Samsung, and currently with LSI.

He is a published author: Serial ATA Architectures and Applications; and patent holder: USPTO 7,007,142 Network Data Storage-related operations.

Mr. Smith successfully managed 25 tech projects, negotiated and executed 15 significant technology-related business deals, was a significant contributor in establishing the Serial ATA industry standards and in establishing the Enterprise Serial ATA market.

Acknowledgements

Theron, John, Darice, Tim ... thanks for making this happen; and happen better. You guys are the best, a joy to work with.

What, Exactly, Will We Accomplish?

The One Reason Every CIO or IT Manager Should Read This

Today we overspend on data center storage and still often fall very short of business needs for storage. This book takes a balanced "business-meets-technology" approach to delivering data center storage service levels while avoiding overspending.

Let's expand that statement. Today, we overspend on data center storage. Business data is expanding fast, therefore our storage-related overspending is accelerating. This book reveals where and why we overspend and how to deliver same or better storage service levels, storage capacity, and data protection at a lower cost to your company.

This book is for those who are motivated to apply financial responsibility when spending on data center storage. This book provides alternatives that exceed business needs and are clear, quantifiable, and understandable by both the chief information officer (CIO) and the chief financial officer (CFO), allowing communication, understanding, agreement, and execution.

At Risk of Ruining the Ending . . .

1. Replace direct attached storage and compartmentalized storage with consolidated storage area network (SAN)-attached storage. Consolidating direct attached storage into shared storage saves money on backup. Consolidation creates the opportunity to create tiers. It creates the opportunity to establish Service Level Agreements (SLAs), which help identify Tier 1 storage and treat it separately from Tier 2 storage. Establish the concept of storage tiering.

2. Use SLAs as a clear and simple way to communicate with your business unit customers. Establish service levels and assign them

to applications. Reserve Service Level 1 for only those applications in which performance impacts user productivity or storage performance impacts the company's ability to earn money. Push all other data to Service Level 2 and Service Level 3 in the interest of avoiding overspending for storage for noncritical applications.

3. Use time and data aging as a tool to work in your favor to save money. Push cooler data to affordable capacity-optimized storage. Implement processes to protect data and to clear data off Service Level 1 storage: Migrate data as it ages from *performance tier* to *capacity tier* to *archive*.

4. Selectively deploy to managed hosting and cloud storage. Steps 1, 2, and 3 change your storage to allow your company to take advantage of managed hosting and the cloud selectively, where it makes sense, is most efficient, and has the least risk.

Put that way, it looks easy. The more aggressively you can apply the storage tiering/service level model, the better off you'll be in your task to deliver storage services that meet and exceed business unit needs and avoid overspending.

The harder questions addressed in this book include overcoming the barriers to change—changing attitudes and behaviors to get these changes implemented in your organization so that you can deliver better quality for a cheaper price. This book includes CIO-relevant analyses to get both the funding and the staffing to implement projects to deliver on service levels, economically.

Business Data

Business data is the lifeblood of our businesses. In data center storage, we underspend or spend wastefully by continued investment in existing systems. Or, we overspend, we overcompensate by treating all data as mission-critical, Tier 1 data; when in-fact, most data is Tier 2. When we overspend, we waste limited money which should be better applied to building a more competitive business. When we underspend, we are left with IT infrastructure which reduces our ability to execute and compete.

Enterprise storage is shifting, we know it's risky and complex to make changes, we also know standing still is often more painful than the risk and difficulties of plunging ahead. We intend to disassemble big problems into smaller problems, which are more readily understood, quantifiable, and fixable.

It is no understatement to say IT is under attack (see Table P.1).

Table P.1   Quotes on Storage Growth and IT Expenses

		Source
Storage Growth	"Intel's storage requirements grow 35 percent per year, driven in part by the need to retain data for compliance reasons and to fulfill e-discovery requests"	Diane Bryant, CIO of Intel, at Computerworld, August 17, 2009
	IDC reports that, with a compound annual growth rate of almost 60 percent, the digital universe is projected to hit 1800 exabytes by 2011. That's a tenfold increase within five years."	Machael Friedenberg, President and CEO of CIO Magazine in CIO Magazine, September 1, 2009
	"The urge to collect is primal."	Hubbert
	"All data is NOT hot data."	Hubbert Smith
IT Expenses	"Most IT departments spend at least 50 percent of their budget on salaries, and up to 70 percent of IT staff time is spent on maintenance, according to analysts."	www.cloudemail101.org/should-i-go-to-the-cloud (accessed September 28, 2010)
	"Taylor Woodrow, a UK-based construction company, has switched its 1,800 employees' e-mail from Microsoft Outlook to enterprise Gmail." "The company's IT director has already seen a cost savings of nearly $2 million by ditching on-premise e-mail."	www.cio.com/article/429863/Cost_Savings_Found_When_Microsoft_Outlook_Ousted_for_Gmail_at_British_Construction_Firm_ (accessed September 28, 2010).

The treadmill never stops. Data center storage demand is relentless and accelerating: more users, more applications, better uptime, faster provisioning, faster transfer rates, and lower latencies. The pinch continues with lower OpX (spending for operations, mostly people) budgets for headcount, consultants, and services; and the crunch is worsened with lower CapX (capital for equipment) budgets for equipment and data center infrastructure.

This book tackles all these issues, but its focus is on the biggest: How to deal with business operational mandates for storage infrastructure with expanded capabilities without breaking the bank and outgrowing existing data center infrastructure. At the core of this book, we are asking how to best solve (or at least ease the pain) the business appetite for data center storage, capacity growth, performance demands, uptime SLAs, and low power consumption.

These issues beg the question: What got us where we are today? Why all the pain? Why this disconnect?

Enterprise storage matured several decades ago. I was in data center storage back in the 1980s and 1990s, and the entire problem space was different: databases were small, e-mail users were few, and traffic was low. Only large businesses invested in IT departments. At that time, small businesses had some PCs, but enterprise computing was the rarified domain of big financial institutions. As enterprise storage matured and began to be a commodity, the world was still mostly paper; the Internet was still a DARPA science project. A typical enterprise storage system involved a 10 MB-to-10 GB database, or all-text e-mail, a server, a RAID controller, and a bunch of disk drives, usually 10K rpm.

Compared to enterprise applications today, those old applications were downright tiny, hugely expensive, owned by a few. The bottom line is that enterprise storage got stuck in the 1980s and 1990s, and it more or less just stayed there as the IT world changed.

Fast forward to today. Since those innocent golden years, the world has changed rapidly—normal business people do not even consider running any major component of their business on paper. In most businesses, e-mail is more important than the telephone as a communications tool. I could go on and on; but to the point: Today, enterprise applications are large, and they are many. IT organizations and those who serve IT organizations are tasked to deliver storage infrastructure that is fast enough, big enough, reliable enough, and affordable. It's that last attribute—*affordable*—that gives us pause. Using approaches from the 1980s and 1990s, we can achieve performance, capacity, and reliability if we throw enough money at the problems. But the point of this book is to deliver efficiently and affordably.

Clearly the approaches formed in the 1980s and 1990s are no longer workable or affordable.

The good news: Financial sanity can be found again, through a clarified view of the problem with a clear and simplified view of the variables: price, performance, power, and capacity. There are alternatives to the approaches matured in the 1980s and 1990s, and we're going to cover these alternatives in the next couple hundred pages.

It is my objective to thoroughly engage you, the reader, with tasks along the way that take the book from the theoretical to the real-world. We want the book framework to help you apply intelligence from your own shop into a meaningful analysis and project plan, enabling you to respond to business demand with a new and workable storage system approach with hard data, which will make sense to both CIOs and CFOs. At the end of the day, CIOs and CFOs write the checks. They'll either spend on approaches from the 1990s (increasingly uncompetitive and unsustainable), or they'll spend on the new approaches, which are workable and competitive in the 2010s and beyond.

If you walk a mile in the shoes of the CFO or CIO, you can see that they're looking for alternatives to throwing money at the Cold War–era approaches—and you can help them. To get as close as possible to your IT world, we will create example analysis exercises. I'll fill in the analysis with industry-typical values. The analyses are structured so that you can apply your real-world data within the same structure to illustrate before-and-after proposals. The desired outcomes are improvement plans that will make sense to CFOs and CIOs. They are clear and compelling enough that these executives will authorize staffing and funding for the improvements.

This book is organized into three parts:

Part I   *Building Blocks, Power, and Consolidation* of many separate server-direct attached storage into shared network storage. Better single-tier storage through consolidation. Service levels.

Part II   *Tiered Storage, SLAs, Managing Aging Data and E-Mail Expenses* by implementing tiered storage and service levels for individual systems. Cost-effective use of solid state storage in a Tiered+SLA operation.

Part III   *Managed Hosting and Cloud* using tiered storage and service level approaches.

This book, by design, is organized bottom-up instead of top-down. Although we might have started with big-picture use cases, service levels, sweeping system architectures with big confusing SAN diagrams, and the like, this is not one of those books that starts at a high level and never gets down to actionable detail. Nor is this a textbook covering information for information's sake. We are interested in getting right to the approaches that yield the quickest return with the lowest risk. Therefore, we start with the basic building block of data center storage: the hard disk drives (HDDs). HDDs are the common denominator in all data center storage systems.

Rest assured that we'll get into the use cases, service levels, systems architectures, and the like. We will definitely cover solid state devices, solid state storage, and cloud storage. But right now, we're starting from the bottom because that's where we can move the needle and get meaningful results.

The approach will hopefully engage you, as a reader, to evolve the content from discussing a theoretical system to discussing *your* system. Hope you'll enjoy the ride.

Part I
Building Blocks, Power, and Consolidation

In Part I, we consolidate server direct attach storage, improve on single tier storage, and discuss unrelenting demand growth for performance capacity and the expenses related to hardware price (CapX), power (OpX), management (OpX), data aging (OpX), and data center outgrowth (CapX). We demystify both the technology and the business aspects of storage performance, replication, backup/recovery/archival, and storage virtualization.

Part I establishes a baseline for single-tier storage using critical ratios for performance, capacity, cost, and power as well as data aging (these same ratios will be compared for multitier and cloud storage architectures).

Chapter 1

The Disk Drive: The Fundamental Building Block of Enterprise Storage

All enterprise storage is based on the basic building block: the hard disk drive or HDD.

We will start with *key* metrics of the hard disk drive: *price, performance, power,* and *capacity.* We're going to identify the important stuff and remove the noise. Once we have a command of foundation and key metrics, the systems, processes, and economic delivery on service levels readily falls into place.

HDDs come in various price/performance/power/capacities and we can remove the complexity to arrive at the right tool for the job at hand. In the real world, enterprise storage is *not* about which system offers the cheapest gigabytes for the money. Enterprise storage is *not* about which system has the highest performance benchmark number. In the real world, enterprise storage is about the balance of adequate performance, adequate capacity, adequate reliability, and data protection, all at the best possible price. And this book is about disassembling the problem into manageable but related components to find that balance for the situation at hand.

Most people, including IT people, consider storage performance as the realm of PhDs: complex and difficult to understand. I am here to tell you, it is much simpler than it may appear. We can overcome the perceived complexity of storage performance by deconstructing this messy, complex problem into easy-to-understand components, focusing on the important, pertinent facts, and eliminating the nonrelevant noise.

Our objective is to remove the mystery, remove the mush, remove the fear, uncertainty, and doubt (FUD), and explore the mystery of storage performance and storage reliability. Everywhere possible, we will focus on the quantifiable and push aside the immaterial. HDDs are the fundamental building blocks of enterprise storage, so that's where we will start. We will continue on to a systems view; we'll address operational improvements; and then we'll review new system architectures with variations (dynamic storage tiering, hybrid cloud, and private cloud, to drop a few names).

1.1   Using a Metrics-Based Approach to Get Past the Complexity

Ever run into one of those personalities who, when you ask the time of day, tells you how to build a clock? We're just looking for the time of day—we don't want or need to know how to build a clock. This metaphor applies well to data center storage. Storage vendors and suppliers have been known to claim leadership based on one (and usually only one) dimension of their product.

My favorite example is when a newbie enterprise solid state product marketing person claimed a high performance number (something like 100,000 IOPS, or input-output operations per second) and then crowed that to achieve that same number of IOPS would require some hundreds of 15K rpm drives. While we can relate to the notion that a vendor needs marketing sound bites—such as the world's best storage performance benchmark—we also know performance benchmarks alone are not the whole story. We know IOPS can be large or small; the workload can be random or sequential; the workload can be some mix of reads or writes. The one-dimensional "market-ecture" above, though factually correct, does not remotely resemble anything in the real world. The benchmark above assumed the smallest possible block size (512 bytes), 100 percent random workload, and 100 percent read 0 percent write workload—a situation never encountered in mainstream data storage.

- In the real world, block sizes vary, but the typical block size is 4,000 bytes (not 512 bytes).
- In the real world, the workload is sometimes random and sometimes sequential (not 100 percent random).
- In the real world, there is a mix of reads and writes; the rule of thumb is a 70:30 read:write ratio (not read-only).
- And obviously, the workload (mix of block sizes, read versus write, and random versus sequential) can vary based on the storage task/application, as well as on the time of day, week, month, quarter, or even year.

Our approach is to focus on real-world benchmarks, real-world use cases, and key components. We make a conscious effort to cull the noise, the irrelevant, and the imponderable from the equation.

We'll discover how to establish your own relevant criteria, applicable to your shop, rather than buying into those one-dimensional talking points. To be fair, to counterbalance the self-serving people; the data center storage industry has no shortage of good folks whose first instinct is to make things right with the customer. The techniques and approaches we'll cover will help you clearly identify those good folks in the industry, in contrast to the other kind.

1.2 Metrics for the Basic Building Block: Hard Disk Drives and Solid State Devices

For HDD building blocks, our approach is to structure a decision-making process around key metrics: price, performance, power, and capacity. As our objective is to turn raw data into useful information; we can take these four key variables (raw data) and evaluate them using key ratios (useful information), as shown in Table 1.1.

Table 1.1   Hard Disk Drive Key Ratios (Bigger is Better)

Key Ratio for Hard Drives	Ratio	Example
Performance/Cost	IOPS/$	300 IOPS, $200 IOPS/$ = 1.5
Performance/Power	IOPS/watt	300 IOPS, 12 watts IOPS/watt = 25
Capacity/Cost	GB/$	300G, $200 GB/$ = 2
Capacity/Power	GB/watt	300G, 12 watts GB/watt = 33

Notice the *benefit* (performance or capacity) is always in the top of the fraction (numerator), and the *expense* (cost or power) is always in the bottom of the fraction (denominator).

This way, *bigger is always better.*

The *key ratios* chart in Table 1.2 serves to simplify the total storage view. It tells us 10K drives are better in GB/$, better in GB/watt, and better in

Table 1.2   Hard Disk Drive Key Ratios Raw Data

	10K	15K	7200 2TB	10K 400G		15K 144G		7200 2TB	
perfor-mance	300	400	120	IOP/$	1.5	IOP/$	1.3	IOP/$	0.7
capacity	400	144	200	IOP/Watt	25.0	IOP/Watt	57.1	IOP/Watt	17.1
power	12	7	7	GB/$	2.0	GB/$	0.5	GB/$	1.1
price	$200	$300	$180	GB/watt	33.3	GB/watt	20.6	GB/watt	28.6

Sources: Vendor HDD data sheets, Nextag.com for approximate price, storager-eview.com for approximate Web server performance.

IOPS/$; but not better in IOPS/watt than 15K rpm drives. It also serves as the underlying data for Figures 1.1 through 1.7.

Storage system engineering is sometimes (but not always) about performance, and it's also important to see the entire picture including price, power, and capacity (Figure 1.1).

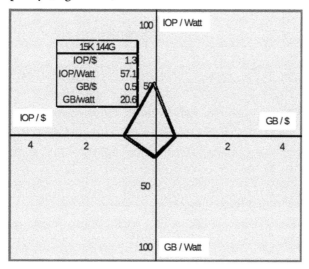

Figure 1.1   Key Metrics for 2.5" Small Form Factor 15K rpm, 146G

Clearly, the strength of this product is IOPS/watt. It's noticeably anemic in the areas of GB/$, GB/watt, and IOPS/$.

The creators of this small form factor 2.5" HDD product were motivated by their IT customers to add more storage performance in over-full data centers with limited power, limited A/C, and limited floor space (sound familiar?).

In situations where slow storage interferes with end-user productivity (and, as a result, this costs the company money), this class of performance-optimized HDD or SSD is the right tool for the job. But in situations where storage performance has a minimal impact on end-user productivity (e.g., e-mail), there are other, more financially responsible tools for the job.

Let's review the same chart for a typical 10K rpm drive (Figure 1.2).

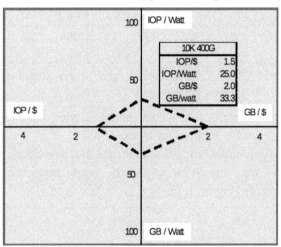

Figure 1.2   Key Metrics for a 3.5" 10K rpm, 400G (Bigger is Better)

The 10K rpm product diagrammed above shows some balance across IOPS/$, IOPS/watt, GB/$, and GB/watt. This characterization is for a 3.5" drive. It consumes more power, but it also has more platter space with better total capacity, better capacity/$, and good sequential performance. The ratios improve our shared understanding of the merits of a specific HDD (the basic building block of storage).

What does Figure 1.3 tell us? We are looking at the tradeoffs between a 10K rpm 450G drive as compared to a 15K rpm, 144G drive. In this example (no surprise) the 10K rpm drive exceeds the 15K drive in GB/watt and GB/$. Also (no surprise) the 15K drive exceeded the 10K drive in IOPS/watt. The interesting surprise, however, is that the 10K drive exceeded the 15K drive in IOPS/$.

So, do we conclude we should use 10K rpm drives throughout your system?

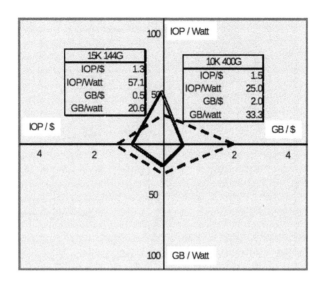

Figure 1.3   Combined Chart for Evaluation of Key Storage Ratios: IOPS/$, IOPS/ watt, GB/$, GB/watt (Bigger is Better)

This analysis indicates we should use 10K rpm drives as the default. But, when performance is the top criteria, *this analysis* leads us to apply 15K rpm drives.

This is just a simple example. And the analysis gets even more interesting when we add enterprise solid state devices (SSDs).

We know some systems should be optimized for performance, and other systems should be optimized for capacity, and still other systems should be optimized for a combination of both performance and capacity. With this insight and structure, we'll be able to objectively compare and buy the right tool for the job. Later in the book, our sections on Service Level Agreements (SLAs) will map to this approach.

Sometimes we need a moving van, sometimes a sportscar, right? This approach balances technology against power and cost of ownership. This metrics/ratio approach will drive closure on the question of "when is *good enough* really good enough?"

It gets better in Figure 1.4.

We could double the scale of this diagram and the GB/watt (almost 300) and GB/$ (11) would still be off the scale.

The capacity-optimized disk drive is an incredible tool to achieve economic delivery of service levels. Capacity-optimized drives are not the right tool for situations where storage performance has an impact on user productivity and therefore costs the company money, but in almost every other

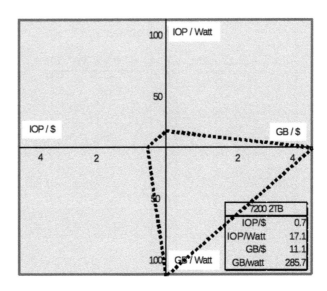

Figure 1.4   Key Metrics for a 5400 rpm, 2000G, 120 est IOPS, est $180

instance the capacity-optimized drive is a tool that truly can save money and still get the job done.

There are data center professionals who have serious reservations regarding the reliability of high-capacity drives in the enterprise as well as regarding the use of SATA (serial advanced technology attachment) as an enterprise drive interface. It's likely these reservations are based on stale information and assumptions. Highly reliable capacity-optimized drives have been shipping for the better part of a decade. They are available in both SAS interface (for dual controller implementations) and SATA (for single controller and server-direct-attached implementations). These enterprise-class capacity-optimized drives (Raid Edition or NL-Nearline) demonstrate 1.2 million hours mean time to failure, consistent with other 10K and 15K drives.

Although there is much more to the subject than we touch on here (we will cover it in later sections on manual tiering and automated tiering), solid state devices make great sense when used in conjunction with capacity-optimized drives. SSDs make limited sense in general IT applications employing single-tiered approaches. But an approach that uses SSDs plus capacity-optimized HDDs properly, in two-tier applications, offers a significant advantage in IOPS/$, IOPS/watt, GB/$, and GB/watt over any single-tier storage system (see Figures 1.5, 1.6, and 1.7).

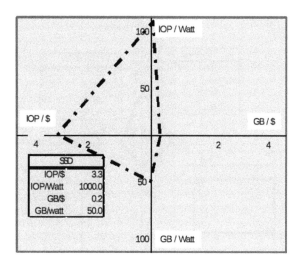

Figure 1.5   Key Metrics Comparison for SSD; Assume 100GB, 2000 IOPS, $600 (Bigger is Better)

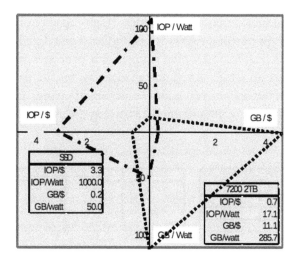

Figure 1.6   Key Metrics Comparison for SSD with Capacity-Optimized 7200 rpm Drives (Bigger is Better)

Notice the storage device classes that are strongest: capacity-optimized and SSD. Everything else is a compromise. For the upcoming sections, we will walk before we run, so I will not mention SSDs for the next few sections, but we'll cover SSDs and where and why they make financial sense later in the book.

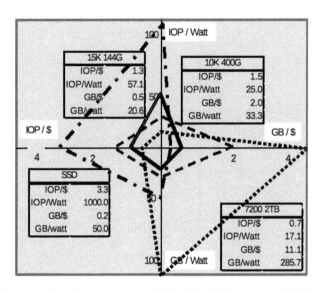

Figure 1.7   Key Metrics Comparison for 15K, 10K, 5400 rpm, and SSD

The bottom line is that these products (high-capacity HDD, 15K rpm HDD, SSDs) align to storage service levels (Tier 2 and Tier 1).

When these technologies, plus people, plus processes, are intelligently applied to deliver on service levels and manage aging data from tier-to-tier-to-tape archival, the operational savings and capital savings are compelling.

Table 1.3 shows the underlying data driving the charts in this chapter.

Table 1.3   Raw Data for Key Metrics Comparison for 15K, 10K, 5400 rpm, and SSD

	10K	15K	7200 2TB	SSD	10K 400G		15K 144G		7200 2TB		SSD	
performance	300	400	120	2,000	IOP/$	1.5	IOP/$	1.3	IOP/$	0.7	IOP/$	3.3
capacity	400	144	2,000	100	IOP/Watt	25.0	IOP/Watt	57.1	IOP/Watt	17.1	IOP/Watt	1000.0
power	12	7	7	2	GB/$	2.0	GB/$	0.5	GB/$	11.1	GB/$	0.2
price	$200	$300	$180	$600	GB/watt	33.3	GB/watt	20.6	GB/watt	285.7	GB/watt	50.0

Source: Vendor data sheets for typical drives, typical performance data (Web server IOPS) from storagereview.com, typical prices from nextag.com

My point is that considering the ratios of IOPS/$, IOPS/watt, GB/$, and GB/watt enables us to avoid getting tangled in information spaghetti. Using key ratios, we trade confusion for clarity as we compare one *class of drives* to another *class of drives*. New HDD products will emerge with improved capacities, improved performance, improved pricing.

I hope that makes sense, and that we can declare "confusion avoided" instead of falling victim to analysis paralysis or stalling our investigation.

A side note on the drives we've examined: You may read this and think, "He said 400 GB, didn't he mean 450 GB?" At the time I put this section together the 400G 10K rpm drive was based on four platters of 100 GB each. Along the way, the platter density changed from 100 GB to 150 GB per platter. Now we see a 450 GB 10K rpm product, not a 400 GB product. That's the nature of the HDD industry.

The 450 GB product is based around three platters of 150 GB each (significantly less expensive to produce; its higher bit density offers higher sequential performance). The raw data will change quickly; it's the ratios that are the main event. Ratios turn data into information.

1.3   About HDD Capacity and Service Levels

The march of disk drive capacity increases over the years is a truly amazing story. Every year, the drives increase in capacity (often doubling year after year). Higher capacity drives basically increase the number of bits on the platters. Two good things result: more capacity for the same power, and improved performance, with bits passing under the head at a faster rate. The incentives for data centers to migrate from many smaller drives onto fewer but higher capacity drives include saving on the power bill, saving drive slots, saving data center power system capacity, saving data center A/C system capacity, and reducing the risk of outgrowing existing data centers. (See Table 1.3.)

When you implement, be conscious of the capacity versus performance trade-off: Higher spin-speed, smaller form-factor drives are great in performance-optimized systems.

For situations where performance is the driving concern, it's financially appropriate to use small form-factor 15K rpm drives. The cost of the storage is small as compared to the cost of the user time and productivity. For stock trading and similar Service Level 1 applications, that's a justifiable use of the company's money. But 15K rpm small form-factor drives are not the right tool for every job.

The other side of that coin: It is irresponsible and wasteful to apply 15K rpm small form-factor drives in a situation where storage system performance has low impact on end-user time and productivity (e.g., Service Level 2 or Level 3 applications).

10K drives are popular for this exact reason: For single-tier storage systems that require a compromise between capacity and performance, 3.5" 10K drives have "good enough" performance and better capacity than 15K drives or small form factor HDD. (See Table 1.4.)

Table 1.4   The Tradeoffs Between Form-Factor, Spin Speed, and Capacity

Drive Type	Common Capacities	
15K rpm 2.5" performance	146G, 73G	Note the tradeoff: smaller form factor = much smaller capacity
15K rpm 3.5" performance	600G, 450G,300G	
10K rpm 2.5" performance	300G, 146G	Note the tradeoff: smaller form factor = much smaller capacity
10K rpm 3.5" performance	400G, 300G	
7200 rpm 3.5" capacity	2TB, 1TB, 750G, 500G	Note the tradeoff: slower spin speed = larger capacity
5400 rpm 3.5" capacity	2TB,1TB	

Source: HDD data sheets

The idea is to apply the right technology to the right problem:

- 15K rpm small form factor drives should be used only for Service Level 1: high-performance applications
- 3.5" larger capacity drives should be used for Service Level 2: active storage applications
- 3.5" capacity optimized drives should be used for Service Level 3: seldom-accessed data

Data center storage tiering and its associated service levels will receive thorough coverage throughout the book.

Also notable is the fact that drive capacities have grown over the years. There is money to be saved by replacing older, lower-capacity drives with similar up-to-date higher-capacity drives At one time, a 146 G 15K drive was state-of-the-art; no longer. Now we have 400 G and 600 G 15K drives, and expect larger ones still. That's quadruple the capacity for the same slot and same power footprint. Upgrading drives in an older system is a straight-forward and obvious way to save money on power and free up slot capacity in your existing single-tier data center storage.

Table 1.5   Brief: Service Levels and Typical Classes of HDD

Service Level 1	$$$$ per TB per Month	For high-performance storage applications (financial databases) and situations where moments lost waiting on the system to respond cost significant money. Typically, use *15K rpm 2.5"* small form factor drives, mirrored, remotely replicated.
Service Level 2	$$ per TB per month	For active data (e-mail, active projects, call center, Web site, content delivery) and situations where moments lost waiting on the system to respond are important, but not overly costly. Typically, use *7200 rpm or 10K rpm 3.5"*; increasingly using a two-tier system with an aging data migration process
Service Level 3	$ per TB per month	For seldom-accessed or stale data (old e-mail, inactive projects, reference materials, regulatory docs, financial history, business intelligence, surveillance) and situations where the cost of the data storage is more expensive than the cost of the user-time and productivity associated with infrequent retrieval. Typically, use *7200 rpm 3.5"* capacity-optimized drives.

Regarding the latest and greatest highest capacity drives: *caveat emptor.* You've probably heard the advice: "Don't buy that new model automobile the first year it's made." The same is true for drives—disk drives undergo a similar maturity curve. Drive manufacturers are ironing out problems with production, quality, factory yields, testing, compatibility, firmware, vibration, and head-to-media interfaces. The first six months of a new drive platform will have noticeably more problems and early failures. It's in your best interest to consciously avoid purchasing HDDs which were produced in the first six months of HDD platform lifecycle. And look out for stale inventory

Key Concept

The early lifecycle (the first six months) of a new drive platform will have noticeably more problems and early failures. It's in your best interest to consciously avoid purchasing HDDs that were produced in the first six months of the HDD platform lifecycle. Caveat emptor!

and storage close-out sales—the reason it's stale inventory or on sale is because few people are buying it. Other current products are a better buy.

1.4   Financial Responsibility and the Tradeoffs between Capacity, Form Factor, and Spin Speed

The economically responsible path is to recognize that the 15K rpm small form factor delivers great random performance, but 15K is the most costly per TB. Apply the Service Level concept to drive responsible behavior. Where there is a real cost to user productivity if the storage is slow, use Service Level 1 15K rpm small form factor drives. Use the more economical Service Level 2 for data (such as e-mail) that has little or no impact on cost of user time. Set up processes to move aging, less useful data from Service Level 1 storage and onto more economical lower tiers.

Key leanings on HDD capacity:

- Recognize that smaller form factor sacrifices capacity.
- Recognize that faster spin speed also sacrifices capacity.
- Be aware of reliability issues associated with early-lifecycle disk drive products.
- 15K drives are expensive. Use service levels to limit expensive storage to expensive problems.
- Use service levels to drive financially responsible choices.

1.5   Demystifying Hard Disk Drive Performance

This book applies a service level approach, which leads us to put hot data on performance storage and everything else on capacity-optimized storage. To establish service levels, we'll need to peel the onion to identify storage performance, capacity, reliability, and cost.

Many IT organizations have gotten into the bad habit of relying on single-tier storage: They put all their data on 10K drives or 15K drives and just grow it without much forethought. In the past, the single-tier approach was the dominant way to do enterprise storage; a single tier for all data was acceptable.

Unfortunately, the world has changed; the alarming expansion of data and overfull data centers mean that it is no longer economically feasible, or even economically responsible, to just keep stuffing more and more data onto the same single-tier storage.

The fiscally responsible approach is

-
- Buy performance storage for performance-sensitive storage tiers
- Buy capacity-optimized storage for applications that can tolerate "good enough" performance

To highlight the contrast . . .

Consider spending on performance. Is it truly required that e-mail storage demonstrate sub-25-millisecond latency? Do we really care if e-mail takes one second or five seconds? We all care whether our e-mail is reliably accessible, but performance? The fiscally responsible thing to do it to shape your various applications into service level tiers: typically Tier 1, Tier 2, and Tier 3. By the way, that's how a really big semi-conductor business in northern California does it.

Now consider spending on reliability. Do we really, *really* need e-mail on systems that are replicated and fully covered for disaster recovery? I kid you not, I read a really good book on storage for Microsoft exchange; the authors devoted a significant portion of the book to engineering storage systems with continuous data replication for e-mail. Spending large amounts of money on reliability where it is not warranted is fiscally irresponsible. So, let's start down the road of data storage service levels and associated performance, capacity, cost, and uptime.

Storage performance is not as complex as it appears. This section is intended to give you the ammunition to defend moving from an inefficient storage system to a more efficient one. You will encounter pushback from individuals who find change hard to handle, and the central objection you will encounter is the topic of storage performance: "The performance will be unacceptable! We run enterprise storage here, and that means everything is in 15K drives!" That is not the best practice. Numerous organizations, including banks, large technology companies, and large hospitality operations, use a combination of performance-optimized and capacity-optimized drives throughout their organization. Fiscally responsible spending embraces a two-tier approach: Spend on performance and disaster recovery where warranted for Tier 1 data. Spend less on performance and on disaster recovery for Tier 2 data.

Storage systems basically read, write, and handle errors. Storage system performance has two important components: *throughput* and *latency*.

1.6   Hard Disk Drive Quick Guided Tour

Have you ever asked someone the time, only to be told how to build a watch? My intention is not to explain the details of the technology, only to impart adequate knowledge to make informed business decisions related to cost, performance, and capacity. I'll keep it brief, I promise.

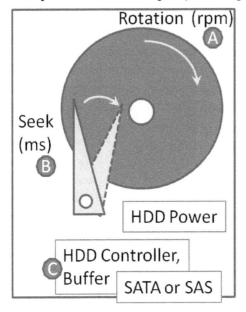

Figure 1.8   A Brief Guided Tour of the HDD

The disk drives (see Figure 1.8 for a diagram) are made of a simple list of building blocks:

- Platters (usually three), and a motor to spin the platters (usually spinning at 7200, 10,000, or 15,000 rpm)—like a phonograph vinyl. (A)
- Read-write heads, one for each surface of each platter. The heads sit at the end of the armature, like a phonograph needle. A "voice coil" positions the heads on the desired tracks. (B)
- A bunch of electronics and a drive buffer (also known as a drive cache), along with an SAS or SATA connection to a storage system, RAID card, or server. (C)

The mechanical limitations of these components determine the capacity, reliability, performance, and cost of the disk drive. Some drives are optimized for performance with faster rotations and faster seek times. Others are optimized for capacity, with bigger platters, more platters, and slower rotation speeds, allowing tighter bit spacing and increased capacity.

Yes, there is a tradeoff between cost, performance, and capacity.

Throughput is determined by the slowest link in the system—usually media transfer, the rate at which the data is read off the disk by the heads. The speed of media transfer is governed by how tightly the bits are packed on the disk and the spin speed.

Latency is determined by how fast the heads can be moved to the right track, by delays for the data to be rotated under the head, and by drive firmware which can intelligently reorder the input/output (I/O) requests for greater efficiency (a process known as *queuing*).

Key Concept

Throughput *is analogous to a speed limit on a roadway when traffic is moving smoothly. Think highways with a speed limit. Usually measured in* MB/*second data transfer rate for data delivered.*

Latency *is basically delay or wait time, analogous to roadway stoplights or traffic slowdowns. It's reasonable to compare latency to traffic with stoplights. The more "hops" and the higher the latency, the poorer the performance will be. Cache is used as a performance accelerator to remove latency, but for cache to work, the requested data needs to be loaded into cache. Latency is most often measured in milliseconds and sometimes microseconds of delay.*

For *random workloads* (lots of users asking for lots and lots of random small bits of information), the latency will impact performance more than throughput. Latency is introduced by things like disk drive head movement, multiple I/O hops on a SAN, or competing data traffic on a SAN. For *sequential workloads* (few users asking for a few large quantities of information), throughput will impact performance more than latency.

We're taking a bottom-up approach, starting with the basic storage system building block: the highly mystical hard drive.

Hard drives are the essence of any storage system; at least for now, and we'll review solid state devices (SSDs) at length later in the book. Right now, we're establishing a baseline for today's systems, and that means hard drives.

There are two very distinct classes of enterprise hard drives: performance optimized and capacity optimized. Sometimes we need a sports car, sometimes we need a moving van; choose wisely.

- *Performance-optimized enterprise hard drives* (typically 15,000 rpm with really fast random I/O: ~3–4 ms [1 ms = 1 millisecond = 1/thousandth of a second]). The sum of seek and rotational latency. Seek is the time it takes to move the hard drive head from track to track. Rotational latency is the time it takes to rotate the platter so the requested data is under the disk drive head. Performance-optimized drives typically offer sequential throughput of between 120–160 MB/s.
- *Capacity-optimized enterprise hard drives* (typically 7200 rpm, with not-so-fast random I/O: ~12–14 ms for the sum of seek and rotational latency). Capacity-optimized drives typically offer sequential throughput of between 100–140 MB/s.

Hard drive performance is gated by two things: seek (also known as latency) and sequential behavior.

- *Seek.* The speed the HDD drive head moves from track to track; this largely determines random I/O performance. Random I/O performance includes movement of the head to the desired track (*seek*) plus time to rotate the platter so the desired data is under the head (*rotational latency*). When reading HDD data sheets, be sure both seek and rotational latency are included in the specs for random I/O.
- *Sequential.* The speed of bits passing under the head (*sequential transfer rates*), determined by spin speed and bit density, this largely determines the maximum data rate for reading or writing sequential data (no seek, no head movement from track to track involved).

This section seeks to demystify storage performance, so let's take a look at the various components of performance, zero in on the components that really move the needle, and consciously eliminate the stuff that does not matter. Let's start by debunking a prevalent myth: Hard drive performance is NOT largely determined by spin speed or by the hard drive interface (SATA, SAS, FC).

1.6.1   Hard Drive Spin Speeds and Latency

Latency is a fancy word for delay or a wait, like waiting on the head to arrive over the right track or waiting for the platters to rotate so the data is positioned under the head.

Performance-optimized drives (15K rpm 2.5") do their appointed mission really well. They spin very fast, reducing rotational latency—the time it takes to rotate the platter so the data is under the head. Average rotational latency is easily calculated: one-half the time it takes for a platter to turn a complete revolution. But there is an inevitable tradeoff between random performance (seek times) and total drive capacity. Otherwise stated, disk drive manufacturers face a trade-off; they can either optimize for capacity or they can optimize for performance.

Capacity-optimized drives have the highest possible number of bits on the platter—bits are packed closely in line on each track, and tracks (like grooves on a vinyl record) are packed closely side-by-side. The challenge is the rocket science required to get the head to seek-settle-track reliably on the track if the tracks are packed so closely. Keep in mind, HDDs are mass manufactured, so there are mechanical variances from drive to drive; the servo tracking firmware and mechanical assembly must compensate for these mechanical variances. We can expect to see higher and higher capacities in all classes of drives through a variety of HDD technologies, which are beyond the scope of this book. We are zeroing in on the really meaningful characteristics of the disk drive, which is the basic building block of the storage system. We'll spend this section demystifying drive performance (using the right yardstick: what matters and what doesn't).

Table 1.6   Demystifying Performance Bottlenecks: Latency and Seek

Where's the Bottleneck? Spin Latency or Seek/Move the Head?	Rotational Latency and Seek (Lower is Better)
15,000 rpm 2.5" HDD typical	2.0 ms rotational latency + 3.3 ms seek = 5.3 ms total
10,000 rpm 3.5" HDD typical	3.0 ms rotational latency + 4.0 ms seek = 7 ms total
7200 rpm 3.5" HDD typical	4.1 ms rotational latency + 9 ms seek = 13.1 ms total
5400 rpm 3.5" HDD typical	5.5 ms rotational latency + 10 ms seek = 15.5 ms total

In Table 1.6, we see an even spread of random I/O performance rotational-plus-seek: 5, 7, 13, and 15 ms across the various classes of HDDs. It's important to correlate random performance to heavy random workloads involving hot data and to use those HDDs for high random performance against a workload that needs high random performance (hot data); alternatively, use more economical and bigger HDDs against a larger workload (cool data). We will discuss hot and cold data much more later in the book.

1.6.2   Interface Speeds: SATA Speeds, SAS Speeds, FC Speeds

In the section above, we were discussing random I/O performance. In this section, we're shifting to sequential (nonrandom) I/O performance.

The short answer is that interface speeds don't determine HDD performance.

The longer answer is that the interface is not the performance bottleneck; the drive performance is bottlenecked where the data comes off the platter. SAS or SATA HDD interfaces (SATA 300MB/s moving to 600MB/s and SAS2 2×300MB/s moving to 2×600MB/s) are much faster than sequential data rates. HDD interface does not have a big impact on performance.

The qualifier here is that although drive interface (SAS, SATA, FC) are not the bottleneck in HDDs, drive interface will become the performance bottleneck with SSDs—a topic we'll return to later in the book.

For HDDs, though, the bottom line is that the interface to the HDD does not determine HDD performance.

For random workloads:
- Moving the head (seek) is the key performance bottleneck.
- In random I/O workloads, pay attention to seek; random I/O performance is very dependent on how fast the head moves.
- Rotational latency (spin) is a smaller component of HDD performance; spin speed is less important.
- Random I/O performance is *not* heavily dependent on disk interface (FC, SAS, or SATA).

Let's cover the same variables of seek and spin for sequential workloads:

- Sequential performance is how fast the bits come off the platter
- Sequential performance is highly dependent on bit density.
- Sequential performance is *not* heavily dependent on spin speed.

- Sequential performance is *not* heavily dependent on disk interface (FC, SAS, or SATA).

The answer to the question "Where is the bottleneck?" is that drive performance is limited by how fast bits can be read or written off the platter (roughly 200 MB/s). Drive performance is not limited by interface speed. In English, that means buying a faster interface does not mean you're going to experience faster drive performance, as shown in Table 1.7.

Table 1.7   Demystifying Performance Bottlenecks: Media Transfer and Interface Speed

Where's the Bottleneck— Interface or Media Transfer?	Media Transfer Rate	Interface Speed
15,000 rpm 2.5" HDD typical	190 MB/s	
10,000 rpm 3.5" HDD typical	155 MB/s	
7200 rpm 3.5" HDD typical	130 MB/s	
5400 rpm 3.5" HDD typical	110 MB/s	
SAS 6 Gb/s disk interface		2×600 MB/s
SAS 3 Gb/s disk interface		2×300 MB/s
FC 2 Gb/s disk interface		2×200 MB/s
SATA 3 Gb/s disk interface		300 MB/s
Media transfer (also known as sequential transfer) is the maximum rate that a drive can read data off the platter (just streaming a big file, with no interruptions for seeking).		
The slowest interface speed is single channel SATA (300 MB/s); the fastest media transfer speed is less than 200 MB/s. Buying a faster interface will not buy faster performance; performance is gated by media transfer rate.		

Drive interfaces have other useful characteristics; for example, they have dual channels, meaning that if one controller fails or hangs, the data will remain accessible through the other channel. This quality is useful in companies that require high availability of their systems and are willing to pay the associated price tag (we'll cover more in the reliability chapters).

- The key spec for disk drive *random* performance is seek performance (not spin speed or interface speed).
- The key spec for disk drive *sequential* performance is media transfer rate (not spin speed or interface speed).

- Interface (FC, SAS, SATA) has very little impact on performance. Interfaces are important for other compatibility-related reasons.

1.6.3   HDD Caching

The short answer is HDD caching—referring to the cache on the disk drive itself—does not make much difference, so ignore it.

The longer answer is that in order for caching to pay off, the data needs to be in cache. If the server or storage array requests data that is already in cache, we get a cache hit, and the performance is improved. If the cache has a really small capacity as compared to the overall capacity of the drive, the chances of cache-hits gets pretty small, pretty fast.

To improve caching and reliability, HDD write caching on HDDs should be turned off for enterprise applications, because if power is abruptly lost the data sitting in cache pending write to platter will be lost.

If only "read" workloads matter, then, let us separate *sequential read* workloads from *random read* workloads. Turning HDD write caching off further reduces the probability of cache hits.

For *sequential read* workloads, caching on disk drives rarely pays off; the cache simply fills up and then doesn't help.

For *random read* workloads, the cache will pay off if the desired data is stilling in cache when requested. However, this also rarely pays off, because today's systems have large amounts of system RAM designed to hold frequently accessed data; if the data is frequently accessed, it's usually already in the system RAM. In situations where the data is not already in RAM, cache hit rates come into play. A typical drive holds 146 GB; a typical cache is 32 MB. That's a 5000-to-1 ratio. Raw math says that is a .002% probability that the data is actually sitting in cache, but drives are rarely 100% full and all data is not equally hot or recently accessed. So the real-world probability of a cache hit is increased, but the real-world probability of a cache hit is also significantly decreased by the chance the data is already sitting in system RAM.

Using HDD cache has a risk—if HDD write cache is enabled, this creates a situation where the system may write data to the disk drive, the data is written to cache. But if the drive powers off unexpectedly before that data is written to disk platters, that data is lost. For that reason, in enterprise applications, HDD write caching should be off. It's okay to have read cache enabled. Most storage systems deliver this properly configured.

The bottom line on disk drive caching is that it does not make much difference, so ignore it. Please bear in mind, these conclusions are all based on the assumption that there is a very small cache compared to a very large overall storage; and there are other ways to do caching than just putting the cache on the HDD.

1.6.4   HDD Queuing

The short answer is that HDD queuing does improve performance, but all HDDs have queuing, so ignore it. SSDs do not require queuing.

The easiest way to understand queuing is by example. Queuing logic is referred to as "the elevator algorithm." Think of a high-rise building with people, floors, and elevators. The people represent the data, the floors represent the tracks on a disk drive platters, the elevators represent the heads on the disk drive. The idea is to efficiently deliver lots of people onto the proper floors. With queuing, the elevator delivers people to the nearest floor. Without queuing, the elevator delivers the people in the order in which the buttons were pushed. Get the picture?

For enterprise drives servicing lots of simultaneous I/O requests, queuing makes a real difference (picture that crowded elevator going from floor to floor in the order the buttons were pushed). For drives servicing few simultaneous I/O requests (archival systems, laptops, desktops) queuing makes very little difference (picture the elevator with one or two people going in the order the buttons are pushed).

There is a difference between SATA queuing and SAS queuing:

- SATA supports a queue depth of 32 and payload delivery priority of high and low (payload is also known as FIS, frame information structure).
- SAS supports a queue depth of 256 and payload delivery priority of one through sixteen.

In some use cases, such as an enterprise database that is capable of setting queue priority on IO requests, the difference between SAS and SATA queuing makes significant difference. In other use cases, where the application is not setting queue priority, the differences between SAS and SATA queuing makes no difference.

Queuing is designed around the concept of HDD spinning platters with tracks (like a phonograph) and a read/write head (like the needle of a phonograph). Therefore, queuing makes good sense for HDDs. Solid state devices or solid state storage do not have platters, tracks or heads. SSDs and SSS have memory addresses and wear leveling algorithms and I/O channels.

They can read and write the storage protocols (SAS, SATA, FC), which include queuing, but since there is no need for SSDs and SSSs to gather and order the I/O based on head location, SSDs and SSSs will ignore queuing instructions and simply send to a memory address.

It is worth knowing that even seemingly sequential workloads like video surveillance still have lots of inputs (multiple cameras) and lots of outputs (several computers reading the surveillance data and analyzing it), so even these streaming workloads can generate a highly random I/O workload for HDDs and SSDs.

The bottom line on queuing is that it's covered; all enterprise drives have queuing.

1.6.5   Drive Performance Summary

When you characterize the performance of the drives within your system, it can be boiled down to random I/O performance (I/O per sec or seek) and sequential performance (MB/s).

Drive specs you should *pay attention to* include:
- Drive random I/O performance (as measured by Iometer with a random workload)
- Drive seek performance (ms)
- Drive sequential performance (MB/s, higher is better)

There is a description on the use of Iometer in Appendix E.
Drive specs you can *ignore with minimal risk* include:

- Drive spin speed
- Drive cache size
- Drive interface (SATA, SAS, FC)

These have limited impact on performance.

These rules hold up uniformly with any disk drive, any capacity, any interface, any platter count.

These rules do not apply to solid state devices (SSDs), which we will cover in another section.

Which drives to use? The simple answer is that it depends on the performance service level, the workload, and the size of the dataset:

- *A highly random workload*: lots of users pounding on a small dataset should use performance-optimized drives (15K rpm with a fast seek time).
- *A sequential workload*: a few users accessing a larger data set should use capacity-optimized drive (Enterprise SATA 7200 rpm or 5400 rpm)
- Workloads that are somewhere in between can use 10K rpm drives

The longer answer is that it's important to operationally separate the hot data from the cool data. Once you do that, you use a small number of 15K drives (or SSD drives) on the hot data; all the cool data goes onto capacity-optimized enterprise SATA drives. 10K rpm drives actually represent a giant compromise, a spork, capable of a reasonable amount of capacity and a reasonable amount of performance, but not very good at either. But that requires significant operational improvements to separate the hot from cool data; we'll cover this subject later in the book.

See, I told you it was simple.

At the end of Part I, we provide an example that compares the costs, capacities, and performance in the interest of showing the financial improvements associated with using the right devices for the right task in your IT shop.

Chapter 2

Power and AC

We are going to make some simplifying assumptions (approximations) to avoid setting ourselves up for failure by including too many variables and going for 100% accuracy. The problem of power becomes unmanageable if we try to understand all the dynamics—data grows over time, situations change depending on time of day or time of month. Rather we will sign up for simplifying assumptions, set up a solvable problem, and generate a useful, informative analysis.

About drive power, *active*, *idle*, and *sleep*, spec sheets for most hard drives show power in three ratings (see Table 2.1).

Table 2.1   The Tradeoffs Between Form Factor, Spin Speed, and Capacity

Drive Type	Common Capacities	Active	Idle (Spinning)	Sleep (Not Spinning)
15K rpm 2.5"	300G, 146G	8 watts	7 watts	1.5 watts
15K rpm 3.5"	600G, 450G, 300G	14 watts	12 watts	2 watts
10K rpm 2.5"	300G, 146G	8 watts	7 watts	1.5 watts
10K rpm 3.5"	600G, 300G, 146G	14 watts	12 watts	2 watts
7200 rpm	21TB, 750G, 500G	9 watts	7 watts	1.5 watts
5400 rpm	2TB,1TB	7 watts	6 watts	1.5 watts

Source: HDD data sheets

Key Concepts

- *Active power is only slightly higher than idle-spinning power*
- *Sleep is considerably lower than active or idle-spinning because the motor is not consuming power, but there is a time-lag and a power spike (also known as a "current inrush") when recovering from sleep to active.*
- *Capacity trade-off: Higher spin-speed is lower capacity. Smaller form (2.5") is lower capacity.*

These are enterprise environments, presumably 24×7, mostly operating in an active state. This analysis use HDD ratings for the *active* state. In your analysis, if your environment has periods of inactivity; it's reasonable to include a derating multiplier on the active HDD power number, but including this will not substantially influence the results.

2.1   Powering Down Inactive Drives, or MAID

Systems that will sleep or spin down HDDs after minutes of inactivity are available. I'm not convinced these make great sense. HDD sleep modes are not typical of performance-optimized 15K rpm or 10K rpm drives. Rather, sleep mode behavior is typical of capacity-optimized 7200 rpm or 5400 rpm enterprise drives. While it is worth knowing that spin-down *does* save power for inactive drives, there is a downside: Once the drives are spun down, it will take some time (typically 10–15 seconds) for the drive to spin back up after receiving a read or write request.

RAID I/O logic make spinning down individual inactive drives infeasible. In RAID (redundant array of inexpensive/independent disks) groups, an I/O request involves all drives in the RAID group. In order to sleep, all drives in a RAID group must be idle for the prescribed time (tens of minutes), then they all sleep. Then if any write I/O to the RAID group is received, the entire RAID group spins up.

All the drives in a RAID group behave as a group. The entire RAID group must be quiet to spin down. And all the drives in a RAID group must spin up to recover from sleep and access the data. This RAID group behavior considerably reduces the potential benefit of power savings. The bottom line is that real-world power savings from MAID (massive array of idle disks) are limited. There are lots of other, higher reward ways to save power.

2.2   Facilities and Power

About controller power: Storage controllers for NAS systems (network attached storage, file data access) and SAN systems (storage area network, block data access) are basically computers, in the sense they consume approximately the same power as typical servers. I/O controllers and servers typically consume 200 watts to 300 watts. If you know the exact wattage rating, by all means plug it into your analysis.

However, our basic simplifying assumption is 250 watts per I/O controller. Dual controllers typically use 250 watts per I/O controller, and servers typically use 250 watts each.

Data center power is the big hitter. For any electrical load in a data center, there are losses and inefficiencies. Power is consumed (bled off) by transformers, wire resistance, less-than-efficient cooling systems, and less-than-efficient thermal transfer systems. The chart in Figure 2.1 illustrates just how lossy data center power consumption is.

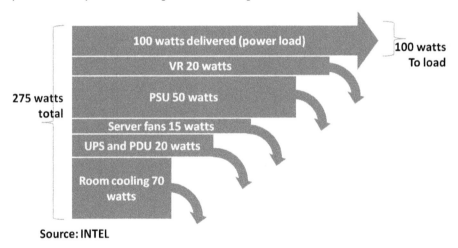

Source: INTEL

Figure 2.1   Estimated PUE Data Center Power Loss Ratios

Source: Intel, via http://download.intel.com/pressroom/kits/research/poster_Data_Center_Energy_Efficiency.pdf

Figure 2.1 shows
- PUE (power usage effectiveness)—total facility power/IT equipment power
- VR (voltage regulator)—shelf-level
- PSU (power supply unit)—shelf-level or rack-level
- Server fans (air movers)—shelf-level

- UPS (uninterruptible power supply)—room-level
- PDU (power distribution unit) —room-level
- Room cooling—data center air conditioning, room level

2.2.1 Facilities: Air Conditioning

This section is intended to provide insight into data center cooling problems, raise opportunities to identify inefficiencies, improve your data center, and know enough to intelligently interact with your facilities A/C guys; all in the interest of delivering IT storage and at the same time being fiscally responsible.

To provide a common vocabulary to communicate with your facilities people, Table 2.2 contains a brief on power and air conditioning load (it's pretty simple to understand).

Table 2.2   Facilities Power and AC Basics

The vocabulary basics:
▪ 1 watt = 1 volt * 1 amp * (power factor)†
▪ 1 KW (kilowatt) = 1000 watts
▪ 1 KWh (kilowatt-hour) = 1000 watts for an hour
Your power bill, depending on location, can be as low as ~$0.08 per KWh or as high as ~$0.16 per KWH. If in doubt, a nice round figure is ~$0.10 per KWh.
Applied:
▪ Facilities engineers will talk in terms of air conditioning BTUs or tons of capacity.
▪ A 24-kilowatt heat load requires 78,000 BTUs of cooling capacity or six to seven tons of A/C capacity.
† A simplifying assumption: the power factor is usually close to one, so in our simplified calculations we can assume KVA (kilo-volt-amp) and KW.

Most computer room cooling systems are over-engineered and provide too much cooling for the load. There are methods to significantly improve the efficiency of computer room cooling.

The design process for normal office areas starts with a calculation of the heat load in the office space (lights, equipment, people, windows, insulation); the process then adds:

- Duct work and air handlers to distribute cool air evenly throughout the space
- Chiller capacity to provide refrigerated water to the air handlers
- Control, in the form of thermostats to turn on the air handlers when the space gets too warm, turn off the air handlers when the space is too cool, and handle simple thermal programming for nights and weekends.

Building design engineers and architectural consultants apply pretty much the same techniques for data centers and computer rooms. The heat loads are higher, so the duct work and chillers are bigger and there are perhaps more thermostats supplemented with alarms and backup cooling capacity. But it's still the same basic approach: heat load, duct work, chiller, and control.

The difficulty here is that data centers are not like office spaces.

Unlike offices, data centers have some areas of very high concentrations of heat loads; some parts of the room house hundreds of processors per cubic yard. People and lights don't generate that kind of heat in that concentrated area. Wikipedia.org indicates the current generation of Intel Itanium2 server processors consumes 104 watts per processor. Multiprocessor blade servers are even more dense in power consumption per square foot.

Data center equipment heat loads are highly concentrated, unlike office heat loads, which spread about larger floor spaces. Data center equipment generates different heat at different times of the day. A server disk drive generates as much as 14 watts in active use, 9 or 10 watts while idle and spinning, and less than 2 watts while in sleep state (on, but not spinning). Lastly, unlike offices, data centers keep adding hotter and hotter equipment, rarely retiring equipment over the lifetime of the data center.

So, that's the rub: Some data centers are cooled like office space, generally delivering the cool air into the big volume rather than delivering the A/C directly to the heat load. This leads to over-designing to account for more and hotter equipment over time, usually with few thermostats.

There are specialized computer room air handlers, which are basically larger air conditioners. Typically they are controlled by thermal sensors located near the air inlets rather than near the air return, the big vent that takes air OUT of the room. Public research indicates that three quarters of all data centers have thermal sensors at the air inlets. Alternatively, thermal sensors can be placed in the cold aisles between racks—an improvement, but still stuck in the old paradigm of office cooling: pump air into the space, but don't worry about specifically what is hot and where it's hot or about delivering and measuring cooling efficiently close to the heat load.

More often than not, data centers are over-designed and run at least 5 degrees cooler than necessary. When delivering cooling directly to the heat load, it's okay to save power and run a bit warmer ambient temperature.

Facilities cooling is not just about CPU-generated heat. Heat is the enemy of hard disk drive reliability. The recommended ambient operating temperature for all hard drives is 40°C (104°F). Running hard drives at anything warmer than 40°C will shorten hard disk lifespan.

To achieve big bang for the buck, cooling must be delivered and measured in a more granular and more targeted way. We now understand that heat loads in data centers are concentrated, and that they get hot and cool at different times of the day or month. The game plan is to implement thermal sensors at the heat loads and let those thermal sensors control air delivery to that specific rack, not the entire room.

In summary, the office cooling design problem, addressed with an office cooling design process and design assumptions, is simply less-than-ideal for data center cooling.

Key Concepts

- *Every watt spent on a server or on a disk drive consumes 2.75 watts in total energy, so add electrical loads to your data center with care. Every data center has a limited amount of power capacity and a limited amount of A/C capacity; sooner or later, these capacities are consumed and the choice is to retire/rework/replace existing storage or build new data centers.*
- *Make sure HDDs are kept at an ambient temperature no warmer than 40°C. Keeping drives cool will reduce failures.*
- *Cooling systems are very inefficient. It is best to deliver the cooling directly to the heat load and control it with lots of thermostats at each load than to deliver the cooling into the room and control it with a single thermostat far from the heat load.*

2.3 Establishing a Baseline for Performance, Capacity, and Power

Table 2.3 contains an example of a *simple* storage baseline for your chosen system, focused on capacity, power, and hot/cold data. (We will touch on performance in an upcoming section). The working assumption is this baseline system will be a few years old and have older drives. We'll quantify and compare the performance, power, and capacity of systems with older vintage drives to systems with newer drives. The differences will surprise you.

Reliability costs money, and not every application requires 5-nines of uptime (99.999% uptime, eight minutes of downtime per year). Some applications are good with lower, more affordable levels of reliability. We'll cover these in sections on Service Level Agreements (SLAs). For right now, we'll assume "acceptable reliability."

Table 2.3   Baseline Storage System

Drive Qty	Drive Type	Capacity per Drive (GB)	Watts per Drive	Total Capacity (TB)	Total usable Capacity (TB) **	Data (Used capacity)	Total Power (watts)	Hot Data / Cold data
System Name:								
16	15K rpm 3.5" 144G	144 GB	13 w	2.3 TB	1.7 TB	1.0 TB	16*14= 208 w *** 208+250= 458 w *** 458*2.75= 1260 w ****	50/50
16	7200 rpm 3.5" 500G	500 GB	9 w	8 TB	6.0 TB	4.0TB	16*9= 144 w 144+250= 394 W 394*2.75= 1083 w	0/100
	totals				7.7 TB	5 TB	2343 watts	

** Calculate total usable capacity; subtract out RAID overhead, warm spares, etc.
*** Power for disk drives plus power consumed by controllers
**** Power for A/C plus power distribution inefficiencies. The formula is HDD power plus controller power X 2.75

2.4   Facilities Cooling Improvements Within Reach

1. Confirm your hard disk drives are 40°C or cooler to improve reliability.

2. Consider replacing arrays of aging 15K or 10K drives with updated higher capacity 15K or 10K drives; alternately, allocate that storage to Tier 2 and migrate to highly power efficient 7200 rpm capacity-optimized HDDs, as shown in Table 2.3.

3. When your data center is approaching over-capacity to cool equipment, deliver cooling to the loads. Rearrange ductwork and rackwork to allow direct (targeted) application of cooled air to the heat load. Add thermal sensors at the heat load and have those sensors control the immediate cool air delivery at the load. Once the heat loads are addressed, it is possible to run at a higher ambient temperature.

Chapter 3

Storage Consolidation

Compartmentalized storage is one of those real-world, commonly encountered, expensive problems that flies below the radar. Reducing compartmentalization is an area where IT departments can both improve service levels and save money in the same motion.

Even in companies with the most advanced IT departments employing advanced technologies for mainstream applications, there is *always* compartmentalized storage that can be found and improved upon.

Information Week's "2009 State of Storage" report states: "The storage used most by respondents is good old-fashioned *direct attached storage.*"

Direct attached storage (DAS) means one server, directly attached to storage. For one server or a couple of servers, direct attached storage is perfectly reasonable and useful means to deploy storage attached to a server. There are several key drawbacks of DAS as compared to SAN (storage area network) systems:

- Over-provisioning (a fancy term for when people buy more than they need)
- Reliability risk, server down time: when the server is down, the data is unavailable until the server is back on line
- Storage manageability
- Sprawl, hardware spares, power
- Backup inefficiencies

DAS is compared to consolidated SAN storage in Table 3.1.

Table 3.1 Comparing Direct Attached Storage (DAS) to SAN Storage

Issue	Direct Attached Storage	SAN Storage
Over-provisioning	Typically 40–50% unused	Typically 20–25% unused
Manageable storage	The task of adding DAS capacity for growth requires additional HDDs that match the HDD type/capacity. Difficult with a variety of different types of DAS equipment.	The task of adding SAN capacity for growth is significantly easier with a consolidated storage pool. Planning is easier to manage, spare hard drives is a simpler task.
Sprawl, hardware spares	A variety of DAS systems consumes more rack space, more floor space, more power, more A/C. The cost and complexity of cabling and cable troubleshooting is increased too.	Consolidated SAN storage consumes less rack space, less floor space, less power, less A/C. Simpler cabling, too.
Backup efficiency	Backups for many individual server DAS arrays are highly labor intensive, and tape management is problematic. Establishing recover point objectives and recover time objectives are significantly more difficult.	Backups for consolidated SAN storage are simpler and less labor intensive. Managing the tape library is lower risk and less problematic. Establishing recover point objectives and recover time objectives is more straightforward.
Reliability and uptime	With DAS, if the server fails or simply needs to be rebooted or updated, the storage is not accessible until the server is repaired or until the storage is manually connected to another server (not a trivial task).	With SAN, if a server fails, reboots, or is updating, SANs can interoperate with servers supporting multipath I/O (MPIO) failover to have another server pick up the load of the failed server. This requires some configuration, but is very commonplace.

Table 3.1   Comparing Direct Attached Storage (DAS) to SAN Storage (continued)

Issue	Direct Attached Storage	SAN Storage
Improved use of IT people	Managing multiple DAS systems is time consuming. People costs are almost always more expensive than hardware costs.	Managing fewer SAS systems is more efficient. Improves efficiencies in tasks such as backup, bringing on new storage, growing storage, training, having a backup person in the case of time off, sickness, vacation, promotion, employee turnover.
Tiering	Tiering (putting hot data on performance-optimized HDDs and putting cooler data on capacity-optimized HDDs) is challenging to do across dozens of different DAS systems.	Tiering is possible for DAS, but tiering in SAN storage environments is much simpler: Configure one or more performance storage pools and one or more capacity storage pools, and map servers to the appropriate performance pool or capacity pool.

According to Wikibon.org, storage consolidation typically results in:

- Reducing storage total cost of ownership by ten to thirty percent
- Increasing the capacity managed per admin by a factor of two to four times
- Increasing disk utilization from typically less than forty percent to typically more than fifty-five percent
- Breaking even within six to eighteen months
- Cutting in half the time required to deploy new or changed storage for applications
- Consolidating training to a single set of courseware, encouraging deeper technical talent within the IT organization

3.1   Cost of DAS versus SAN: Overprovisioning

The typical cost analysis compares cost per GB, which DAS usually wins. But over-provisioning is typically overlooked. Every storage system, including both DAS and SAN, has some amount of excess, unused capacity.

Typically DAS arrays typically have 40 to 50 percent capacity in use, and 50 to 60 percent capacity unused. Compare this to SAN systems, which typically have 75 to 80 percent of storage in use.

The "brain" icon indicates RAID-smarts; this is important as we look at several use cases.

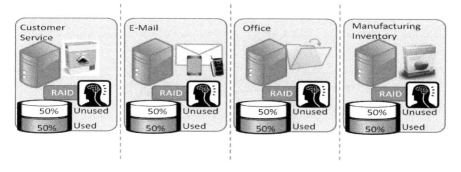

Figure 3.1   Baseline DAS System Schematic

In DAS (see Figure 3.1), the RAID brain is in each server. This is good because it's relatively simple, relatively high performance. It's not good because only one server can access the data at once; and so storage tends to get over-provisioned. Direct attached servers tend to often be over-provisioned and wasteful. Direct attached storage is offline whenever the supporting server is down, so uptime is a concern. And it's much simpler and cheaper to back up and protect data (and, most importantly, reliably recover data) from one consolidated system as opposed to lots of little systems that are often ineptly maintained and backed up. Over-provisioning, uptime, and backup recovery are significantly improved with SAN storage (as shown in Figure 3.2).

Based on a simple TCO calculation (just focusing on over-provisioning), Table 3.2 compares break-even costs of DAS versus SAN in simple, round numbers:

- In approximate numbers for a 15-drive array, DAS will cost $2,000 plus drives
- In approximate numbers for a 15-drive array, SAN will cost $10,000 plus drives
- There is a crossover point where cost of the over-provisioned DAS drives will overcome the savings of the cost of the $2,000 DAS array versus the $10,000 SAN array.
   (yes, I did the math so this would break even)

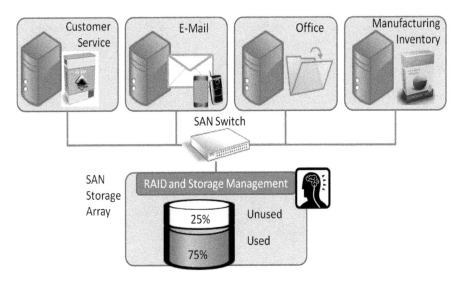

Figure 3.2   Baseline SAN Storage System Schematic

Table 3.2   Baseline Storage System Financial Estimate

Simple utilization comparison DAS to SAN	DAS	SAN
Array	$1,900	$11,939
Drives: 20 × 2TB at $700 each (40TB)	$14,000	$14,000
Total	$15,900	$25,900
$/GB	$0.40/GB	$0.65/GB
Utilization Rate	50%	80%
Business Cost $/GB adjusted for utilization	$0.79	$0.81

In this model, with these assumptions (same drive type, same drive capacity, utilization percentage, costs), the break-even is *solely on the topic of utilization*. If there are fewer than twenty drives, then DAS is more cost effective, but if there are more than twenty drives, SAN is more cost effective. Obviously, if you transition older storage on older smaller drives to new storage with higher capacity drives, there is a big difference in the breakeven point. And obviously, this simple analysis does not take into advantage the other benefits of SAN storage: consolidated backup, tape library improvements, failover, and opportunity to implement tiered storage.

Key Concepts

- *Pushing the RAID "smarts" from the server into the storage array improves performance, reliability (server failover).*
- *Storage consolidation significantly reduces over-provisioning (typically from fifty percent DAS utilization to seventy percent or more for SAN). Getting an additional twenty to thirty percent utilization changes the TCO as we compare DAS to SAN.*
- *Consolidated storage makes growth easier to predict and provision. Lots of little DAS systems growing at inconsistent rates are harder to predict than fewer, larger SAN storage systems.*
- *Storage consolidation improves reliability and uptime with multipath I/O.*
- *Storage consolidation improves backup efficiency and simplifies tape library management. Improves RPO (recover point objective), the time since the last snapshot and RTO (recover time objective), the time needed from taking the request to recover to the delivery of recovered data.*
- *Storage consolidation creates an opportunity for storage tiering: putting the hot data on fast drives and putting the cooler data on higher performance drives.*

3.2   Cost of DAS versus SAN: Backup Efficiency

Backups cost money. It's not unlike an insurance policy: you spend money on insurance and it rarely gets used. We'll examine backups, just like you review your insurance policies to ensure you're getting the coverage you need (no more, no less) and paying the best price. The cost of backup for consolidated storage is less expensive than cost of backups for lots of smaller compartmentalized storage.

It's obvious that there should be frequent backups or snapshots of mission critical information. It makes less sense to apply the same rigor of frequent backups to less important information. Applying a service level approach to drive the right business behavior and spending is the advisable approach.

The typical compartmentalized storage system (as shown in Figure 3.3) is usually a server with direct attached disks. It works, but it's highly inefficient and can be very expensive:

Figure 3.3   An Example of Compartmentalized Storage

is an icon for the tape backup treadmill—a repetitive task. Tape backup is messy, and costly, with lots of moving parts. It involves people, materials (tape), technology (tape archival hardware and scripts), moving targets to backup (new volumes, expanded volumes), and tape library management. Tape backup is costly; if multiplied across several functional areas, it can be very expensive.

This is a situation where consolidated backup will reduce overall costs. The expense is hidden in the people and the repetitive tasks. In this typical situation, each administrator separately manages the storage, storage growth, new hardware, backup, and archival. Incremental backups of data that has changed typically are conducted each 24 hours, and full backups typically are conducted each week.

Additionally, each administrator manages tape and responds to the inevitable support calls when some file or record or e-mail was accidentally deleted, misplaced, or otherwise lost in the wilderness. Each administrator deals with problems relating to tape and tape drives.

Risks related to silo tape backup are significant: if the tape library is managed in a less-than-professional way, risks include infrequent backups, inconsistent backups, no backups, invalid backups, malfunctioning recovery attempts, misfiled or lost tape, and the risk of sensitive information leaks.

It would be a better place, and a better use of company money, if one storage group was put in place to handle the task of incremental backups, full backup, managing tape, and managing recoveries—as shown in Figure 3.4. And this would free up time for the application administrators to do something more valuable, right?

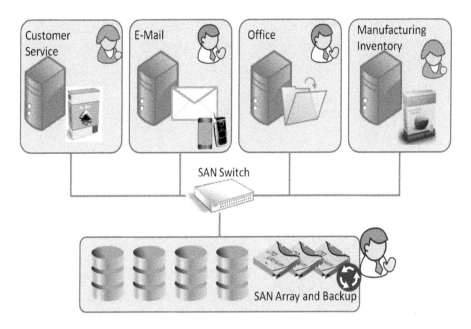

Figure 3.4   Consolidated Storage: Improvement over Compartmentalized Storage

The tape backup treadmill is consolidated from many servers to one (or few) storage arrays. Incremental backups are more efficient and better managed; full backups are more efficient and better managed; and the cost of tape is reduced (use fewer full tapes instead of lots of partially full tapes). But most important is the task of recovery.

When I was a young man, I attended a speech by a NASA astronaut. His speech started with the following statement:

"We sent three men to the moon, and back. Let's not underestimated that 'and back' part."

As we deal with backup, let's never lose sight of the main goal: to recover data in the case of:

- Accidental deletion
- Data corruption, file system problems, or similar
- Virus
- Hardware failure
- Regulatory compliance

The biggest upsides to consolidating backup are improvements in recovery. By consolidating recovery tasks and recovery library management, IT is better able to:

- Quickly locate desired data
- Quickly and reliably recover data (offer good recovery time objectives or RTOs)
- Recover recent images (offer good recovery point objectives or RPOs)

Table 3.3 shows a comparison, before and after.

Table 3.3   Consolidated Storage: Improvement over Compartmentalized Storage

	Separated Storage	Shared Storage	Comment
Daily incremental backup	Finance: 1 hour (per day) E-mail: 1 hour Office: 1 hour Mfg/Inventory: 1 hour	3 hours per day	One SAN array and backup administrator can back up 4 GB more easily than four people can separately backup 4 GB.
Weekly full backup	Finance: 2 hours (per week) E-mail: 3 hours Office: 3 hours Mfg/Inventory: 2 hours	3 hours per week	One SAN array and backup administrator can back up 20 GB, easier than four people can separately backup 20 GB.
Tape cost and tape management (per month)	Finance: $1000 E-mail: $2000 Office: $1000 Mfg/Inventory: $2000	$4000 per month	One backup task uses tape more efficiently: six full tapes rather than fifteen half-full tapes.

Table 3.3   Consolidated Storage: Improvement over Compartmentalized Storage

	Separated Storage	**Shared Storage**	**Comment**
Costs of recovery			One backup admin can more consistently efficiently file and find the right tapes
Archive	Push older full backup tapes sent to archive	Push older full backup tapes to archive	

The simple example shown in Table 3.3, focused on recurring expenses, estimates a monthly savings of twenty-eight staff hours plus $2,000 in expenses. This analysis of recurring expenses makes for a straightforward cost justification of a SAN for consolidation.

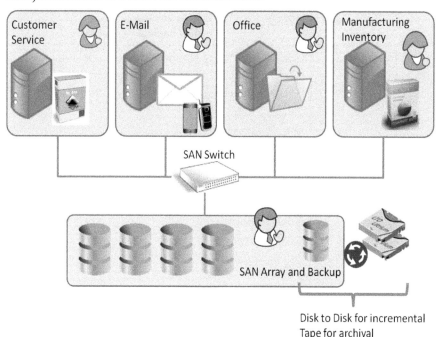

Figure 3.5   Consolidated Storage with Disk-to-Disk Backup and Tape for Archival Only; Improvement over Compartmentalized Storage

If we automate, it saves more. Figure 3.5 illustrates a big additional benefit by conducting incremental backup to disk-to-disk. This approach relegates tape solely to archive purposes and eliminates tape for incremental backup.

Using disk-to-disk backup for incremental backup eliminates the expense associated with having human beings deal with scheduling incremental backups, handling the resulting tape, and maintaining tape libraries, as well as the cost of the tape media and the tape drives for incremental. Tapes and tape drives are only for archival, and we can be selective about what we archive and when.

Consolidation provides the economies of scale that make disk-to-disk backup and tape for archival-only possible. Table 3.4 shows a before and after comparison with automated disk-to-disk.

Table 3.4   Consolidated Storage and Disk-to-Disk Backup: Improvement over Compartmentalized Storage

	Separated Storage	Shared Storage with disk-to-disk backup	Comment
Daily incremental backup	Finance : 1 hour (per day) E-mail: 1 hour Office: 1 hour Mfg/Inventory: 1 hour	Automated disk to disk	Limited time to administrate disk-to-disk
Weekly full backup	Finance: 2 hours (per week) E-mail: 3 hours Office: 3 hours Mfg/Inventory: 2 hours	Automated disk to disk	
Tape cost and tape management (per month)	Finance: $1,000 E-mail: $2,000 Office: $1,000 Mfg/Inventory: $2,000	$4,000 per month	One backup task uses tape more efficiently: six full tapes rather than fifteen half-full tapes.

Table 3.4   Consolidated Storage and Disk-to-Disk Backup: Improvement over Compartmentalized Storage

	Separated Storage	Shared Storage with disk-to-disk backup	Comment
Costs of recovery	Recover from tape	Recover from drive	On the drive, it is easier to find and easier to recover lost information.
archive	Push older full backup tapes sent to archive	Only archive tape $500 per month	

The simple example outlined in Table 3.4 indicates a monthly savings of 120 staff hours plus $6,000 expenses. It includes only recurring costs. Consolidation also serves to reclaim unused or inactive wasted space.

With compartmentalized backup, it's as if the functional administrators each live in a separate log cabin in the wilderness. They do everything themselves: raise sheep to make wool to make sweaters, render fat to make soap, cut firewood to make heat and cook. Sometimes you need to move near a town and depend on others for basic stuff like soap and yarn. It's okay to rely on others.

Implementing changes is a messy situation which is more about people than technology. Silo tape backup originates from organic growth over time. It's uncomfortable for application administrators to give that area of comfort and control to others. They prefer to be in control of supporting their own users—and their users are trained to come to those administrators. Putting the backups into the hands of someone else is not comfortable. The core issue is that application administrators, responsible for the smooth operations of systems for finance, or e-mail, or office apps, or manufacturing, fight fires day in and day out. Responding to a request to find a missing or accidentally deleted file, document, or record is a normal part of their day; a routine problem that will turn into a big problem if the request is not fulfilled, and quickly. That's the underlying reason for the control: Keeping the little problems manageable so they don't turn into big problems that may be outside their ability to resolve. Reputations are on the line.

The advisable method to deal with this perceived risk is an implementation plan that runs backup systems the old compartmentalized way and the consolidated way, in parallel. After several successful recoveries, the old compartmentalized backups will quickly be phased out and disappear. And the functional administrators can focus on improving applications and service, rather than spending time, effort, and limited money on the backup treadmill.

3.3   Hot Data, Cool Data, and Consolidation, a Single-Tiered Systems Approach

The key concept of this section is a theme you'll hear throughout this book: *All data is NOT hot data.*

Money, power, and data center capacity can be saved by moving that cooler data off the performance-optimized drives and onto capacity-optimized drives.

Single-tiering refers to the practice of having a single pool of high-performance storage systems, usually on high performance (15K rpm) drives. All data is put on these drives. When data gets old, it's eventually retired to tape. Back in the day, that worked well; incoming data arrived at a modest rate, and there was an adequate time window to allow tape backups to run against unchanging data. Increasingly, this approach is impractical: Data arrival rates are increasing, the amounts of data to backup or archive are alarmingly large, and there are no backup windows, no periods of time where the data is unchanging and backups can be performed against an unchanging dataset and without creating an I/O load that will lead to significant performance drops.

During the IT data center's day-to-day firefights, it's easy to let the urgent shout down the important. The path of least resistance is to let that single-tier data grow, add more 10K drives, add shelves, add controllers. The problem is that the stale data is taking up valuable space on fast (small) drives, occupying rack-space, occupying floor-space, consuming power, and imposing a load on data center air conditioning. This is the central problem with single-tier storage: without migration in some form, data will grow, data will get stale, data has nowhere to go (tape archival is becoming increasingly inconvenient, impractical, and expensive). Sooner or later, you are at risk of outgrowing your data center, and that's an expensive scenario.

So, when you've got lots of data coming in, no good way to make data go away . . . you have a case of data constipation.

Back in the day, data growth was manageable. Databases were small, expansion was modest; you dealt with growth by adding more drives. E-mail was all text, and not all people had e-mail accounts; again, you dealt with growth by just adding more drives.

If you are reading this book, you know firsthand that in today's world, data growth is accelerating. Throwing more disk drives (even the high-capacity disk drives) at the problem is not workable in the long run.

Increasingly, there are solutions to relieve this problem:

- Static tiering
- Dynamic (or auto) tiering
- Improvements to backup-archival systems

Static tiering refers to the practice of manually locating cooler data on bigger, slower, less expensive storage.

The most important advantage to storage tiering making room on the performance systems for new, hot data is that it means getting cooler data off the small, expensive, power-hungry drives and onto bigger, cheaper, and more power-thrifty drives. Otherwise, it's really about managing cool data: tending the garden to make room (migrate and cleanup to create available capacity) on performance storage by clearing off the cool data.

Storage tiering, information lifecycle management (ILM), and hierarchical storage management (HSM) are (or have been) hot topics in the industry. The general idea of ILM and HSM is to solve an expensive business problem related to cost of storage and data aging. When data is new, it's accessed frequently, and therefore it has a place on the high-performance storage tiers. Once data ages, it's accessed less frequently, but often that "long tail" of stale data stays on the fast (expensive) storage.

As Figure 3.6 illustrates, "time is money." There are certain applications where time literally is money . . . if the application is slow, it gets in the way of executing the main business and directly effects company earnings. Examples include point-of-sale checkout, reservations, banking transactions, stock trades. Performance and reliability are the main events.

And there are applications where the performance just needs to be "good enough," and reliability is the main event. In Figure 3.6, we identify the *finance* application as "Time is Money" important; the others—e-mail, office, manufacturing/inventory—are not. Calling these *critical* and *noncritical* is not appropriate. If e-mail goes down, it's equivalent to having the phone service go down. Having e-mail that runs slowly, but still runs, is inconvenient but will not result in significant business impact. For convenience, let's refer to these categories as Tier 1 (time is money) and Tier 2.

This model points out the obvious but expensive problem: Silo storage leads us down a path of overspending for storage. We keep too much cool and inactive data on expensive hardware, and we keep too much spinning

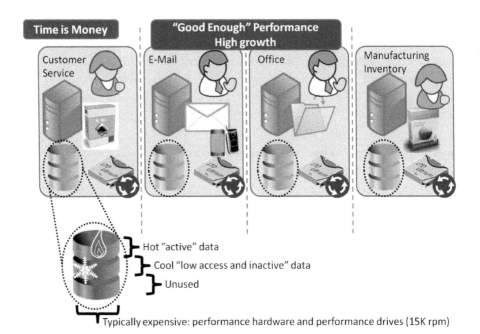

Time is Money

"Good Enough" Performance
High growth

Customer
Service

E-Mail

Office

Manufacturing
Inventory

Hot "active" data

Cool "low access and inactive" data

Unused

Typically expensive: performance hardware and performance drives (15K rpm)

Figure 3.6   Silo Applications with Mix of Hot (Active) Data, Cool (Inactive) Data,
and Unused Space

spare capacity "just in case". Just in case is expensive and adds up fast when multiplied over several functional areas.

Inhibiting change is the fact that each of these functional areas (separately) is not in a position to address migrating cool data to cost-efficient storage, and spare/unused capacity will be a higher percentage of the smaller functional approach to storage. Consolidation of storage eliminates that inhibitor to change. Consolidation of storage creates the opportunity to add cost-effective tiers for cooler data, as well as to retain a lower chunk of spare and unused storage "just in case." However, multiple groups are in a position to work together and consolidate, thus saving major money for the company.

Worth noting is the not-so-obvious by-product: the critical "time is money" application is bogged down by cooler data. Dragging around cooler data has the effect of slowing performance, because seeking data in larger datasets take longer, backing up data impacts performance, and backing up larger datasets takes more time and more tape (and is accordingly slower to restore). The remedy is getting the cooler data onto a different array. And there is a way to migrate that cooler data without high risk.

3.4   Consolidation for Noncritical (Tier 2) Applications

Our consolidation stepping-stone project (see Figure 3.7) consolidates storage for several not-so-critical (Tier 2) applications. Consolidation will serve to relieve costs of backup and storage administration. Consolidation will also serve to reduce consumption of floor space, power, and A/C in the data center (or computer room). In this plan, we are intentionally leaving the "time is money" application for last.

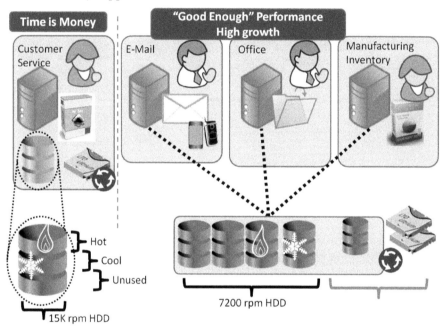

Figure 3.7   Staging Consolidated Storage for Noncritical Applications, in Preparation to Help the Critical Application

In this phase, we don't directly transition the critical "time is money" customer service application. This staged approach, focusing on noncritical applications, gives the entire storage system and its supporting processes the ability to demonstrate uptime, recovery, performance, ability to expand capacity (also known as provisioning). And if for some reason the storage system or supporting processes are not living up to expectations, address the issue and move on to the next stage to help the "time is money" customer service system by addressing the data constipation problem in noncritical, usually high-growth situations.

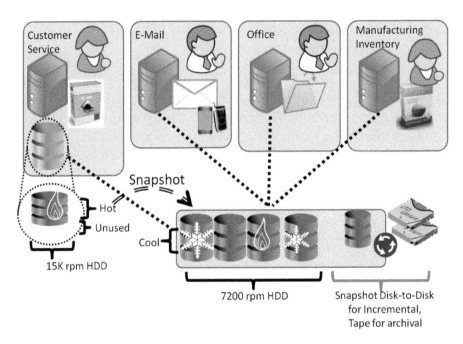

Figure 3.8   Consolidated Storage Maintaining Separate High Performance Storage, Making Use of Shared Array for Snapshots and Offload Cool Data (Help the Critical Application)

The next step is to offload the mission-critical application without messing with a full transition.

Notice, in Figure 3.8, that the mission-critical application's cool data is moved to the shared storage array. This serves to improve the overall performance of the critical application by lessening the amount of data to seek through. Taking frequent snapshots of smaller datasets, rather than making incremental tape backups of bigger datasets, does many good things: It improves the frequency of the snapshot, shorter-time windows to capture changes, and provides quicker time-to-respond to user requests for recovery. Increasing automation reduces the workload of application analysts, allowing them to do more gainful work. And this creates a situation where data can be migrated offsite and to archival storage for really complete data protection.

3.5   More Silo System Avoidance

IT Silo—there's a phrase with negative associations: lack of economy, lack of scalability, lack of interoperability/integration with other applications. related required ongoing human experts to keep operational, dedicated resources for backup and restore, usually costly tape-based backup and restore, often less-than-reliable restore, RPO, RTO.

The root cause of silo'd IT systems is typically that a business unit or functional department needed some capability and was unsuccessful in engaging IT to take care of the system. Perhaps the department was unsuccessful in getting IT to execute, perhaps the department did not attempt try to engage IT but instead assumed it was simpler/cheaper/faster to fly below the radar and do the system without involvement from IT (I've done this myself, personally). Once the basic system is up, populated, and running, the hidden expenses surface: training new users, answering support calls, running backups, and updating/scaling the software and hardware.

3.5.1   Corrective Action for Situations Where Silos Are Not Yet Deployed

You can take corrective action for situations where silos have yet to be deployed. Have IT and the business unit collaborate, and draw out a roadmap (think stepping stones).

- On paper, capture the core system functionality and general idea of the information.
- Define today's end users (both information creators and information consumers). Often the system is focused on creators, and additional focus on information consumers will provide clarity on integration with other IT systems. Estimate users, both creators and consumers, now and in the future. Just guess at annual growth; a rough estimate will suffice early in the process.
- Define infrastructure: How much storage is needed today? Estimate data growth to determine storage needed for tomorrow. Just guess at annual growth, a rough estimate will suffice early in the process. Estimate data retention: How long is the data to be retained on primary storage (or secondary storage)? What happens to aging data?
- Define data protection: How often is the data to be backed up? An incremental backup each 24 hours? A full backup each week? When can the data be accessed to allow a backup during a time when no files or records are being edited? Is there a database that links to another database, creating a need for consistency groups?
- Define structured access and search: How do users find information? Is there a need for indexing and search?

It's a lot to bite off, isn't it? No wonder that it takes IT more time to get all this in place than most business units have patience.

No wonder that it gives business units a headache to even try to think about all this themselves. As a result, they don't; they just concentrate on Job One—getting the system up, populated, and running—and worry about all those other details later. Silos.

The cure for both parties (IT and the business unit) is to generate a roadmap (a series of stepping stones) to take care of the entire project. A stepping-stone approach allows focus and a short timeline for getting the system up, populated, and running. It also deals with all that other yucky stuff—backups, recovery, consistency groups, data growth, data retirement/ archival, integration with other applications.

3.5.2   Corrective Action for Situations Where the Silos are Already in Place

The process for situations where the silos are already in place is much the same as the process outlined for situations where silos are not yet deployed. First, take a look at the existing application, existing data, existing users, and so forth.

Next, recognize that this costs the business in some form or fashion. Their own people do the backups, deal with data integration, deal with growth, and have to think about software updates and hardware expansion. Put together an estimate of those costs as performed by the business units. Compare to a comparable estimate if the job were done by IT. It's highly likely that your IT team can outperform and will cost less than the business unit estimate we just mentioned. (That's why IT departments exist in the first place.) If the estimates do not fall in your favor, peel the onion and find

Table 3.5   Template for Estimating Silo Applications

Task	Scenario 1 (BU Implementation)	Scenario 2 (IT Implementation)
Application End Users Information Creators Information Consumers	Simple example: 2 servers	2 servers, 1 shared storage array

Table 3.5   Template for Estimating Silo Applications (continued)

Task	Scenario 1 (BU Implementation)	Scenario 2 (IT Implementation)
Storage Infrastructure Today Total Usable Capacity What Tier	Server 1: 20 HDD, 300 G each 6 TB raw, 5 TB usable, 3 TB used Server 2: 20 HDD, 300G each 6 TB raw, 5 TB usable, 3 TB used	Assuming storage array has same (300 G HDD). 40 HDDs, 12 TB raw, 10 TB usable, 6 TB used (leaving 4 TB capacity for growth Going to updated 600 G HDD 20 HDDs, 12 TB raw, 10 usable, 6 TB used (leaving 4 TB capacity for growth)
Storage Infrastructure Tomorrow Data Arrival Rate Data Retention What Happens to Aging Data	Data growth (assuming two years' data is kept online) Server 1: 30% per year ■ After year 1: 5 TB usable, 4 TB used (buy HW) ■ Year 2: 7 TB usable, 5 TB used (buy HW) ■ Year 3: 7 TB usable, 6.5 TB used (buy HW) ■ Buy more hardware when we reach 4 TB in 15 months, and again every year Server 2: 15% per year ■ Year 1: 5 TB usable, 3.5 TB used ■ Year 2: 5 TB usable, 4 TB Used (buy HW) ■ Year 3: 7 TB usable, 4.7 TB used ■ Buy more hardware when we reach 4 TB in 30 months, and again every 2 years	Arrival rate 22% (average of 15% and 30%) and online retention of 2 years Array 1: 22% per year, used, in 24 months, ■ Year 1: 10 TB usable, 7.3 TB used ■ Year 2: 10 TB usable, 8.9 TB used (buy HW) ■ Year 3: 14 TB usable, 11 TB used Consolidated storage can run with a lower total percentage of spare capacity. buy more hardware when we reach 80–90% utilization

Table 3.5   Template for Estimating Silo Applications (continued)

Task	Scenario 1 (BU Implementation)	Scenario 2 (IT Implementation)
	These predictions assume that aging data stays on servers for 2 years. The key cost drivers are data growth rates, how long data stays online, burdened cost per GB, cost to backup (cost analysis is covered in an upcoming chapter). Right now we are concentrating on consolidation; we'll get to tiering shortly.	
System Maintenance and Expansion Software Updates Storage Hardware Updates	More frequent service events add drives; expansion volumes on multiple separate systems (managed by separate departments) costs more time and money, requires training, and sometimes requires troubleshooting when things go wrong. Higher administrative costs of doing lots of little separate approvals, purchases, and installs.	Consolidated storage requires fewer service events, performed by better-trained individuals. The administrative costs are lower, due to fewer approvals, purchases, and installs. Better planned and executed service events and expansions.
CAPEX Storage Hardware Cost Optimal Equipment/ $$? Space in Data Center	Lots of small capital expenses that add up to big capital expenses, starting with over provisioning and high risk of under-buying or over-buying.	Consolidated storage, less over-provisioning Opportunity to do tiered storage.

Table 3.5   Template for Estimating Silo Applications (continued)

Task	Scenario 1 (BU Implementation)	Scenario 2 (IT Implementation)
OPEX People to Support Hardware People to Support Storage Software Optimal People/$$ Facilities: Energy, AC, Floorspace	Expenses associated with lots and lots of backups Questions about technical support: ▪ Who provides 24×7 technical support? ▪ Who fixes things when they break? ▪ Who upgrades the hardware, software and firmware?	Consolidated backup is more efficient and more reliable 24×7 support is possible and affordable Upgrades, and expansions to hardware, software, and firmware can be conducted by highly skilled people (not BU people with less IT training/experience).
Integration with Other Systems Data Integration IT Expenses Data Integration Business Expenses	What application data integrates to what other applications? How is data integration being done today? What are the IT costs? What is the business impact of nonintegrated data?	With consolidated storage, there is some possibility for integrated applications (multiple servers access the same data).

out about failures, cost of failures, and costs of manual data exchange relating to lack of integration.

Once you're got the side-by-side estimates together (an example is shown in Table 3.5), it's straightforward for the business unit to turn over the application and hardware to IT, and to allocate budget to IT.

3.6   Consolidation Conclusion

The benefits of migration and consolidation are many. We'll offer techniques to quantify the benefits in the project section. Benefits include:

- OpX: Getting onto fewer servers and fewer storage arrays, lowering costs to support and administrate
- CapX: Avoiding outgrowing the existing data center
- OpX: Lowering energy consumption
- OpX: Improving system performance and reliability
- OpX: Lowering costs of ongoing support
- OpX: Avoiding downtime with aging hardware

But migration has typically been problematic.

The root cause is often because, when systems are initially deployed, system administrators pound on the configuration until the application starts to run. Frequently, the admins fail to document precisely what configuration changes were done to coax the application to work. Once the application is running, the "if it ain't broke, I'm not fixing it" thinking kicks in. Fast-forward two or three years—it's time to migrate the application storage. Oh gee, we get to come in on the weekend, take the application down, migrate to new hardware and hope we can get the darn thing running again . . . lost in the wilderness without a map or compass.

Not surprisingly, this is more about people and processes than about technology. The recommended techniques and processes are:

- *Keep a configuration log*: The log should be a digital lab notebook for all IT supported systems. Capture a written map of the configuration—you'll definitely need it in a year or two.
- *Plan*: Do your prep work prior to taking the system down. Don't let day-to-day urgent stuff get in the way of the important migration planning and execution.
- *Practice*: As much as possible, dry-run the new system prior to imposing any risk to operations.
- *Manage risk*: Make a list of all the bad things that can go wrong, add things you can do to mitigate or avoid risk, and review the list with the team.
- *Perform methodical troubleshooting*: Change one thing at a time, make sure that the change behaves as intended, then proceed to the next change.

Migration inevitably happens. Hardware ages, business requirements change, applications expand, and people come and go. In most IT departments, migration techniques and processes are not business-as-usual. If your migration capability is starting from scratch, pick a low-risk migration project from server direct attached storage to a storage array. Plan out a desired outcome: one set of configuration logs, one successful migration with the supporting best known methods (BKM). Build on that experience for the next migration.

Chapter 4

Service Level Overview

Why do service levels? This is more than just an academic exercise, right?

The short answer is that our task is to avoid overspending while delivering services to meet/exceed business needs—so YES, service levels are more than just an academic exercise! Using service levels will improve what you spend and what you get in return.

The longer answer is that Tier 1 service levels cost significantly more than those for Tier 2 or Tier 3. Reducing the amount of data stored on Tier 1 will save the company money (back to that fiscal responsibility thing).

The first step is to establish service levels with price tags. The second step is to improve processes to minimize the amount of data stored on the higher service level storage.

Otherwise stated, we save big money when data can be pushed off Service Level 1 and onto Service Level 2, while still delivering services to meet/exceed business needs.

Let's disassemble a big messy problem into smaller components and manage risk:

- *How do we establish service levels?*
- *How do we enforce service levels?* Bill-back, mock-bill-back, know about data and application classification
- *How do we confirm we're delivering to BU needs and reduce complaints?* Search/pointers, backup/recover

The benefits of tiering are many, and we offer techniques to quantify the benefits in the project section. Benefits include:

- OpX: More data is stored on less hardware. Getting cool, less-valuable data off expensive Tier 1 performance-optimized storage and onto Tier 2 or 3 capacity-optimized storage lowers the costs required for support and administration.

- CapX: Having more data on less hardware reduces risk of outgrowing the existing data center.
- OpX: Having more data on less hardware lowers the total cost of hardware and software maintenance and support contracts.
- OpX: Having more data on less hardware lowers energy consumption.
- OpX: Having more data on Tier 2 or 3 improves the performance of Tier 1 performance-optimized storage (less I/O to compete with).
- OpX: A tiered approach lowers the costs of backup. Hot data must be backed up and/or replicated frequently. Backing up less data reduces costs.

4.1 Service Level Agreements (SLAs)

In some circles, the term *SLA* carries negative baggage. It's either too wimpy or it's unrealistic. Or real life happens and SLAs are forgotten. We will quickly get past that and recognize that the business is almost always spending too much on IT and getting too little in return. There *must* be reasonable expectations set in writing, some standard to compare the spending to the benefit, some standard to manage to. Every business measures what's earned and what's spent; IT is no different. Every business knows something about what their customers need. Again, IT is no exception.

In the Service Level Conceptual diagram in Figure 4.1, capacity and growth for Service Levels 1, 2, and 3 are represented by relative diameter. Cost, performance, and uptime requirements are represented on horizontal and vertical axis.

The diagram's purpose is to help us separately recognize where the cost, performance, and uptime requirements are (Service Level 1) and separate needs for high capacity and high growth (Service Levels 2 and 3). The fiscally responsible approach is to aggressively push data out of Service Level 1 storage into Service Level 2 storage, and also to aggressively push data out of Service Level 2 into Service Level 3 storage.

The five components of storage SLAs are:

1. *Uptime*—storage availability, employing some mix of RAID, mirroring, replication, failover, and updating/upgrading systems and processes

2. *Recovery (RPO and RTO)*—the time since last snapshot (recovery point objective) and the time required to respond to a recovery request (recovery time objective)

3. *Provisioning*—bringing additional capacity into service

4. *Performance*—the quality of service in throughput (MB/S) and in latency (ms delay)

5. *Cost*—the department bill-back per month

Our task is to create two or three storage service levels with the appropriate metrics, the appropriate price tag, and (the tough part) the right applications on the right service levels.

Basically, if we stop treating Tier 2 data like Tier 1 data, your data center efficiencies improve—and so does your cost structure.

4.2   Reviewing SLAs with Business Unit Customers

Table 4.1 is an example brief you can review with your business unit customers to communicate annual per TB costs, the associated protection (and risk), and the service levels you will deliver accordingly.

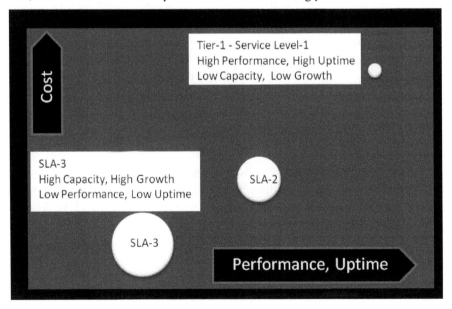

Figure 4.1   Service Level Conceptual Diagram

Table 4.1   Basic Service Level Agreement (SLA) Structure

Service Level Agreement to Present to your Business Unit Customers		
Service Level 1 Typical applications: order entry, banking, reservations, e-commerce	Uptime: 99.999% (5-nines, 8 minutes downtime per year) Recovery: ■ RPO snapshot window no longer than 30 minutes ■ RPO restore within 30 minutes of request (trouble ticket) Performance: At least 20 MB/s and not more than 60 ms latency Provisioning: Bring on additional storage on-line within five working days of request	Cost: $$$$ per TB per year
Service Level 2 Typical applications: inventory, purchasing, e-mail, sharepoint	Uptime: 99.99% (4-nines, 80 minutes downtime per year) Recovery: ■ RPO backup window no greater than 12 hours ■ RPO restore within 60 minutes of request (trouble ticket) Performance: At least 10 MB/s and not more than 2000 ms latency Provisioning: Bring additional storage online within two working days of request	Cost: $$ per TB per year

4.3 Delivering on SLA Commitments

Not all data has equal levels of business relevance: Key business data, such as sales orders and accounts receivable, is far more important (and far more consequential if lost) than some casual PowerPoint or e-mail. And not all protection schemes are of equal expense. Costs vary considerably between Tier 1, Tier 2, and Tier 3 levels of protection.

Perhaps the key point of this entire book is to spend money where it is warranted for protection, recoverability, and performance—and to avoid wasting money by spending on storage capabilities not warranted by the data being stored. Some data is super important, but most is not.

Table 4.2   Basic Service Level Agreement (SLA) Implementation Plan, Optimize Expenses

Achieving Service Levels: Implementation Plan, Optimizing Expense		
SLA Level 1 Typical applications: order entry, banking, reservations, e-commerce	Performance-optimized 600 G 15K drives or SSDs. RAID level 1+0—Stripe plus mirror (mirror drive failures recover faster) Local array-to-array mirroring or local snapshots (every 30 minutes) or remote replication Performance—At least 20 MB/s and not more than 60 ms latency. Achieved with fastest FC, system cache, server memory and load isolation (avoid overloading the storage and SAN with extraneous traffic load) Provisioning—Once we're isolated this top performance/uptime tier. Analyze the growth, should be small compare to the other tiers. Pre-planning for capacity	Cost: $$$$ per TB

Table 4.2   Basic Service Level Agreement (SLA) Implementation Plan, Optimize Expenses (continued)

SLA Level 2 Typical applications: inventory, purchasing, e-mail, Share-Point, LotusLive	expansion should be significantly simpler, purchasing hardware should be significantly simpler. Very large capacity (2TB) enterprise SATA drives 0+1 stripe plus mirror RAID level 1+0—Stripe plus mirror (mirror drive failures recover faster) Local array-to-array mirroring or local snapshots (every 24 hours); complete image backup every 7 days Performance—At least 2 MB/s and not more than 2000 ms latency. Economically achieved with lower performance arrays, iSCSI rather than FC. Provisioning—Once we're isolated this second performance/uptime tier. Growth is expected to be higher, but pre-planning for capacity expansion should be significantly simpler, purchasing hardware should be significantly simpler. Sets up a situation where Tier 2 can be moved to cloud-managed hosting in the future.	Cost: $$ per TB

To manage Service Level Agreements with your customer, demonstrate your ability to deliver by preparing for these questions:

- Can you deliver the SLA-specified uptime?

- Show that you deliver the uptime prescribed by the SLA. If your SLA for a specific service is 4-nines, then measure every outage, measure the duration of every outage, and be able to demonstrate the history and trend is less than eighty minutes per year.
- Can you deliver the SLA-specified recovery?
  - Show that the SLA for recovery can be met. Test-run the recovery, show your customers that the SLA is within your capabilities. Use trouble tickets to capture recovery requests, and time-stamp both the ticket receipt and its resolution. The Recovery Point Objective (RPO) defines the longest period of time since last backup or snapshot. The Recovery Time Objective (RTO) measures how long it will be from the time a request to recover data is logged until the data is again available to the user.
- Can you respond to provisioning requests as specified by SLA?
  - Show that you can respond to user requests for more capacity and deliver within prescribed time limits. Typically, capacity for 3-nines can be provisioned in hours; 5-nines storage, which is presumably remotely mirrored, can be brought online in days. Use trouble tickets to log requests for provisioning, and time-stamp both the ticket receipt and its resolution.

By establishing SLAs for business units or for CFOs, this approach associates the costs of data storage to the classes of data storage.

Chapter 5

Uptime, Reliability, and SLAs

The fundamental storage building block is the disk drive, so we start with drive reliability.

Disk drive spec sheets show two reliability-related specs: Mean Time Between Failure (MTBF) and Annual Failure Rate (AFR).

MTBF is a statistical measure of preproduction drive families. MTBF is defined as the mean time between failure of a group of disk drives. In English, that's the statistical likelihood of how long it will take for half (50%) of a group of drives to fail. MTBF is established before drives go into high-volume production, using a process called the Reliability Demonstration Test (RDT). RDT involves putting 1000+ drives into test chambers, running them hard, 24×7, one hundred percent I/O, at elevated temperature, for about six weeks. Inevitably, some drives in these test chambers fail. From these failures, the MTBF is statistically calculated, all before a single drive is shipped to the field. MTBF is a useful litmus test to determine whether a new drive is reliable enough to ship, but it's preproduction use, not real-world. Spec sheets show values, typically between 1 million to 1.5 million hours. It's meaningful for disk drive manufacturers or a big system OEM who will buy drives in large quantity, but for an IT department, it's not so meaningful—1.5 million hours is 170 years.

So ignore MTBF. Just be sure to buy enterprise drives; all enterprise-class drives have about the same 1.2 million hours for MTBF anyway.

The Annual Failure Rate is more interesting. AFR is defined as the percentage of the installed base of drives that fail in a given year. Drive vendors publish a target AFR on their data sheets. The actual AFR calculation counts drives returned and found to be failed over the course of a year, compared to the installed base. The typical value is a 0.7 percent annual failure rate.

Sure, these tests involve some estimations and inaccuracies. But the 0.7 percent annual failure rate gives us something real-world to examine. In rough numbers, if you have 1000 drives installed, you can expect 7 of them to fail within a year.

There are things you can do to improve that 0.7 percent annual failure rate in your shop:

- Keep drives cool, below 40°C (104°F) ambient temperature
- Turn drives off when not in use (applies to branch office and capacity-optimized)

No surprise, this makes a pretty strong case for system design that can compensate for drive failures. So let's explore the various approaches.

A wealth of technical information is available about RAID levels, so rather than repeating all that, we'll focus on the business side of RAID instead.

5.1   SLA Uptime: RAID Levels

RAID—Redundant Array of Inexpensive/Independent Disks—is protection against disk drive failure.

Described in business terms: RAID protects against HDD failure, but RAID is not backup. Backup is most often used to recover from accidental deletion, operator error, corruption, or virus. RAID does not protect against any of these things.

Nested RAID terminology—the basic, commonly used RAID levels—is outlined and described in Table 5.1. There are additional terms for nested RAID levels. RAID-10 (also known as RAID-1+0) is the practice of establishing multiple drives into a single large striped RAID volume, making a carbon copy, then mirroring those two striped volumes for redundancy. RAID-51 (also known as RAID-5+1) is similar: Create a RAID-5 volume, create a carbon copy RAID-5 volume, then mirror these two together.

This approach pertains to Service Levels, as we will compare typical baseline single-tier RAID-6 to a Tier 1 plus Tier 2 with several different RAID approaches.

5.2   SLA and Point in Time Copy: Avoiding the Backup Window Problem

Tape is a data protection staple in the IT world, with good reason: Tape does stuff that RAID cannot. RAID does a great job of protecting against drive failure, but it does not protect against accidental deletion. If a user

Table 5.1 RAID Levels, Pros, Cons, and SLAs

	How it Works	**Advantages**	**Disadvantages**
Striping: RAID-0 and Mirroring: RAID-1	Striping (aka RAID-0) makes multiple disks appear as a single disk to the system. Mirroring (aka RAID-1) writes twice, so if one drive fails, the data is available on another mirrored drive	Best reliability. Mirroring is simple, imposes no additional CPU load and no performance penalty. If a drive fails, the mirrored drive immediately takes over. When the failed drive is replaced, the new drive automatically remirrors in the background. Near-zero performance impact in the case of a failure or rebuild. Expanding volume is straightforward: add devices to the stripe.	Expensive. The cost of mirrored storage is the highest, as the usable capacity is 50% of the raw capacity. Mirroring consumes the most disk space and the most drive slots. In the unlikely event that a drive and its mirror pair fail simultaneously, data is lost. RAID does not protect against accidental deletion, corruption, or viruses. Snapshots or backups are the smart way to protect against these things (for all RAID levels)
Parity: RAID-5	RAID-5 uses a mathematical parity calculation to recreate a volume in the case of a single drive failure.	Most economical. Usable capacity varies based on how many drives are in the RAID volume (n–1), but usable capacity is typically around 90% of raw capacity.	Lowest level of protection. RAID-5 can recover from a single drive failure, but if a second drive fails, all data on the volume is lost.

Table 5.1   RAID Levels, Pros, Cons, and SLAs (continued)

	How it Works	Advantages	Disadvantages
			There is a significant performance penalty after a drive is failed. The system performs additional reads/writes/calculations to respond to I/O requests. There is a significant performance penalty when rebuilding. Once the failed drive is replaced, the system performs additional reads/writes/calculations to rebuild data on the new drive
Double Parity: RAID-6	RAID-6 is much like RAID-5, but can tolerate two simultaneous drive failures. Uses a mathematical parity calculation to recreate a volume in the case of a one- or two-drive failure.	Good compromise. RAID-6 offers economy and protection against drive failure. Usable capacity varies based on how many drives are in the RAID volume (n–2), but usable capacity is typically around 80% of raw capacity.	Mid-level protection. RAID-6 can recover from one or two drive failures, but if a third drive fails, all data on the volume is lost. There is a significant performance penalty after a drive fails. The system performs additional reads/writes/calculations to respond to I/O requests.

Table 5.1 RAID Levels, Pros, Cons, and SLAs (continued)

	How it Works	Advantages	Disadvantages
			There is a significant performance penalty when rebuilding. Once the failed drive is replaced, the system performs additional reads/writes/calculations to rebuild data on the new drive

deletes a file or folder or record, the RAID array will work as designed and delete the data. Tape (or a similar point-in-time copy) is required to recover an accidental deletion. And replication, despite all its advantages, will replicate the deletion—so replication cannot fix all maladies. Similarly, if there is a virus, RAID will not protect against that; a point-in-time copy is the only way to recover a previous version of the system. And lastly, if there is a physical disaster—fire, or a flood that could be anything from hurricane damage to a broken pipe or an overflowing sink from a floor above—a point-in-time copy stored offsite is the means to recover the data.

In short, backup or similar point-in-time copy is required.

The problem is that backups create I/O, and bigger datasets increase the amount of time that the I/O load competes for resources in a 24×7 workday. As data grows, the backup task is getting bigger and bigger, and the backup window (best time of day) to conduct backup is getting smaller and smaller. Tiering for hot and cold data provides some relief. If cool data is not accessed or written often, then logically it requires less frequent backups. Any approach that reduces backup load saves the company time and money and frees compute and storage resources for real work.

A key advantage of the hot data, cool data approach is the choice the approach offers in context of backups and backup windows. Very important applications require point-in-time incremental backups or snapshots frequently. Less important applications with lower data churn, lower risk, and lower impact if data is lost can accept less-frequent point-in-time incremental backups or snapshots.

SLAs should include backup service level commitments:

- *SLA for Tier 1* should include aggressive RPO/RTO and a fairly high price-tag.
- *SLA for Tier 2* should offer a less aggressive RPO/RTO (after all, it is less important data by definition) and a modest price tag.

Reducing the total backup load by reducing repetitive backups of cooler Tier 2 data serves to reduce the total time, effort, tape, library, I/O resource usage, and backup window.

5.3   SLA Uptime: Failover

Failover is a Tier 1 SLA capability.

Information Week, in February 2010, stated that " just 17% do not have a BC/DR plan." The quote is true, but it misses the key concept of selectivity in applying Business Continuity/Disaster Recovery, or BC/DR, to specific data, not to all data. The tiered SLA approach helps us selectively apply the tools of local failover and remote replication and failover selectively and economically.

A remote replication Pilot program creates redundant system initial setup, approached as stepping stones:

1. *Staged Test/Deployment*:

    a.   Offline Test: nonredundant, local replication, remote replication

    b.   Online Pilot (live data, but not critical data): nonredundant, local replication, remote replication

    c.   Offline key application

    d.   Live key application

2. *Offline test.* Establish a test system, a real application—but not a critical application—that can be tested. Keep a copy of production live data but not critical data (you'll be practicing failover on this system).

3. *Offline test with local replication.* Create a carbon-copy local storage system identical to the offline test system. Establish local replication to another storage array in the same location. Local replication is most often a carbon copy of the primary storage system hardware, drives, and RAID configuration. Test to confirm the data replication is working (compare the size of primary

data to the size of secondary data; spot-check with an artificial change to the primary data and confirm the change is made to the secondary data). Configure servers to failover from primary pilot data to secondary pilot data. Conduct a mock failover to confirm that server failover will function properly if there is a failure of the primary array. Take that opportunity to confirm failover time for the pilot system and calculate failover time for larger production system.

4. *Offline test with remote replication.* Server failover depends on a domain name system (DNS) capable of redirecting client IP traffic from the failed server to the failover target destination. Virtual private LAN services (VPLS) are a commonly applied approach to redirect IP traffic. VPLS allows clean reassignment of IP addresses within a virtual private LAN. VPLS is mesh compatible and can work with the network's own routing system, routing around many network problems via alternate paths. Mobile IP is a lower cost alternatives for VPLS, but mobile IP is a little more complicated. Once in place, exercise a test plan to simulate all single points of failure: pull data cables, pull power supplies. Exercise failover and failback.

5. *Online live data trial with remote replication.* In this phase, the objective is to prove the SLA can be delivered on a key application. Be prepared to run the online data trial for a period of months, perhaps as long as a year. Collect and review key metrics: uptime, performance quality of service, and simulated events.

6. *Offline key application.* Welcome to the big dance. Grab a copy of production data, deploy on a local system, then deploy the carbon-copy local system, configure the server failover, deploy remote replication, reconfigure and test server failover. Successful deployment of the offline system sets the stage for the deployment of the live key application.

Key points include:
- *Local replication storage* in one location is much easier to troubleshoot.
- *An offline test of remote replication* works out the problems with wide area replication as well as people and processes, and establishes whom to call if/when things go wrong. Have a training and system book at both sites.

Use SLAs to control the expense to build and maintain. In the interest of fiscal responsibility, it's best to drive every application possible onto lower-tier SLAs. Remote replication and failover is expensive, so use it only when warranted. Local replication is a viable (and affordable) alternative. Another cost-avoiding alternative to deliver the SLA is to replicate and failover to a managed hosting service provider.

5.4   SLA Cost and Billing

It's critical that some price tag be placed on costs of storage to:

- Establish a baseline of expense, to demonstrate improvement over time
- Provide a basis for making fact-based decisions regarding outsourcing and managed hosting
- Instill a discipline of avoiding overspending and curb costly storage consumption
- Specifically curb storage consumption in the expensive tiers (remember the old rule: that which gets measured, gets done).

Storage bill-back is based on the sum of hardware and software initial purchase; the cost of hardware and software maintenance fees; the cost of people to manage, maintain, and support; and the cost to replicate-snapshot-backup-archive.

We're embarking on a total cost of ownership comparison between single tier and multi-tier (static).

Static tiering means we pick a storage tier and assign an application, and the application and data stay on that storage tier until archived.

- Tier 1: procurement and inventory and reservations
- Tier 2: e-mail
- Tier 3: shared folders

In upcoming chapters, we will cover an advanced variation of storage tiering: *tiered dynamic storage*, meaning the data moves from tier to tier. For example, aging Tier 1 data moves to Tier 2. This task can be done manually or with scripts, and it sets the stage for systems where we can implement our own dynamic storage tiering, employing SSDs and capacity-optimized storage and system software to manage hot data on the SSDs and put cooler data on capacity-optimized drives. This approach sets us up for a tiered system where we manage hot data locally in our data center and the cooler aging data is pushed to storage in the cloud, where it can be searched, retrieved, protected, and eventually archived. One step at a time.

Let's proceed to the cost analysis, so we can save the company some money to save limited budget to be used for the higher-value dynamic and cloud stuff down the road.

5.5   Performance and SLAs

Establish your storage performance monitoring to look at something approximating a real-world workload. A workload is defined by the mix of reads versus writes, with the mix of sequential versus random and the mix of I/O sizes, usually 60 percent being 4KB I/O with the other 40 percent being a mix of very small and very large I/O requests. Then, monitor that storage workload over time.

Watch out for storage system benchmarks: It's usually describing a storage system with a maxed out hardware configuration, all the drive slots filled with the highest performing drives, maximum cache, maximum host connections, running a workload that is often one hundred percent read, one hundred percent small block, and one hundred percent sequential. So you're usually looking at a workload that will never be encountered, running on a system that you will never own.

Typical performance monitoring is central office–biased; in other words, most performance monitoring tools start at the central office and look outward at the remote servers. The important aspect is not performance experienced by the central office, but rather the performance experienced at the end nodes, where the users are. Any performance monitoring should have end-user agents out at the servers.

Storage performance monitoring tools can monitor lots of different things. I suggest you select some simple and meaningful metrics, enter these into the SLA, and monitor them closely.

One popular storage profiler offers the following list of metrics. I have italicized the ones I believe appropriate for SLA. I urge you not to indulge in adding ALL the metrics to the SLA, as too many metrics are unmanageable and lead to spending that may not deliver the right service.

- Total IO
- Percentage write IO
- Average read size (MB)

- Average write size (MB)
- I/O response (sec)
- MB transfers
- MB transfers/second
- MB read
- MB read/second
- MB write
- MB write/second
- Queue depth
- Read hit I/O
- Read hit I/O/second
- Write hit I/O
- Write hit I/O/second
- Service time
- Total I/O

This storage profiler tool can generate reports over time. The three highlighted metrics can be used for an SLA: I/O response (maximum latency), MB read/second, and service time. If you hit these three you will deliver acceptable service to your business unit customer. If you have problems, this tool can also create reports that indicate the busiest and least busy logical unit numbers (LUNs), this offers a way to look for busy LUNs and identify performance bottlenecks. It also offers a way to identify mostly idle LUNs that are not required to offer high performance, and put that data onto capacity optimized Tier 2 storage.

It is important to avoid getting lost in the tool or the data just for the sake of academic insights. The tool should be focused on the task of affordably delivering storage performance, spending enough so the business task can complete smoothly, delivering on the SLA, and quickly identifying and resolving problems that get in the way of delivering the SLA, all the while avoiding overspending.

Chapter 6

Storage Tiering and SLAs

Every Service Level Agreement has a price tag attached. The point of Service Level Agreements is to spend wisely: spend more on hot data and important data, spend less on cooler, staler, less important data. We'll ruin the punch line by cutting directly to the answer:

You will save money and/or improve service by replacing single-tier storage with two-tier storage; and either offer the same service levels with significantly lower total cost; or offer significantly better service levels at the same cost (as shown in Figure 6.1).

Comparison of Single-Tier versus Two-Tier Storage Total Costs

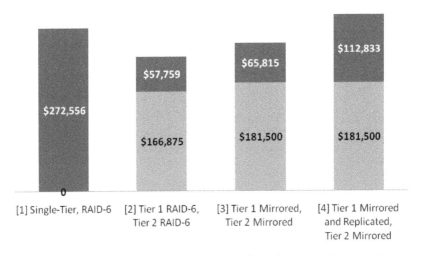

Figure 6.1   Single Tier Total Costs Compared to Alternative Two-Tier Storage Approaches (Map to SLA)

6.1   Comparing Scenarios

Our total cost analysis of single-tier versus two-tier solutions is of necessity a simplified comparison, based on a list of assumptions which may or may not apply to your specific situation. As always, your mileage may vary.

6.1.1   Scenario 1: Single-Tier Baseline

Our starting point is a baseline of a very typical 100TB single-tier storage system, built with 600GB 15K drives protected with RAID-6 and usually frequently backed up because of the presence of hot data. This is a commonplace configuration that compromises between capacity, performance, reliability/uptime, and cost. I am definitely *not* suggesting this be implemented; it is presented as a baseline for comparison to multitier. We compare this single-tier 100TB system to tiered systems with 20 percent on Tier 1 and 80 percent on Tier 2, plus room for growth.

Let's walk through the reasons why.

Table 6.1   Scenario 1: Baseline of Total Costs for 100TB Single Tier Storage Protected by RAID-6

	Scenario 1. Baseline 100TB of Single Tier Storage, Protected by RAID-6		
1	100TB—Single Tier—600G—15K—RAID-6		
2	Usable Cap (TB)		100
3	RAID level	RAID-6 overhead 80%	80%
4	Type HDD	600G 15K in RAID-6	600
5	#HDDs		208
6	HDD Price Each		$1,500
7	HDD Total Price		$312,500
8	System HW (excluding HDD)	assume $10K/tray	$180,000
9	HW maintenance (typically 18% per year)	18%	$88,650
10	Storage SW		$20,000
11	People per Year	0.5	$60,000
12	Cost of full backups per year		$20,000

Table 6.1   Scenario 1: Baseline of Total Costs for 100TB Single Tier Storage Protected by RAID-6 (continued)

13	Cost of Incremental or Snaps per year		$52,000
14	Communications for Replication		$ -
15	Added Capacity per Year		$35,000
16	Total Initial HW/SW		$512,500
17	Total Yearly Expense	assuming 4-year life	$295,125
18	Yearly Cost per TB		$2,951
19	Performance Score	600G 15K in RAID-6	4
20	Power Score		4
21	Reliability-Uptime Score	big rebuild times	4

The key assumptions for the Scenario 1 baseline are listed in Table 6.1. We all know disk drive prices and storage systems prices vary wildly, so your mileage will definitely vary. We're using the same round numbers consistently, in all scenarios, to illustrate the *relative* total costs of single-tier versus two-tier systems.

At the heart of the matter is wasteful practice of using performance-optimized (in this case 600 G 15K HDDs) for everything. We get good performance for both hot and cool data. We back up frequently—and we back up both the hot and the cool data.

6.1.2   Scenario 2: Two Tiers

In Scenario 2 (Table 6.2), we analyze Tier 1 RAID-6 and Tier 2 RAID-6. The key assumptions: Tier 1 is 20 TB of 600 G 15K RAID-6, and Tier 2 (for cool data) is 90 TB 2 TB 7200 rpm in RAID-6.

Comparing Scenario 2 to our Scenario 1 Baseline, we can see that Scenario 2 offers a considerable estimated $70,000 per year total cost saving. The big change is moving approximately 80 percent of the cooler data to capacity optimized 2TB 7200 rpm drives. The obvious advantages are significantly lower spending on hardware and hardware maintenance fees, because only the hot data is on that 20TB Tier 1 storage; the remainder of the cooler data is on the Tier 2 storage. The less obvious advantages include less rackspace (18 trays in Scenario 1, reduced to 9 trays in Scenario 2) and

Table 6.2   Scenario 2: Two-Tier, RAID-6, Same Service Level, Save Money

Scenario 2. Same Service Levels, Use 2-Tier Approach to Save Money			
1	20TB—Tier 1—600G 15K—RAID-6		
2	Usable Cap (TB)		20
3	RAID level	RAID-6 overhead 80%	80%
4	Type HDD	600 G 15K in RAID-6	600
5	#HDDs		42
6	HDD Price Each		$1,500
7	HDD Total Price		$62,500
8	System HW (excluding HDD)	assume $10K/tray	$40,000
9	HW maintenance (typically 18% per year)	18%	$18,450
10	Storage SW		$10,000
11	People per Year	0.2	$24,000
12	Cost of Full Backups per Year		$2,000
13	Cost of Incremental or Snaps per Year		$5,000
14	Communications for Replication		$ -
15	Added Capacity per Year		$5,000
16	Total Initial HW/SW		$112,500
17	Total Yearly Expense	assuming 4-year life	$64,125
18	Yearly Cost per TB		$3,206
19	Performance score	600G 15K in RAID-6	4
20	Power score		4
21	Reliability-uptime score	big rebuild times	4
1	90 TB—Tier 2—2 TB 7200—RAID-6		

Table 6.2 Scenario 2: Two-Tier, RAID-6, Same Service Level, Save Money

2	Usable Cap (TB)		90
3	RAID level	RAID-6 overhead 80%	80%
4	Type HDD	600 G 15K in RAID-6	2000
5	#HDDs		56
6	HDD Price Each		$750
7	HDD Total Price		$42,188
8	System HW (excluding HDD)	assume $10K/tray	$50,000
9	HW Maintenance (Typically 18% per Year)	18%	$16,594
10	Storage SW		$10,000
11	People per Year	0.4	$48,000
12	Cost of Full Backups per Year		$20,000
13	Cost of Incremental or Snaps per Year		$52,000
14	Communications for Replication		$ -
15	Added Capacity per Year		$15,000
16	Total Initial HW/SW		$102,188
17	Total Yearly Expense	assuming 4 year life	$160,547
18	Yearly Cost per TB		$1,784
19	Performance Score	600 G 15K in RAID6	4
20	Power Score	TB/watt	7
21	Reliability-uptime score	big rebuild times	4

less power used. The overall reliability and risk of losing data is nearly the same between Scenarios 1 and 2, as both have RAID-6 throughout. The downside is that, in the case of losing a 2TB drive, the RAID-6 rebuild can take a long, long time—sometimes more than 10 hours, depending on the amount of data actually on the drive, the performance of the storage processor, and the demands of the regular I/O load. This rebuild time can be avoided by using mirroring instead of RAID-6. And while mirroring is definitely more expensive than RAID-6, in the overall picture (Scenario 3, shown in Table 6.3) the additional annual expenses are modest (roughly 10 percent more than RAID-6) and the advantage is that when a mirrored disk fails, there is no degraded performance and the rebuild times are very short. Scenario 3 is a great example of how to improve service levels while still reducing annual expenses, in this case by roughly $50,000 per year.

6.1.3   Scenario 3: Two Tiers, Better Service Levels

Scenario 3 offers better service levels (mirroring, but not replication); this is a good balance between better service levels and annual expense.

Table 6.3   Scenario 3: Two-tier, Mirrored, Better Service Levels, Save Money

Scenario 3. Better Service Levels, Still Save Some Money		
1	20 TB—Tier 1—600 G 15K—Mirrored		
2	Usable Cap (TB)		20
3	RAID Level	RAID-1 overhead 50%	0.5
4	Type HDD	600 G 15K in RAID-6	600
5	#HDDs		74
6	HDD Price Each		$800
7	HDD Total Price		$59,529
8	System HW (excluding HDD)	assume $10K/tray	$50,000
9	HW Maintenance (Typically 18% per year)	18%	$19,667
10	Storage SW		$10,000
11	People per Year	0.2	$24,000
12	Cost of Full Backups per Year		$2,000
13	Cost of Incremental or Snaps per year		$5,000
14	Communications for Replication		$ -

Table 6.3   Scenario 3: Two-tier, Mirrored, Better Service Levels, Save Money

15	Added Capacity per Year		$5,000
16	Total Initial HW/SW		$119,259
17	Total Yearly Expense	assuming 4-year life	$65,815
18	Yearly Cost per TB		$3,291
19	Performance Score	600 G 15K mirrored	7
20	Power score	TB/watt	2
21	Reliability-uptime score	good—mirroring	6
1	90TB—Tier 2—2TB 7200—Mirrored		
2	Usable Cap (TB)		90
3	RAID Level	RAID-1 overhead 50%	50%
4	Type HDD	600 G 15K in RAID-6	2000
5	#HDDs		120
6	HDD Price Each		800
7	HDD Total Price		$96,000
8	System HW (excluding HDD)	assume $10K/tray	$80,000
9	HW Maintenance (Typically 18% per Year)	18%	$31,680
10	Storage SW		$10,000
11	People per Year	0.4	$48,000
12	Cost of Full Backups per Year		$20,000
13	Cost of Incremental or Snaps per Year		$52,000
14	Communications for Replication		$ -
15	Added Capacity per Year		$15,000
16	Total Initial HW/SW		$186,000
17	Total Yearly Expense	assuming 4-year life	$181,500

Table 6.3   Scenario 3: Two-tier, Mirrored, Better Service Levels, Save Money

18	Yearly Cost per TB		$2,017
19	Performance Score	cool data on 7200	5
20	Power Score	TB/watt	6
21	Reliability-Uptime Score	mirrored, no rebuild times	7

6.1.4   Scenario 4: Two Tiers, Significantly Better Service

The big advantage of Scenario 4 (outlined in Table 6.4) is replication of the 20TB Tier 1 data to a remote site. Scenario 4 is roughly the same annual expense as Scenario 1, but provides considerably better service levels and data protection levels. Replication has the distinct advantage of substantially replacing need for frequent incremental backups while still offering significantly better Recovery Point Objectives (RPO) and Recovery Time Objectives (RTO) over incremental backups onto disk drives or incremental backups onto tape. If there is a request to recover a file or folder, replication- or snapshot-based systems can more quickly recover the data (RTO) and within a tighter time window (RTO).

Table 6.4   Scenario 4: Two-Tier; Tier 1 is Mirrored and Replicated; Tier 2 is Mirrored; Significantly Better Service Levels at the Same Price as Single-Tiered

Scenario 4. Add Replication Best Service Levels, Same Price		
1	20 TB—Tier 1—600 G 15K—Mirrored, Replicated	
2	Usable Cap (TB)		20
3	RAID Level	Mirrored and replicated. Usable/raw = 25%	25%
4	Type HDD	600 G 15K in RAID6	600
5	#HDDs		148
6	HDD Price Each		$900
7	HDD Total Price		$133,33
8	System HW (excluding HDD)	assume $10K/tray	$110,000

Table 6.4   Scenario 4: Two-Tier; Tier 1 is Mirrored and Replicated; Tier 2 is Mirrored; Significantly Better Service Levels at the Same Price as Single-Tiered

9	HW Maintenance (Typically 18% per year)	18%	$43,800
10	Storage SW		$40,000
11	People per Year	0.2	$24,000
12	Cost of Full Backups per Year		$2,000
13	Cost of Incremental or Snaps per year		$5,000
14	Communications for Replication	assume $500 per month	$6,000
15	Added Capacity per Year		$5,000
16	Total Initial HW/SW		$283,333
17	Total Yearly Expense	assuming 4-year life	$112,833
18	Yearly Cost per TB		$5642
19	Performance Score	600G 15K mirrored	7
20	Power score	TB/watt	2
21	Reliability-uptime score	best money can buy	10
1	90 TB—Tier 2—2 TB 7200—Mirrored		
2	Usable Cap (TB)		90
3	RAID Level	RAID 1 overhead 50%	50%
4	Type HDD	600 G 10K	2000
5	#HDDs		120
6	HDD Price Each		$800
7	HDD Total Price		$96,000
8	System HW (excluding HDD)	assume $10K/tray	$80,000
9	HW Maintenance (Typically 18% per year)	18%	$31,680
10	Storage SW		$10,000

Table 6.4   Scenario 4: Two-Tier; Tier 1 is Mirrored and Replicated; Tier 2 is Mirrored; Significantly Better Service Levels at the Same Price as Single-Tiered

11	People per Year	0.4	$48,000
12	Cost of Full Backups per Year		$20,000
13	Cost of Incremental or Snaps per year		$52,000
14	Communications for Replication		$ -
15	Added Capacity per Year		$15,000
16	Total Initial HW/SW		$186,500
17	Total Yearly Expense	assuming 4-year life	$181,500
18	Yearly Cost per TB		$2,017
19	Performance Score	600 G 15K in RAID6	4
20	Power score	TB/watt	6
21	Reliability-uptime score	mirrored, no rebuild times	7

To conclude our total cost analysis of single-tier versus two-tier solutions, we note that this is a simplified comparison based on a list of assumptions which may or may not apply to your specific situation.

6.1.5   From Scenario to Reality

The improvements in spending and service levels delivered are definitely available (though we reiterate that the scenarios presented in this chapter form a simplified comparison, based on a list of assumptions which may or may not apply to your specific situation). The IT challenge is to overcome the personalities who resist change and want to stick to what they have, or the personalities who think that all data is hot data, or those who insist that every single bit be protected by quadruple redundancy and instantly available.

To these personalities, we say, "Great! If you really need it, we can deliver it. But you write the check."

All right, I realize this is not always realistic or possible, but sharing the costs and sharing the alternatives will go a long way in making shared and informed decisions involving the business unit and the storage services required to compete.

The four scenarios illustrate the approaches and relative expenses of single-tiered storage as compared to two-tiered storage. The next step is to communicate the service levels and costs to the business units and collaborate with them to classify the data and applications that belong on Tier 1 and those that belong on Tier 2. Attach a price tag, in the interest of making informed decisions.

Chapter 7

Service Level Agreements and IT Bill-Back

Based on the substantial body of available storage industry market information, it's easy to conclude that most (not all) business units are unaware of the expenses associated with storage. Single tier is the prevalent option, and because of that, rolling up actual storage costs and assigning those costs to various business units was not a gainful use of time or energy. Understandably, few IT departments captured expenses and even fewer communicated those expenses to business units. There are a few rare and exceptional IT departments who do roll up storage costs and bill-back departments. These IT groups are basically saying to the business units, "Here is the amount of storage you use, please use less of it." They offer no tools or approaches for a business unit to take substantial action to reduce storage-related expenses. "IT Bill-Back" turns into an exercise in accounting, not motivation to use less or motivation to intelligently manage expensive storage resources.

Change boils down to spending and risk. Give the business units insight into spending, accompanied by real and meaningful alternatives to reduce spending at acceptable risk, and they'll cooperate. IT departments should know the cost of the storage they consume. They should be presented with options to reduce storage-related spending.

Help business units with clear information and alternative approaches to improve. Present business units with a before-and-after picture of their storage-related spending today, compared to storage-related spending relating to tiered storage. Spending is dynamic and changes with time, so a supporting bill-back system tracks spending and (hopefully) spending reductions.

Regarding risk, it must be said that there is no such thing as a risk-free storage system. It's all about how much risk is tolerable versus the amount of money that can be applied to reduce the risk. Business units should understand associated risks if they are to cooperate. It's useful and appropriate to present business units with a before-and-after picture of risk. Give business units insight into the risk they have right now. And show the business units how tiered storage will enable them to spend on risk reduction selectively—where it matters most—and therefore spend on risk effectively and frugally.

7.1   IT Bill-Back Example of SLA

Even if the IT bill-back does not actually happen, it is worthwhile to publish a mock IT bill-back to communicate storage spending to business units, giving them the information they need to make informed decisions, to spend only where necessary, and to avoid consuming limited funds wherever possible.

Earlier in this chapter, we established approximate unburdened annual costs per TB and for several two-tier alternatives:

Scenario 1. Single-Tier RAID-6 $3,000 per year per TB

Scenario 2. Tier 1 RAID-6, Tier 2 RAID-6
$2,000 per year per TB
(assuming 20/80)

Scenario 3. Tier 1 Mirrored, Tier 2 Mirrored $2,300 per year per TB
(assuming 20/80)
Tier 1 $4,000 per TB
Tier 2 $2,000 per TB

Scenario 4. Tier 1 Mirrored & Replicated, Tier 2 Mirrored
$2,800 per year per TB
(average)

Table 7.1 contains an example IT bill-back. Of course, your mileage may vary—storage system pricing and drive pricing are very dynamic and change all the time; soon enough, these estimates will be stale and inaccurate. The point is to get a feel for the comparisons of the total costs of typical Tier 1, compared to typical Tier 2, compared to typical Tier 3 total costs. As this is discussed, you can expect pushback and objections, probably along the lines of "this is not just about TB/$; this is about reliability, data protection, and performance suited for the job at hand." And they will be correct; the point is to correct overengineering and common financial abuses that occur as a result of keeping Tier 2 data on Tier 1 systems and Tier 3 data on Tier 2 systems.

Expect resistance to change. IT technical folks will likely push to avoid work and risk by keeping single-tier storage. To get their skin in the game, they can go and present the business units with the bill for $4,000 per year per TB. Additionally we can expect IT technical folks to push for putting more than twenty percent of the storage on Tier 1. Again, this is a way to

Table 7.1   Example IT Bill-Back

Costs and Bill-Back Example Calculation for Tier 1, Tier 2, and Tier 3 Storage Arrays		
Single Tier SLA (today's solution)	All data is on 600 G 15k drives, protected by RAID-6	Annual cost per managed TB: $6,000
	Today's single-tier bill:	$600,000 per year
Tier 1 and Tier 2	Tier 1 mirrored 600 G 15K rpm drives Point in time copy every 4 hours	Annual cost per managed TB: $8,000
	Tier 2 Mirrored 2 TB 7200 rpm drives Point in time copy every 24 hours	Annual cost per managed TB: $4,000
	The proposed two-tier bill: Both are mirrored with better service levels Assume 20:80 ratio of Tier 1 to Tier 2	$480,000 per year

get their skin in the game; they can go and present the business units for the bill for a much larger number.

The last and most desirable solution, is to push as much data as possible to Tier 2; reducing the data stored on the expensive Tier 1 storage. This serves to reduce the total pricetag and improve performance and protection for Tier 1 data, where it matters most. And present the business units with a lower bill for better service in the areas where it matters most.

A low risk, high value pilot project will take a not-so-critical system and convert it to two-tier, track the total costs, and then develop best-known methods for future projects.

Chapter 8

Demonstrating Delivery on SLA Service Levels

Earlier in this book, we identified the key SLA attributes : uptime, recovery, provisioning and cost. These are the components of SLAs that you should prepare to capture and periodically review with your business unit customers.

- *Uptime.* Your IT staff should track planned and unplanned downtime, including which system, which department, which application and root cause. Plan on a downstream pareto analysis to improve your quality. The pareto process will expose chronic problems if there is one specific array that keeps failing, a chronic power or cooling situation, or a network- or application-related problem. A pareto analysis will bring the recurring problem to the surface so that it can be addressed.
- *Recovery.* This attribute can be easily tracked by using IT trouble tickets to capture requests, including timestamping both the receipt and the resolution. A trouble ticket report specific to recovery tickets will enable you to demonstrate your RPO and RTO, or raise any problem areas so they can be addressed.
- *Provisioning.* This attribute can also easily be tracked by IT trouble tickets. Capture the initial request, and timestamp it. Then add the requested capacity, and timestamp it, too.
- *Cost.* Use a configuration log to track the capacities consumed by different departments

8.1 Customer Feedback and Service Levels

In the interest of being fiscally responsible, we try to be frugal everywhere possible and spend money only where appropriate to deliver the necessary service levels. A good start on determining where to be frugal and where to spend is to gather structured customer feedback.

Here, our objective is to efficiently gather baseline customer perceptions and customer feedback, and chart progress in improving the things that are important to your customers.One way to do this is through a survey.

Google Docs, Survey Monkey, and many other sites offer easy cheap or free survey tools. To use Google Docs, for example, use your Web browser to go to docs.google.com, and then select *Create New Form.*

You'll want to sort results based on which users, which applications and key values, as they change over time. Your survey will include pull down lists for what application, and type of user, and date stamp. I prefer user surveys formatted on a scale of 1 thru 7, where 1=hate it, 4=neutral, and 7=love it. Keep the survey to a short list of important questions, deliver the survey with an unchanging list of questions at several points in time. This provides visibility on what components are improving, staying the same or degrading over time.

About you:

1. your department (pull down list)

2. the application you use (pull down list)

3. About your experiences:

4. Your experience with storage performance (scale of 1-7)

5. Your experience with storage downtime (scale of 1-7)

6. Your experience with recovery from backup (scale of 1-7)

7. Your experience with storage helpdesk (scale of 1-7)

8. Your experience with training and knowledge exchange (scale of 1-7)

9. Your experience with storage tools (scale of 1-7)

10. Your experience with data migration and equipment updates (scale of 1-7)

11. Your experience with storage related processes and policies (scale of 1-7)

12. Anything else on your mind? (open text paragraph to capture input)

Once you have gathered your survey responses, diagram your customer satisfaction survey results to identify trouble areas. Run the same survey several times to chart improvement.

8.2   SLA Conclusion

Unfortunately, it's human nature to be wasteful of things which seem infinite. And it's human nature to place higher value on and take better care of scarce and limited things.

Like every resource, IT resources are not infinite. Service Level Agreements are a healthy and constructive way to attach value to finite and costly IT resources. SLAs are a great way to have that "inconvenient truth" conversation with those who consume the organizations IT resources.

Chapter 9

Planning for Growth and Storage Tiering

Dealing with storage growth scenarios is where SLA approaches and tiered storage show extraordinary advantages over single-tiered storage. For the sake of easy comparison (see Table 9.1), I'll use a total single tier of 100 TB, and compare that to 20 TB Tier 1 and 80 TB Tier 2.

For this single tier, let's assume a typical single-tier, middle-of-the-road (compromise) configuration with mirrored drives, not replicated.

Table 9.1   Growth Planning for Tiered Storage and SLA

Single Tier and Growth Planning	Capacity Configuration	Cost
Total Available Storage Capacity	100 TB	
Total Used Capacity	75 TB	
Capacity Growth Rate	25% per year ~20 TB per year	$3,000×20 total = $60,000
Tier 1 and Tier 2	Capacity Config-uration	Cost
Total Available Storage Capacity in Per-formance-Optimized Storage (Tier 1)	20 TB	
Total Used Capacity in Performance-Optimized Storage (Tier 1)	15 TB	
Capacity Growth Rate in Perfor-mance-Optimized Storage (Tier 1)	10% per year ~1.5 TB	$3,000
Total Available Storage Capacity in Capacity-Optimized Storage (Tier 2)	80 TB	
Total Used Capacity in Capacity-Optimized Storage (Tier 2)	60 TB	

Table 9.1   Growth Planning for Tiered Storage and SLA (continued)

Single Tier and Growth Planning	Capacity Configuration	Cost
Capacity Growth Rate in Capacity-Optimized Storage (Tier 2)	30% per year ~20 TB	$40,000
		Total $43,000

The simple concept of two-tier storage pays off in multiple ways, including growth planning. Planning for expected growth, using mostly 2 TB drives in fewer drive slots, is considerably easier and cheaper than attempting to plan for growth using 600GB drives and lots of slots.

Additionally, there is a less obvious advantage of two-tiered storage: if your Tier 1 is nearly full, you can move some of that data from Tier 1 to Tier 2. With single-tier storage, there are only two choices to deal with growth: add more 600 G drives (and possibly more shelves) or push that data to an offline archive, a painful decision.

9.1   Storage Growth, and SLA for Provisioning

Regarding SLA and business unit requests for more capacity, your SLA can (and should) include service level commitments to your business units to execute on requests for new storage. The commonly faced problem by IT organizations is how to respond to business unit requests for new storage capacity. One very common approach is to add storage to existing servers (DAS); this approach is simple but has well-documented high total costs of ownership (unconsolidated backup and overprovisioning, as discussed). The next approach is adding storage capacity to single-tier consolidated storage. This is also a high-priced response, because the assumption is that every-thing requires performance-optimized (expensive) drives, usually in very expensive storage hardware. The advisable approach, as shown in Table 9.2, is to offer an SLA for adding capacity on Tier 1 and a separate SLA to add capacity for Tier 2.

Table 9.2's SLA for provisioning gives you time to respond to capacity expansion, so you can order additional capacity from your vendor rather than guess at capacity expansion, prepurchase and tie up company money, manage inventory, or experience stale and aging inventory. It alleviates the financial burden for stocking expensive hardware of all different types. It will help you in your longer-term efforts to establish standard storage hardware.

Table 9.2   SLA and Provisioning: Response to Requests for Adding Capacity

Service Level Agreement	Cost per GB	Provisioning SLA (to add capacity)
Tier 1 Capacity Replicated	$$$$	21 business days after request Capacity will be online, configured, available for use, protected by replication and snapshot-per-hour
Tier 1 Capacity Non-replicated	$$	15 business days after request Capacity will be online, configured, available for use, protected by snapshot-per-4 hours
Tier 2 Capacity	$	2 business days after request Capacity will be online, configured, available for use, protected by snapshot-per-12 hours

Thin provisioning is a new twist on an old problem of poor utilization rates (i.e., not putting the storage resources you own to good use). Overprovisioning is commonplace in IT storage; it is amplified in situations where lots of little silos all have an excess fifty percent of unused storage (usually spinning, consuming power and A/C). Thin provisioning is a way around that problem; by using larger centralized storage, thin provisioning enables virtual volume storage capacity to be assigned to servers. Storage capacity can be allocated to servers quickly and easily. The net effect is thin provisioning, allowing expensive storage resources to be utilized at closer to eighty percent rather than the typical fifty percent of the "thick provisioned" traditional storage allocation.

An interesting benefit of thin provisioning in SLA and IT bill-back situations is that thin provisioning allows a storage administrator to allocate (for example) 500 GB to a server, but physically allocate 300 GB to that server. This creates a situation for IT bill-back in which a business unit requests and gets 500 GB assigned, but the actual storage consumed is 300 GB. Does IT bill the department for 500 GB? For 300 GB? Or for something in between?

SLA is an important tool. Even if the business unit is not actually billed, the SLA shares critical information: that storage is not free, and conservation is required.

Chapter 10

Wrap-Up: Projects Within Reach

- *Improvement 1.* Use the right drives and better static single-tier storage.
- *Improvement 2.* Improve facilities; replace "office" cooling with datacenter cooling.
- *Improvement 3.* Consolidate. Replace server direct attached storage and multiple silo'ed storage systems with fewer consolidated storage systems and consolidated backup.
- *Improvement 4.* Improve backup methods: replace tape with snapshots, relegate tape to archive only.
- *Improvement 5.* Implement tiered storage and SLAs.
- *Improvement 6.* Migrate cooling data to Tier 2. Get stale data out of Tier 1 storage.
- *Improvement 7.* Base your IT bill-back system on SLAs; sensitize business units to the company money they consume
- *Improvement 8.* Track results and improve service.

10.1 Improvement 1. Improve Efficiencies with Static Tiering

Getting big data (and seldom accessed data) onto big drives is a great step toward improvement, and it is key to our approach.

Candidates for moveable data include anything more than six months old, any records archival, old e-mail, old running shared folders, SharePoint, and Web sites. If you have storage performance profiling tools, look for LUNs that have a low I/O burden. If this stuff is stored on 10K rpm or 15K rpm drives, limited rack space and floor space are being wasted, as well as power. We have all dealt with facilities departments, and we know that wasted power bites in multiple ways : higher power bills, limited air conditioning, over-capacity auxiliary generation, increased risk of outgrowing existing data centers, and others.

Table 10.1   Improvement 1. Improve Efficiencies with Static Tiering

Drive Qty	Drive Type	Capacity per Drive (GB)	Watts per Drive	Total Capacity (TB)	Total Usable Capacity (TB) **	Data (Used Capacity)	Total Power (watts)	Hot Data/ Cold Data
Before								
16	15K rpm 3.5" 144G	144 GB	13 w	2.3 TB	1.7 TB	1.0 TB	16*14= 224 w *** 224+250= 474 w *** 474*2.75 = 1300 w ****	50/50
16	7200 rpm 3.5" 500G	500 GB	9 w	8 TB	6.0 TB	4.0TB	16*9= 144 w 144+250 = 394 W 394*2.75 = 1083 w	0/100
	Totals				7.7 TB	5 TB	2383 watts	
After								
5	15K rpm 3.5" 400G	400 GB	13 w	2.0 TB	1.3 TB	0.5 TB	5*13= 65 w *** 65+250= 315 w *** 315*2.75 = 866 w ****	50/50
5	7200 rpm 3.5" 2TB	2000 GB	9 w	10 TB	10 TB	4.5 TB	5*9= 45 w 45+250 = 295 W 295*2.75 = 811 w	0/100
	Totals				11.3 TB	5 TB	1677 watts	

** Calculate "total usable capacity" subtract out RAID overhead, warm spares etc
*** power for disk drives plus power consumed by controllers
**** power for air conditioning plus power distribution inefficiencies. The formula is HDD power plus controller power multiplied by 2.75

Three Steps:
1. Move cool data off of 15K drives, put onto 7200 rpm capacity drives
2. Replace 16x 144 G 15K drives with 5x 400 G 15K rpm drives
3. Replace 16x 500 G 7200rpm drives with 5 x 2TB 7200 rpm drives

Table 10.1   Improvement 1. Improve Efficiencies with Static Tiering

Results:
Reduce consumed HDD slots from 32 to 10
Reduce consumed power from 2500 watts to 1677 watts (706 watts off power bill, 706 watts of data center power and A/C capacity free for other uses, avoid outgrowing the existing data center)
Free up ~2000 BTU capacity in Data Center Air Conditioning system
Increase spare capacity for growth from 2.7 TB to 6.3 TB available for growth

Recall your baseline from Chapter 6? Table 10.1 provides a before and after analysis of static tiering improvements.

10.2   Improvement 2. Improve Power and Air Conditioning

Computer room A/C always seems to be under strain. One solution is to improve the facilities: replace "office"-style cooling with cooling designed specifically for a data center. Replace the few room-level thermostats and unfocused delivery of cooling with separate thermostats at each major heat load controlling focused delivery of cooling directly to heat loads.

Establish a baseline TCO for all costs: power, A/C, people, administrative costs, and leasing fees.

Have your facilities team scope the data center computer room project to better direct cool air delivery to the heat loads, including local thermostats to reduce waste. That project should include an energy and A/C improvement calculation which can be compared to the initial TCO for approval.

More efficient delivery will create capacity headroom in your chillers and air handlers and save money on the energy bill too.

10.3   Improvement 3. Consolidate and Reduce Server-Attached Storage

As a pilot project, pick a specific group of servers to consolidate onto SAN storage.

Next, establish a baseline for existing TCO: utilization percentage, power, A/C, time/effort to back up, time/effort to provision and manage growth, quality metrics (uptime, service record, maintenance costs). Consolidating storage creates an opportunity for multiple improvements: less expensive backup, using snapshot instead of tape, offloading the backup burdens from servers, and reducing wasteful overprovisioning. Most importantly, storage consolidation is the first step toward SLAs, improving service levels while reducing expenses. Storage tiering is the first step toward taking advantage of managed hosting and cloud services (covered in the upcoming sections in this book).

10.4   Improvement 4. Better Backup—Replace Tape

Replace tape with disk to disk and snapshots, and relegate tape to archive use only.

1. Start with a specific system. Capture a baseline cost to conduct the backups, purchase tape, manage tape . . . include everything: people, tape, etc. Also, capture the existing RTO and RPO and quality information regarding failed backups and lost tapes.

2. For that specific pilot system, implement a trial system to handle snapshots.

3. Snapshot frequency should be at least twice as often as incremental tape backup (this approach cuts your RPO in half). Also, prove your RTO by random testing recovery—e-mail, database, files, etc.

4. Review the new TCO and the snapshot total costs, and compare them to the previous total costs of the tape system.

5. Roll out to other systems.

10.5   Improvement 5. Establish Tiered Storage and Service Level Agreements

1. *Better static single-tier storage.* Migrate data off old drives onto new (fewer), more economical drives. Establish a baseline for total costs of storage before and after the old hardware is retired and replaced with more efficient hardware—power, backup, quality issues, your staff costs to maintain, vendor maintenance fees, uptime, etc.

2. *Establish separate tiers.* Separate real Tier 1 data from real Tier 2 data. Establish separate Tier 1 storage systems and Tier 2 storage systems.

3. *Retire old hardware.* Migrate from older 10K or 15K drives onto capacity-optimized drives on Tier 2 storage, wherever possible.

4. *Consolidate.* Replace multiple silo'ed storage systems with fewer consolidated storage systems with consolidated backup.

5. *Improve backup.* Replace tape with snapshots, and relegate tape to archive use only.

6. *Establish SLAs.* Include price tags for each tier ($/GB/month).

7. *Segment storage into tiered storage with supporting SLA.*

8. *Establish a new TCO.* Compare it to the previous TCO and consider additional tiering projects.

10.6   Improvement 6. Migrate Cool data onto to Tier 2, Release Tier 1 Resources for Critical Applications

1. Create an option to migrate some Tier 2 and Tier 3 to Managed Hosting

2. Characterize the data. Is it in active use? How many readers/writers? What departments? Is it mission-critical or security sensitive? Is current data mixed in with older, stale data?

3. Assign a cost to the data, using the TCO baseline.

4. Assign a (hopefully improved) cost to the migrated data.

5. Assign the TCO comparison to a business unit (make them understand and share the pain).

6. Catalog what data will be moved.

7. Catalog what servers attach to that data.

8. Catalog what storage/systems administrators have privileges.

9. Archive some data (are there legal constraints?).

10. Lower-tier some data and ensure future access.

11. Set up for future migration (virtual name spaces).

12. Communicate with stakeholders (business unit people and support) and involve them in the process. Plan their interaction into the schedule, and plan risk and testing into the schedule.

13. Follow risk management procedures. On MAP day (mock migration), copy the data—test everything without actually moving

production data. Make one change at a time, confirm it works, and document (we'll do this again soon).

14. Complete failover testing.

15. Test server access and account access and permissions prior to migration.

16. Plan for rollback/undo (test undo).

17. Don't create too much risk (don't couple the migration with major database upgrade, operating system upgrade, or network upgrade; do these one at a time).

18. Set up monitoring for future capacity growth.

19. Establish new TCO, compare to previous TCO, and consider additional migration projects.

10.7   Improvement 7. IT Bill-Back

With SLAs in place, produce a bill for each business unit and review the bill with them.

No doubt there will be some thrash and some criticism (both warranted and unwarranted). Have some confidence. This is how we improve.

10.8   Improvement 8. Track and Improve

We use a financial TCO comparison model throughout this book. We always start with a baseline Cost of Ownership, and we always run a pilot or trial project to measure our improvements against the baseline TCO.

The resulting data will either provide the confidence to continue with additional deployments or give insight into a course correction.

Poll your customers. Capture their feedback in a structured way (I like Google Forms for Surveys). Think ahead about the ways feedback will be analyzed over time; we want to review the same questions with users over time to show improvements. It's not a one-shot deal.

Conclusion

We started Part I with a close look at hard drives and the "why" of retiring old drives and replacing them reduces consumption of floor space, power and A/C. We reviewed facilities power and A/C and achieved additional improvements in power and cooling. We reviewed consolidation and found that some backup consolidation results in reduced expenses, frees up staff time, and considerably reduces risk related to relying on tape backups.

We achieved clarity on Service Levels and embraced the use of SLAs as a tool to *both* reduce IT spending and improve service.

Using SLAs and segmenting data into three tiers of storage sets up a situation where we can take advantage of managed hosting. In the industry press, there is no shortage of discussion about the pros and cons of cloud computing; while these discussions are useful, interesting, and often exciting, they often skip right past the profoundly significant managed hosting trend. IT organizations are increasingly faced with a problem of continued growth and overfull data centers. And IT departments are increasingly turning to managed hosting services to solve this problem. Managed hosting offers either shared or nonshared dedicated servers and storage with supporting management services. IT departments now have the option of using servers and storage at managed hosting services, instead of buying hardware and installing it in their own data centers. The concept of managed hosting has been around for decades, and the advent of the Internet, security, and affordable, high-performance network capacity has put significant money, talent, and credibility into managed hosting.

For those of you who may be skeptical, consider that Daimler-Benz outsources their worldwide SAP operation to a company called T-Systems. SAP controls parts inventory, supply lines, work orders, change orders, and on and on. If Daimler's SAP has an outage, factory production comes to a full stop. And they source the managed hosting to T-Systems. To me, this is nothing short of amazing.

The SLA and tiering approach sets you up to take advantage of managed hosting as a highly affordable option—and we'll be covering that option in Part II.

Part II
Managing Aging Data and E-Mail Expenses

Part II offers additional tactics and insights on delivering data center storage service levels while avoiding overspending. The main event is balancing business and technology.

In Part I, we warmed up with storage basics, HDD building block foundation, facilities issues, data consolidation, and backup improvements, all cumulating with a Service Level Agreement (SLA) business approach that overlays cost of business with applied technologies.

In Part II, we dig into approaches for specific problem areas: dealing with aging data, dealing with aging shared folders, dealing with aging e-mail. We review where and how to spend responsibly on reliability, where and how to spend responsibly on performance. We get into storage tiering, storage virtualization, storage infrastructures.

Part II leads into an essential Part III that covers managed hosting and cloud computing and storage—a brave new world with significant risk and significant reward. Part III emphasizes risk management as we begin to selectively employ and enjoy the advantages of managed hosting and cloud computing and storage.

Chapter 11

Migration and Retiring Aging Systems

Why migrate? If it's not broken, don't fix it, right? Wrong. Sooner or later, we must migrate: User demand grows, application demand grows, the use of the data expands as it integrates with other applications, data itself grows, and hardware ages. It is in your best interest to organize the task of migration well and use it frequently. The cost of the hardware is a fraction of the costs of maintenance, people, backup, and so forth of the total cost of the system.

- *Replace aging server or storage hardware.* Aging hardware becomes outgrown and can become increasingly unreliable; it must be replaced eventually.
- *Standard IT platforms are good.* Hardware and applications age and become nonstandard. IT hardware and software standardization serves to improve uptime, reduce risk, and reduce expenses in people and service contracts to manage a multivendor environment. Employing standard configurations and processes will improve uptime, improve your ability to fix problems quickly, and reduce expenses for people and service contracts. Improve service levels reduce server and storage sprawl and reduce expenses.
- *Replace servers using direct attached storage (DAS) with consolidated storage.* Improve server performance by offloading server-backup or snapshot workloads onto storage-array-based backup or snapshot workloads.
- *Improve performance of primary storage.* This can be accomplished by load-balancing several systems or by migrating aging or nonessential data to Tier 2 of the system to offload and improve performance.
- *Reduce costs of storage and costs of backup.* Using a tiered storage approach and SLAs will help achieve this goal.

- *Consolidate data.* This will reduce overprovisioning, improve RPO/RTO with snapshots, and save expenses on consolidated backup.

Migrating from DAS (direct attached storage) to SAN (external shared storage) is the first place to improve where and how you spend on storage. It's harsh reality time: To achieve these benefits, not only will you need to buy and install the new systems. You must also retire *olde* systems (yes, I used that spelling intentionally).

The challenge is coaching your people to not repeatedly indulge in bad habits, such as leaving lots of data on Tier 1 storage and, whenever demand grows, simply buying more Tier 1. At the core of any business are people, processes, and tools (also known as technologies). Frequently, once the people and processes are established, they become habits, usually bad habits. IT operations people simply carry out the migration, backup, or expansion without considering the alternatives, such as migrating stale data to cheaper systems or retiring aging data to archive. These alternatives could improve operations in many, many ways:

- Removing aging data from Tier 1 systems reduces the time to backup, and coincidentally creates an opportunity for improved SLA for the remaining (non-stale) Tier 1 data. A smaller capacity Tier 1 can be backed up more frequently; the Tier 2 data needs to be backed up much less frequently.
- Removing aging data from Tier 1 storage systems also reduces the total I/O workload and can improve performance for (non-stale) Tier 1 data. A modest reduction of I/O workload from a overfull server or storage array can deliver a pronounced improvement in performance. For instance, reducing an I/O load by ten percent on a fully loaded system can offer dramatically better system performance and response.
- Removing aging data from Tier 1 systems also serves to avoid overhead for replication and WAN data charges, and reduces competition with other WAN traffic for limited bandwidth.
- Moving data from the Tier 1 infrastructure and onto affordable (GB/$) Tier 2 storage system hardware creates further cost efficiencies. Archival to tape completely removes stale data from spinning disk drives that take energy to run and to cool and that consume limited data center floor space. Putting that data onto tape means that it will consume no power, generate no heat, and occupy significantly less expensive floor space.

Without question, there are justifiable situations which merit Tier 1 storage spending. But all proposals to spend more money on Tier 1 storage should—must—be accompanied by a matching plan to conserve Tier 1 storage capacity, moving data to Tier 2, or archiving stale data.

Migration projects fall into two very separate categories:

- *File*: Network attached storage (NAS), shared folders, anything using a file system such as New Technology File System (NTFS), Zettabyte File System (ZFS), or ext, accessed over a NAS protocol such as Network File System (NFS) or Common Internet File System (CIFS).
  - NTFS (New Technology File System) is Microsoft's NT file system
  - ZFS (Zettabyte File System) is a Sun/Oracle-developed file system
  - NFS (Network File System) is a network attached storage protocol originally developed by Sun Microsystems to share files
  - CIFS (Common Internet File System) is a network attached storage protocol developed by Microsoft to share files, printers, and more
- *Block*: Databases, e-mail, SharePoint, and similar projects in which the application includes its own data structure instead of a file system.

11.1   File Migration Project Planning

The goal (as always) is to reduce storage expenses and improve storage service levels. To overcome resistance to change, risk avoidance, and the like, it's important to set the goals in front of the team. Make sure they all understand that leaving the file data (the shared folders) in place and simply expanding the storage increases both risks and costs for the company. To motivate the team, the project plan should include a review of current costs compared to new costs and should plan for both growth of incoming data and retirement of aging data.

Expect both end users and frontline IT people to resist moving any of the shared folders. Moving data usually results in end users not finding the data they seek, and that leads to calls to the IT help desk, yucky for everyone involved. However, the alternative of leaving the data in its current location (assumedly Tier 1 storage) and simply expanding is highly costly.

Moving the data itself is not such a big task. The central problem is all the users have static NFS or CIFS mount points to their data. To better understand that, simply look for that shared folder on your PC and click *properties* to see the mount point (basically a server and folder). Moving the static pointers involves changing every client and every server to no longer point at the old mount point, but rather point at the new mount point.

This causes the IT people to think, "What happens when I break the client side? What happens if I mess up the server setup or permissions? What is this going to do to performance? What is this going to do to the network? What is this going to do for backup and restore? I'll mess it up and look stupid and incompetent."

And then the IT people think, "This task will go on forever, more servers and repeated relocation of aging data off Tier 1 and onto Tier 2—there is just too much work and risk!"

Expect resistance.

11.1.1   File Migration Plan, Discover, Test, QA, Provision, and Cut-Over

- Size the current growth (capacity (GB) growth, growth in numbers of active users, and growth in increased demand for scalable performance), have a plan for expanding storage to accommodate. Usually a spreadsheet with past-present-future capacity-user-performance loads for each application will suffice. The plan doesn't need to be perfect; it can (and should) be revisited and updated.
- Plan on ongoing data retirement. If end users really need to keep data online longer, then include that in the SLA and show the cost to the company. Avoid migrating forward all your stale and unused data. Retire it to archive media, or, if that's not possible, demote it from Tier 1 to Tier 2.
- Perform risk management. Take a look at what might go wrong and determine a remedy or workaround. Make conscious decisions regarding acceptable risk or change the plan when encountering an unacceptable risk. The risk of someone complaining or making a fuss is very different than a risk of real business impact; separate the perception/emotion from the real, concrete issues. For those emotional end users (and we all have them), have a discussion prior to the migration to reduce the drama.
- Establish a plan of record that includes scope, schedule, and resources. If there needs to be a change of plan, do that consciously; communicate a change of plan of record and update the

written project plan. Make that plan of record well known, review it with key stakeholders, make it accessible to your end users. Making a migration go smoothly with low drama will make the next migration easier to accomplish.

- Prior to executing the project, establish a quality assurance plan with well-understood acceptance criteria. Review the acceptance criteria and the plan of record with the team up front. Review the acceptance criteria again, immediately prior to the migration, as a final approval.
- Perform discovery, classification, and cleansing. Discovery can be conducted manually with spreadsheets plus scripting. Every system has stale, obsolete, or otherwise useless data. Either make it useful or get rid of it; involve your end users in the process. Only migrate data that is in use. Migration should first retire stale data. Use the migration as an event to do some housekeeping.
- Do a practice or "dry run." Without disrupting production, do a test run of sample production data, then confirm the pilot run pulled the new data properly. Compare before and after log files and directory listings and file sizes to indicate folders/files were moved successfully. Compare dry run results to acceptance criteria.
- Discover clients, discover storage. Catalog the old servers: IP addresses, folder structures, user/workgroup permissions, systems software (including versions).
- Have a full backup and plan to recover if things go drastically wrong.
- Provision and set up new storage: hardware, RAID volumes, LUNS, and folders.
- Conduct a premigration test before moving the data itself. Conduct a pilot project, followed by phase 1, phase 2, and phase 3.
- Create test scripts for clients and servers to change mount points. Prepare a rollback script in case things go wrong.
- Define acceptance criteria and provide quality assurance. Establish an acceptance checklist, then conduct a QA review to walk through the plan and testing results and confirm the acceptance checklist is met.
- Perform the cutover: move the data and run the scripts.
- Leave the old data in place on the old hardware. Once we are convinced the new migration is properly operating, back up and archive data from the old server and storage.
- Retire or repurpose old servers and storage.

Key considerations to pave the way to the future:

- Improve migration automation. Scripts to update clients, scripts to automate discovery.
- Drive to an IT operation based on standardized configurations. Retire that weird hardware. Use migration to improve consistence and reduce complexity in the IT infrastructure.
- Use migration to establish a two-tier storage infrastructure. Manually migrate aging data (usually LUN level) from Tier 1 to Tier 2.
- Use file abstraction to ease future manual migration and automated tiered migration. On the server side, replace hard-coded pointers to storage mount points with dynamic pointers. File abstraction allows you to move the data and then update the pointer, with no touching of the clients or servers involved. It also allows you to automatically move aging data from Tier 1 to Tier 2 without administrator involvement (huge savings), we'll cover in this section.
- Use migration to set up adoption of managed hosting or cloud storage in the future.

Expect resistance. But providing an alternative is the financially responsible thing to do. Allowing unfettered growth of unstructured file data (especially on Tier 1) is not financially responsible.

See sections on static tiering and dynamic tiering for more important and related information before finalizing your migration plan.

11.1.2   Aging Data and the Role of Near-Line Archive and Search

Perhaps the central problem of shifting data from Tier 1 to Tier 2 to Archive is the issue of end users and access to that data. The end users rely on the data to do their jobs, so moving it to places where they may have trouble finding the data has a big downside. Establishing a search capability (like a private Google) can largely mitigate that risk.

11.1.3   Block (Database, Email etc.) Application Data Migration

There is good news here. Block applications, such as database, e-mail, and the like, (e.g., Oracle, Exchange) all have tools to manage data and manage user access to that data. Most importantly, applications have tools and information about the data to separate the hot data from the aging cooler data—in other words, applications like Oracle have built-in archiving features.

The only open question is your approach to keep all the data piling up on Tier 1; or your approach to push the aging data more aggressively to Tier 2 and then to Archival. (See Table 11.1.)

Table 11.1   Before and After Migration: Tier 1 to Tier 1 and Tier 2

	100% on Tier 1	25% on Tier 1 74% on Tier 2	Comment
Performance	30,000 IOPS peak 5 MB/s peak	Tier 1: 20,000 IOPS peak Tier 2: 10,000 IOPS peak Tier 1: 2 MB/s peak Tier 2: 3 MB/s peak	Notice Tier 1 is heavier random I/O (higher IOPS) and Tier 2 is heavier sequential I/O (higher MB/s) due to the different workload. The hardware can be selected/ configured for each.
Data Growth	20 TB total growing at 2 TB/ yr	Tier 1: 10 TB, growing at 0TB/ yr Tier 2: 15TB, growing at 2TB/ year	Notice the Tier 1 has zero growth. The growth is in the less expensive Tier 2 storage. Adding Tier 2 capacity costs 10% to 20% of the cost of adding Tier 1 capacity.
Power	20 TB on 7-watt 300 G drives is 84 HDD. 588 watts unburdened. 1470 watts burdened	10 TB on 7-watt 300 G drives is 84 HDD. 294 watts unburdened. 740 watts burdened. 10TB on 8-watt 2 TB drives is 6 drives. 48 watts unburdened. 120 watts burdened. 860 watts total	After migration, consumes around half the power.

Table 11.1   Before and After Migration: Tier 1 to Tier 1 and Tier 2

	100% on Tier 1	25% on Tier 1 74% on Tier 2	Comment
Backup/ Recovery Cost	20 TB incremental backup every 12 hours is $4,000 per month in staff-time and $2,000 per month tape and tape management $6,000 per month total	10 TB incremental backup every 12 hours And 10 TB incremental backup every 24 hours $4,500 per month total	

11.2   Migration Overview (Virtualized Storage)

Your starting point with a virtual machine (VM) is an associated home folder with a virtual machines disk file.

Create a new home folder in the new target location. Most virtualization systems have tools to migrate virtual servers and virtual disks with automation; migration still involves small quantities of downtime. The process is as follows: Move virtual machine operating files, Swap, Scratch, Config, and Log Files. Then copy the entire virtual machine storage disk file to the new target location home folder. Compare the contents of the old and the new target folder (same file names, same file sizes, same permissions). Then bring the applications back online targeting the new location.

There is an alternative method that involves only a few moments of downtime. The alternative method employs snapshot technology, and the applications are left online. Use snapshot technologies to establish a point-in-time copy. Copy the data to the new target location, while the applications continue to read and write to the original folder. Snapshot technologies keep track of the changed storage on the original location. Once the copy is complete, the VM and applications are momentarily shut down while the snapshot technology updates the target location with the changes to the original storage since the initiation of the copy. Delete the original virtual machine home folder.

Chapter 12

Shared Folders and Content Management

The urge to collect and hoard is primal.

We know and love shared folders. They are hugely useful for employee collaborations and storing any type of content development, documents, specifications, scanned forms, photos, mechanical designs, electronics designs, or software.

The problem is keeping pace with overall data growth. Specifically, as shared folder content (the stuff connecting to PCs with NFS or CIFS; you see it as your Z drive) continues to grow unabated, the lack of tools to manage the data means more hard drives, more servers, more stuff to back up, more stuff to find when a user forgets that he/she intentionally renamed or moved a project folder. Data grows unobstructed in shared folders and files usually without any cleanup or purging of stale data. Like a neglected closet, end users stuff shared folders full and keep stuffing, and the IT administrator has no way to know whether the data is being used or is just riding around and around on the disk platter, never to be read or changed or removed (sadly laughable: write-once, read-never data).

The source of the shared folder growth problem is that unstructured data growth is accelerating, and there is no obvious way to archive data. But once the data is out there, there are to tools to keep it cleaned up.

The answer is a content management system (CMS). There is a long long list of CMSs. Some are highly integrated with office and mail systems—for example, Microsoft SharePoint. Some are totally generic, such as Google sites, and Blogspot. Some CMSs that are worth looking at include HyperOffice, Alfresco, O3spaces, and the list goes on. Microsoft SharePoint's installed base can be measured in tens of millions of copies. The most obvious reason is intranets and employee collaboration (replacement of shared folders). I should be clear, SharePoint does lots of other things above and beyond replacing shared folders, but this section is about saving money by replacing shared folders, not about the capabilities of SharePoint (a great product, by the way; I use it every day).

The issue is how to manage aging data. Files and folders have no metadata or structure to flag data to keep and data to migrate or retire. The benefit to your organization of CMS is that it will enable you to intelligently clear off aging, useless data to make room for new incoming data without constantly expanding hardware.

CMS has metadata that tracks who created a document, who edited it, when it was last edited, and when it was last opened/read. The "when it was last opened/read" is particularly important. Knowing what data is in frequent use and what data is not accessed offers a means to intelligently migrate and retire aging data.

And no matter how well we plan, there will always be times then end users want to retrieve data that's been retired or archived. Aggressive migration depends on end user ability to search and retrieve archived data. As you evaluate content management systems, pay attention to the CMS's capability not only to intelligently migrate, retire, and archive data, but also to search and retrieve aging data.

Replace your (unmanageable) shared folders system with SharePoint, Alfresco, or another structured data management solution. The hard reality is that the cost savings do not materialize without retiring the older servers and older shared folder system (as shown in Table 12.1).

12.1   Content Management System Cost Analysis, Before and After

Table 12.1   Content Management versus Shared Folders, Before and After

Shared Folders	In-House Shared Folders without Data Management	In-House Shared folders or Content Management System with Data Management and Archiving	Hosted Shared Folders or Content Management
Cost per Month	Not applicable	Not applicable	$3,000 per month
Hardware Costs	2 servers, no quota, with total 45 TB storage capital: $80,000 over 4 years: $20,000/yr	2 servers, w/ total 25 TB storage capital: $50,000 over 4 years: $12,000/yr	Included
Software Costs	Microsoft Server 2007: $2500 includes CIFS over 4 years: $800/year	Microsoft Server 2007: $2500 SharePoint: $4500 clients: $10,000 over 4 years: $4,400/year	Included
Backup	$15,000 per year	$7000 per year	Included
Help Desk	$20,000 per year	$20,000 per year	Included
Admin	$10,000	$10,000	$10,000 per year
Totals	$66,000 per year	$53,000 per year	$46,000 per year

Chapter 13

Storage Strategies for E-Mail

The urge to collect and hoard is primal.

E-mail keeps coming; it is never, ever deleted. E-mail creates more and more data stored on spinning drives, taking up space in the data center, consuming power and A/C. More stuff to back up. E-mail is accessed 24×7. If e-mail is not accessible, it's as bad as the phone system going down. To sum up, e-mail, perhaps more than any other application, creates an ever-increasing pile of unmanageable, undeletable data. There are a few tricks to dealing with it.

End users and business units can be expected to always take the path of least resistance. Without additional restrictions, expense-pass-downs, or tools, end users will allow e-mail folders to grow and grow. It's simply too much trouble to delete old e-mail, as there is a remote possibility that some ancient e-mail might be needed for some unspecified reason, sometime in the unspecified future. . . *sigh.*

13.1   E-Mail Quotas, PC Folders and PC Backup

This problem is easily remedied: Set an e-mail in-box quota. Your users will complain. And you can provide them with a workaround:

- If an end user needs to keep old e-mail, he/she can simply select and drag older e-mail into personal folders on their personal computer.

Establish an automated backup for PCs; that way end users are protected against HDD loss. And turn ON the e-mail search tool, which will return hits from both the in-box and personal folders.

The combination of e-mail in-box quotas, PC personal folders, PC backup, and end-user search tools will significantly reduce the alternative approach, in which the data is piled up in e-mail servers that must be

Table 13.1   E-Mail Hosting, Before and After

E-Mail	In-House E-Mail with No Quota or Big Quota	In-House E-Mail with Quota and PC backup	Hosted E-Mail
Assume 2000 users			
Cost per Month	Not applicable	Not applicable	$2 to $11 per month, per account
Hard-ware Costs	2000 e-mail accounts 2 servers, no quota w/ total 45 TB storage Capital: $80,000 Spread over 4 years: $20,000	2000 e-mail accounts, quota of 1 GB 2 servers, w/ total 25 TB storage Capital: $50,000 Spread over 4 years: $12,000	Included
Software Costs	Microsoft Server 2007: $2,500 Microsoft Exchange Server: $1,500 Spread over 4 years: $1,000/year	Microsoft Server 2007: $2,500 Microsoft Exchange Server: $1,500 Spread over 4 years: $1,000/year Remote PC Backup: $55 per year x 2000 users $110,000 per year	Included
Backup	$15,000 per year	$10,000 per year	Included
Help Desk	$60,000 per year	$60,000 per year	Included
Admin	$10,000	$10,000	$10,000 per year
No PC Backup	$186,000 per year	$103,000 per year	$30,000 per year
With PC Backup		$213,000 per year with backup	$140,000 per year with PC backup

expanded and backed up and supported on systems that take up limited valuable room in usually overfull data centers. See Table 13.1 for a comparison.

13.2   E-Mail Hosting Providers

Managed hosting provides servers, networks, storage, backup, and facilities power and A/C. Taking that approach one additional step, e-mail hosting providers simply charge by the month per account.

As I write today, I see hosting services from Google, Rackspace, Mail-Street/Apptix and many others available from $2 to $11 per month per user. Hosted e-mail usually has some capacity limit (often generous limit) on e-mail storage. It is very feasible to employ public e-mail services rather than in-house.

If this feels too daunting or high risk, the workaround is to push some portion of your e-mail users onto the Web. Later in the book we'll cover more on managed hosting and cloud. Shifting e-mail providers from in-house to outside is a straightforward and high-reward activity.

13.3   Checklist for E-Mail Project

1. Reference accounts and history of SLA delivery (both performance and uptime)

2. Review the service level agreement: uptime, performance, data protection, support SLA. Determine how to confirm that SLA is delivered and what happens if SLA is not delivered.

3. Check to see who actually owns the hardware and who owns the facility.

4. Ask what happens if e-mail hosting provider goes out of business or gets acquired.

5. Ask if there is any lock-in or penalty for leaving.

6. Determine what migration service is offered by the e-mail hosting provider. Is that service included or at an extra fee?

7. Ask about the backup recovery point objective, or RPO (what is the maximum gap for lost data? 24 hours? 12 hours?) and the the recovery time objective, or RTO (time from service ticket to data restored).

8. Ask which data protection measures are in place, such as backups or mirroring.

9. Ask what data security measures are in place, such as physical security, card access, password management, employee screening.

10.   Obtain a catalog of existing e-mail accounts and folder sizes.

11.   Reduce active mailbox size: Archive everything more than a year old and push e-mail to private folders, leaving an active inbox of less than 10MB. This will streamline the data transition from the old system to the new.

12.   Back up and archive e-mail (be prepared to roll the transition back in case there is an unresolvable problem).

13.   Hold a trial run: migrate and test without going live.

14.   Perform the live cut-over.

Chapter 14

Spending Wisely on Performance

Performance is one of those tough emotional issues.

This section focuses on existing storage systems and resolving performance problems, rather than on performance engineering/sizing for new systems. Resolving performance problems on systems you already own is significantly less expensive than buying new systems.

Performance problems can be just annoyances that are felt to be larger than they are due to emotional/perceptual issues. In the absence of facts, people make guesses or listen to vendors motivated by commissions. The responsible approach is to assess the real performance need (in simple, SLA-based terms) prior to throwing random money at a perceived problem.

14.1 Establish Clear Performance Criteria (in SLA Terms)

Performance problems can and do impact business revenues or customer service. From the other side of the table, performance problems often receive spending in areas that don't significantly improve performance. Systems can be over-engineered for the performance needs of the largest and most demanding applications, then overdesigned to account for future growth and increased application demand on the system. Next, that heavy design will get reapplied like a cookie cutter for all applications, demanding or not.

Facts are our friends, so let us ask ourselves: Exactly what problem are we solving? Exactly what is the measure of success? Exactly why is it a good use of company money? Improving a bank or travel agency's ability to efficiently and quickly process customers reduces customer queuing, improves customer satisfaction, and allows the company to offer better customer support for a lower price. That's a good place to spend money. Conversely, a modest improvement that will only help a few people is not a good place to spend money. Storage systems are routinely overengineered. Overengineering on performance is commonplace. This is rooted in obsolete company cultures where squeaky wheel behavior is rewarded more than fiscally responsible behavior. The straightforward approach is to establish a performance SLA with a price tag. Even if the SLA is never actually billed, it shows the requestor that there is a big difference in cost to the company to deliver 30-second response versus 10-second response versus 1-second response and performance. No doubt there is some reasonable level of performance is required for sensible business operations. We'll take a look at common demands for performance and cost-effective remedies.

If you manage data center budgets, or if you are on the business side of IT, you get frequent requests for spending "to improve slow performance." In the interest of spending wisely on performance, you can use the following approaches to make limited company money go further:

- Determine the requirements. How much performance is enough? What response times are really needed? Measure response times today, establish a baseline, and include breakout by users and locations. Establish an SLA for maximum response times.
- Communicate three SLAs for good, better, and best performance, with three different price tags. If an end-user insists on higher performance, then you insist on higher price tag.
- If the task is to solve a specific performance issue, spend intelligently. Base your spending decisions on facts, not guesswork. Know the root cause of performance issue before throwing money at the problem.

14.2   The Yardsticks of Storage Performance

- *IOPS*, the number of input/output operations per second; measured in I/O per second. Typically, published IOPS are for lab or tradeshow workloads: 512 Byte I/O size, read-only, and sequential. That's a useful corner case in the lab, but there are no real-world workloads which are 100% small, 100% read, 100% sequential. That's not the real world. Real world workloads have a mix of large and small transactions, a mix of random and sequential transactions, a mix of read and write transactions. This book's appendix includes instructions for a free, simple, and commonly used tool called IOmeter. If you are dealing with a performance issue, insist on profiling the real-world workload and using that profile as a baseline, then using that profile to establish a metric for acceptable performance.

- *Latency*, the amount of waiting; usually measured in milliseconds (ms). Most often latency is incurred over slow or overtrafficked storage area networks (SANs) or wide area networks (WANs). It is not typical that high latencies have a root cause within the storage array.

- *Throughput*, the amount of data moving from point A to point B per second; most often measured in megabytes per second (MB/s). Throughput is relevant for workloads of big files, file transfers, backups, replication, and similar "data mover" tasks.

Key Concept

In conversations and spending on performance, insist on clarity.

Be clear if the measure is megabits (Mb) or megabytes (MB).

Be clear on exactly what they mean by IOPS.

Be clear if the IOPS represent a profile of your workload or if the IOPS discussion is about "tradeshow IOPS." Mentions of "tradeshow IOPS" is a giveaway that the profile is not known. "Tradeshow IOPS" is a storage-vendor arms race for the largest possible performance number, usually obtained with a non-real-world workload and tuning: all read, all small block, all sequential.

Establish a baseline with your profile, including a metric for what is acceptable and what is unacceptable to avoid mission creep and its associated expenses.

14.3   Resolving Performance Issues in Production Systems

In this section, we assume there are existing storage systems that need performance updates.

14.3.1   Paging

Paging-related performance problems result from too much I/O and too little server RAM. A server application will load information off a disk drive into server RAM. Excessive paging occurs when a large number of user requests create an I/O load that is too large for the available server memory size. Excessive paging also occurs when creating a load that exceeds the ability to get that information off the disk and into memory. For example,

Exchange 2007 has lots of advantages, but it does place a heavier load on memory.

Remedy: A smart fix is to add server memory and/or spread out multiple Exchange databases across multiple servers. Make sure to determine the root cause of performance problems before writing a big check for whole-server upgrades or whole-storage upgrades. Fortunately, basic server performance monitors and application-specific performance monitors for Oracle, VMware, or Exchange can identify paging-related performance problems. If there are performance problems, the first thing to check is: "is there enough server memory?"

14.3.2   I/O Size

Applications group I/O into chunks to be sent to the storage or requested from the storage. Storage arrays can be adjusted to handle I/O in different I/O sizes: 8KB, 64KB and 256KB are common. Smaller sizes (8KB) are typical for small transactions like databases. Typical size I/O for e-mail is 32KB, a compromise between small messages and large PowerPoint messages. Typical size I/O for large-scale data movement, such as backup and streaming media, is 64KB. These are just examples; performance situations can arise from a storage array being initially set up for a database, configured for 8 KB I/O size, and then used for e-mail. And when e-mail and backup is run simultaneously, the concurrent load and the overhead of misaligned I/O size can create slow performance.

Remedy: Check the I/O size configured on the storage as compared to the I/O size of the application. Performance issues may be resolved by simple performance tuning, changing the I/O size configured on the external storage.

14.3.3   Fragmentation

Look for fragmented disk space. As time passes, and data is added, deleted, and modified, the data layout on the disk platters will become noncontinuous, broken up, or fragmented. When a disk drive encounters a continuous read, the disk drive head stays on the same track (like a phonograph record) and the data is read without drive head movement. When the drive encounters noncontinuous data, the drive head must move, there is a seek latency (like moving the phonograph stylus to another song on the phonograph record) and there is rotational latency (waiting for the platter to spin around so the data is under the head). Drives are fast, but thousands of simultaneous requests can cause the system to bog down with a high number of I/O requests waiting in line.

Remedy: Look for the root cause first and spend money to fix it; check storage for fragmentation. Use server-level or application-level defragmentation (this is much like the defrag on your PC). Storage array–level defragmentation can also help. Storage arrays know about disks, volumes, and virtual volumes; storage arrays do not know about files or databases. Storage array–level defragmentation typically involves rearranging storage to eliminate empty blocks and to store all the data for a virtual volume together, rather than scattered across the drives. Additionally, splitting one large data store (I thinking here about e-mail) into several separate data stores can help.

14.3.4   Individual Account Problems

Determine whether performance problems are for all accounts or for individual accounts (typically e-mail).

Remedy: If specific accounts are problematic, this can be addressed by identifying those problem accounts and separating them onto e-mail databases on faster storage, on a faster server, with more memory. Spending low amounts of money to solve specific targeted problems is fiscally responsible, while spending large amounts of money on across-the-board improvements is not so smart.

14.3.5   Resource Contention

The root cause of performance problems often involve multiple loads (other applications, other backup-snapshot-replication I/O loads). There are situations where belt-and-suspenders approaches get in the way. Exchange and other applications have their own snapshot-backup-replication capability, and storage administrators often zealously apply storage array–based snapshot-backup-replication, doubling the consumption of resources.

Remedy: Check for other I/O loads on the storage and the servers. Moving loads to other storage arrays or other servers is simpler, easier, and orders of magnitude cheaper than wholesale replacement of storage hardware.

14.3.6   Time of Day

Time of day issues are related to resource contention, as described in the previous section. Often the root cause of a performance problem can be linked to the time of day. This is a clear indicator of resource contention. It's likely that other I/O or applications are overconsuming memory, storage I/O, or the CPU all at once.

Remedy: Find the root cause by identifying the time of day during which you have performance problems. Identify the servers and storage systems involved, and look for overconsumption of resources.

14.3.7   Storage Array Misbehavior

Performance problems can be generated by storage array misbehavior. Some vendor-specific enterprise storage systems write anywhere on the drive (wherever the disk head happens to be when the write comes through), which can lead to very high levels of fragmentation that require a scheduled defragmentation every 24 hours. In a 24×7 world-wide operation, there are no times in the day where defragging I/O won't compete with user I/O requests.

In a different system from another vendor, dynamic (automated) transition between RAID types is a "feature." In automated RAID transition, for example, the array will decide that a RAID-5 is better off as RAID-1 and the array will initiate that conversion, resulting in lots of I/O and lots of fragmentation. It's advisable to check for storage array–initiated fragmentation and for RAID-type conversion prior to spending money to buy more of the same gear that's causing the problem.

Remedy: Find the root cause: Is automated server array defragmentation occurring? Are automated RAID-type transitions happening? These are behaviors which are architecturally fundamental to two specific storage hardware platforms; the remedy is to migrate data off of those problematic arrays and onto different arrays without those architectural problems. If you are one hundred percent sure that this is the root cause, it is advisable to take steps to retire that hardware early and replace it with storage hardware that does not exhibit the (frankly stupid) behavior of automated RAID level migration or frequent forced automated defragmentation.

14.3.8   Storage Caching

If all signs point to slow storage arrays, consider storage caching. It's important to know how and why caching works, and the risks inherent in the approach. In caching, a server sends a "write" request to a storage array, and that data is written to cache. The storage array cache is like RAM on your PC—it's really fast, but needs power to store anything;

therefore, it is considered "volatile memory" because it will lose data if power is lost. Once data is written to cache, the storage system responds to the server with a "write successful" acknowledgement. The server thinks the write is complete and proceeds merrily on its tasks. Meanwhile, back in the storage array, the data still sits in cache (volatile memory) until the slower drive has time to complete the write onto magnetic HDD or flash (permanent or nonvolatile storage). Figure 14.1 illustrates the process.

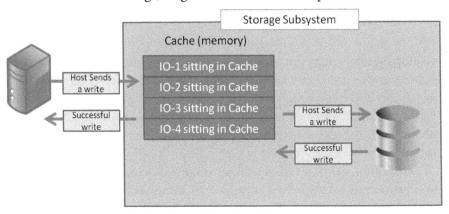

Figure 14.1   Storage Caching

Storage arrays include cache to speed up performance. Caching and data integrity for storage is not an easy computer science problem, and typically, storage caching is turned off. Performance may be improved by turning caching on (if it is off) or adding more cache. Additionally, disk drives have cache. For enterprise applications, turning on the write cache creates a risk of data-loss and is not advisable, but turning on disk drive read caching is safe and useful if there is specific data that is needed often. It's advisable to confirm that disk drives have write caching turned off and read-caching turned on.

For caching to successfully improve storage performance, the write cache must be big enough to buffer the I/O so disk drives don't become overwhelmed with I/O requests. Read caching must be big enough to have "cache hits," meaning a server will request to read a chunk of frequently read data and that data is sitting in cache. The storage subsystem serves the data to the server from cache; the I/O never hits the disk drive. The response time is 10–20 microseconds, rather than 10–20 milliseconds. That may not sound like a lot, but in situations with lots of I/O, these delays can add up.

To deal with the risk of data loss, cache must be protected in case bad stuff happens, such as a power outage or a storage controller malfunction. The better storage arrays include robust, protected caching, including mirrored caching across duplex storage array I/O controllers to deal with single I/O controller failure without data loss. And battery-backed cache can deal with power failure without data loss. Without mirrored or battery-backed cache, write caching is high risk, so performance improvement should be restricted to read caching only. If the application encounters a high percentage of read requests and a low percentage of write requests, read caching may solve the problem.

Performance can be improved by increasing storage cache. But before spending money, ask for data to show the system exceeds cache limits and can actually benefit performance.

14.3.9   Storage Rearrangement

If signs still point to slow storage arrays there are a number of improvements possible:

Remedy: The data can be reorganized. Mirroring, also known as RAID-1, is faster than RAID-5 or RAID-6; it is also more expensive. It is possible to move some hot data off of RAID-5 or 6 and onto mirrored RAID. Performance can be improved by moving to a faster drive (10,000 rpm to 15,000 rpm).

Performance can be improved by reducing competing I/O request (and fragmentation) by partitioning drives for specific high I/O activities like paging, scratch, or swap files.

14.3.10   Fibre Channel Zoning

Fibre channel is an amazing technology; however, as with most amazing technologies, it is possible to misconfigure or misapply it. One common but easily fixed issue with fibre channel is zoning. FC is designed with zones, so I/O for one application can be separated to avoid interfering with another application's I/O. If FC zoning is misconfigured. it can result in performance problems.

Remedy: It's advisable to recheck existing zoning for FC prior to going after a massive FC hardware upgrade. However, it is very possible that the newer 8Gb FC will improve performance, so leave that as an option (selectively).

14.3.11   Latency

Latency is a fancy word for *delay*. Even with the fastest available wire speed (8Gb/s FC), performance problems will be encountered if there are delays along the way. An appropriate metaphor for latency is automobile traffic: The highway speed limit is like wire speed (8 Gb/s FC), but if there are delays, such as stoplights, the trip will take longer. If there is other traffic in addition to the stoplights, the trip gets even longer and can eventually turn into gridlock. Every little delay adds up and is compounded by the amount of I/O traffic competing for bandwidth. Latency can be particularly evident in Internet applications; stuttering audio or video is evidence that too many waits along the way have exceeded the amount of data locally cached (or buffered) locally. The same principles apply to data storage, it's just less visible/obvious; the end user simply sees poor response.

Remedy: The root cause of latency is (generally) too many little delays and too many I/O requests. Look for little delays from end to end. Start with the disk drives; are they capable of responding to the I/O load? Perhaps so, if we spread the I/O load across multiple disks (in geek-speak, "more spindles"). Alternately, the storage can be rearranged to put cooler data elsewhere, taking some of the load away. Putting really hot data on SSDs is increasingly an option.

Key Concept

Performance improvement based on guessing leads to spending lots of money on the wrong stuff.

Make data-driven decisions: How much measurable performance is adequate?

Use tools to measure performance, isolate and address the root cause.

Know the root cause of below-acceptable performance, and make decisions based on facts.

Remedies may involve adding server memory, tuning packet size, rearranging RAID and HDDs, and rearranging the locations of data and storage hardware (hot-data, cool-data approach).

In summary, there is a tendency to overengineer and overspend. The resulting injection of complexity and overengineering can disguise simple problems. Keep it simple. If complexity (e.g., replication, thin provisioning, and the like) is warranted, then use it sparingly, only where merited in Tier 1 storage. Other storage should be addressed with simple, maintainable, scalable solutions.

14.4   Solid State Drives (SSDs) and Solid State Storage (SSS)

I'm going to jump to the end and ruin the punch line on solid state drives (SSDs) and solid state storage (SSS): Simple approaches prevail. Use caching, and use SSDs as a front end to HDDs. Cache the hot data (which needs the performance) on SSDs. The cooler, less accessed data (the stuff that consumes all the capacity) need not go on SSD; it can stay on HDDs.

All the debate about wear-out, wear-leveling, and SLC versus MLC does not matter, or is about problems that have already been solved.

- SSDs are faster than hard drives, especially in random-read workloads.
- SSDs are *more* expensive than hard drives on a cost per GB.
- SSDs are *less* expensive than hard drives on a cost per IOP (performance).

To repeat: Simple approaches prevail. Put the hot data (needing the performance) on SSDs. Put the cooler data (the stuff that consumes all the capacity) on HDDs.

Because solid state storage offers far and away the best performance and best power/performance compared to any HDD, SSS has earned a place in enterprise storage (see Figure 14.2).

It's like the question of a sports car or minivan: There are many examples of enterprise storage where spending on performance is warranted (like the sports car). But mostly, enterprise storage is where good-enough performance is adequate (like getting from A to B in a minivan).

Our focus is on spending less and delivering better service levels. And SSD and SSS, if intelligently applied, have the best potential to do just that—provide better service for less money.

Without taking too deep a dive into the various SSD technologies and industry dynamics (which are fascinating, by the way), we'll cover the how, where, and why of using SSDs.

The big criticism of SSDs is the high cost of GB/$ as compared to hard disks. But SSDs have advantage of very high IO, SSDs, when applied intelligently are a huge performance-price advantage, over HDDs.

14.4.1   Where and How to Use SSDs

SSDs are a new technology—sort of. Solid state storage has been with us for decades, just in a different package. There are many useful solid state storage

Figure 14.2   Solid State Drive and Hard Disk Drive

products—they usually look like a box with a storage interface (SCSI, SAS, FC, Infini-band, or something similar). These products served a useful purpose, usually in scientific or similar settings with large data sets and big computational simulations; using solid state storage for the dataset reliably speeds up the I/O, and the simulation finishes faster. And speed-ups of simulations allow the organization to do the task at hand, be it oil field exploration or finite element analysis for aircraft, spacecraft, or automotive applications. For those types of scientific applications, there is success and immediate payback!

SSD adoption for traditional IT is a different story. Compare the total market for SSDs as compared to the total market for enterprise performance HDDs—the market and total revenues for solid state storage fell significantly short of market and total revenues for performance-optimized hard drives (15K rpm HDDs). The underlying reasons for the lack of traditional IT adoption of SSD are easily understood: It's the wrong tool for the job; too costly, with less than bulletproof reliability and real-world performance that was less than compelling.

The key assumption is that all data should be on SSD, and therefore SSD is unaffordable. Let's challenge the assumption! If we apply SSDs as cache or dynamic tiered storage in front of HDDs, then that changes the price-performance-power comparisons significantly.

There are a short list of variables when applying SSDs:

- Use SSDs to completely replace HDDs or use SSDs to front-end?
- Use SSDs in RAID configuration to protect data?
- Use HDDs in the server or in the storage array?
- Use solid state disks (SSDs) or solid state storage (SSS)?

Figure 14.3 shows examples of the different approaches. Use Case 1 starts with the typical server direct attached storage; the arrow indicates data being read off the drive RAID array into the server. Since this situation requires good performance, the drives will be 15K rpm. When the phrase "Enterprise SSDs" is spoken, Use Case 2 immediately jumps to mind, and the next thought is a very expensive price tag: "If my current system uses 5TB raw capacity 15K drives, that will be big money, $80,000 to $100,000. I think I'll wait."

Use Case 2 requires some sort of RAID protection in the case of failure or replacement.

Use Cases 3 and 4 show SSD or SSS as a fast front end to slower HDD. With the proper storage-tiering software, this approach is financially feasible for the simple reason that only the hot data is on SSD or SSS. There is a payoff for IOPS/$ and GB/$, as long as the money is focused on the hot data. Data movement in Use Cases 3 and 4 can be either caching or tiering.

Simply put, caching *copies* hot data from disk drives (3a, 4a) onto fast SSDs (3b, 4b); specifically leaving a copy of the data on the disk drives. Tiering *moves* hot data from disk drives (3a, 4a) onto fast SSDs (3b,4b), specifically leaving no copy of the data on disk drives.

So, that was our examination of SSDs in direct attached storage model.

When we talk about tiering, our results (and therefore the financial payoff) are dependent on how the data is moved. Let's begin with a terminology refresher: a LUN (logical unit number) is a group of disks; it can contain one or more volumes. When you start looking at products, you can expect to encounter LUN-level tiering and sub-LUN tiering.

A typical LUN-level tiering use case consists of create a LUN for each month of financial transactions. As the months go on, each LUN gets moved to slower storage and eventually archived to tape. LUN-level tiering is better than no tiering; it's workable, but far from ideal. Problems arise when cooler data is demoted, and later in time (like quarter-end or year-end) the data becomes momentarily hot again, and the entire LUN is

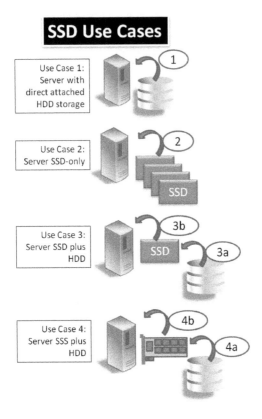

Figure 14.3   SSD Use Cases, Direct Attached Storage

promoted from cooler tier to the performance tier. The bigger the granularity of the data movement, the more unwieldy that movement becomes, the more likely cooler data is intermixed with hot data, and the less likely the financial payoff will be realized.

Tiering at the sub-LUN level will involve migrating groups of blocks. (Another terminology refresher: a block is a loose term referring to a chunk of data.) Sub-LUN tiering involves moving (not copying) blocks from one tier to another tier of disks (both demotion and promotion). One key task is SSD housekeeping to demote the cool data to Tier 2 storage, making room on Tier 1 for the incoming hot data. Smaller granularity is better than bigger granularity of data movement. This begs the question: What happens in tiering if something breaks? What is the serviceability? Where is the data? You should definitely cover these questions with your tiering product suppliers, and make sure they have clear, feasible answers.

The preferred approach is caching, in which data is copied onto the solid state drive or solid state device and a backup copy remains on the hard drive. This approach also raises questions: What happens when things go wrong? Is there a scenario in which data is written to SSD but not yet written back to the HDD storage array, and something breaks? That is a very real risk, but the risk is substantially lower than in tiering. If a write occurs to SSD, that data is relatively safe. Power can fail and the data will be present on the SSD when the power is restored. If something breaks in the caching software itself, removal of that caching software is a significantly lower risk and more straightforward situation than removing tiering software. Simply remove the caching software; the original data will still be available on HDD.

We've covered the model of direct attached storage with SSDs. Let's move onto the model of SAN storage and SSDs, as illustrated in Figure 14.4.

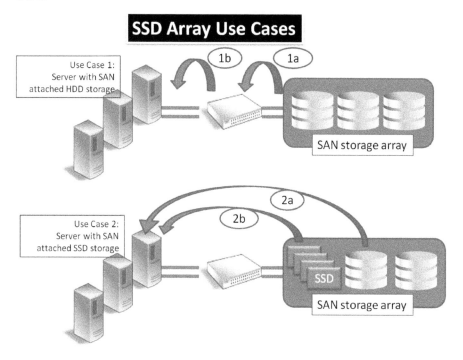

Figure 14.4   SSD Use Cases, SAN Attached Storage

In Use Case 1, the typical SAN attachment, there are latencies (waits). Yes, there is a big pipe, such as 8Gb/s FC, between the server, the switch, and the array. But an I/O involves a request from the server to the switch (delay), an I/O from the switch to the array (delay), retrieval of the data from HDD (delay), an I/O from the array to the switch (delay), and I/O from the switch to the server (delay). Too many delays, poor performance—*yuck*. FC zoning can keep lower-priority traffic from interfering with high-priority traffic, but even with a FC SAN free of competing traffic, the delays described above will inevitably happen, and it only gets worse with competing traffic.

Use Case 2 applies SSDs, but not in an intelligent way. In this example, the SSDs are just another LUN, a group of devices organized in a RAID array. They potentially serve data faster than the 15K drives organized in a similar way. But the SSDs in Use Case 2 are still victim to the SAN latencies.

In Use Case 3, the SSD (one or more) is installed in a disk drive slot in the server. This model depends on caching software to put the hot data onto the server SSD. A few SSDs are employed selectively, serving hot data and not wasted on cool data; SSDs deliver significantly improved random performance. This model does not involve wholesale replacement of lots of HDDs. And (best of all), since the SSD is close to the server, SAN delays will only be experienced the first time the hot data is used; at subsequent times, the hot data will be in the SSD in the server, without the multiple latencies of a SAN.

In Use Case 4, a solid state storage device is employed; the device is installed in the server connecting to the high-speed PCI bus. Therefore, it connects to the south bridge without traversing a disk drive interface (such as SATA or SAS). In some cases, having that drive interface has no impact, if the drive interface doesn't get in the way. But depending on the speed of the SSS, the drive interface may get in the way; in these cases, the SSS is the ideal way to deliver high performance without all the overhead of a protocol written under the assumption that there was a mechanical storage device on the other end of the wire. Otherwise, this Use Case grants the same benefits as Use Case 4—the first time the hot data is moved, it encounters latencies, but subsequent access is faster because the data is right there in the server with no sequential latencies. And with caching (not tiering), the caching software and solid state device can be removed from the system without high risk and the system will continue to serve data, just off the HDD array.

When running your first pilots, you'll run into the question, "How much SSD or SSS capacity should we buy?" The academic answer involves estimating how many read requests will find the data in the cache (or tier) versus how many read requests will need to access data on the storage array. That *hit-ratio* will be affected by the quality of the algorithm that sorts out the hot data to be cached onto the solid state or simply left on the storage array. In other words, the problem becomes intractable (i.e., your mileage may vary). The practical answer is to follow the example set by normal memory caching: size your SSD or SSS as no less than ten percent of your total used capacity on the storage array. If your pilot runs 1 TB of used capacity, then apply SSD or SSS storage of no less than 100 GB.

14.4.2   SSD Endurance, Life Cycle, and Warranty

I'll cut to the chase and ruin the ending: SSDs have adequate wear-endurance.

Wear-endurance has been the topic of significant discussion with the introduction of enterprise SSDs. One type of flash, multi-level cell (MLC), has longer wear endurance: typically, 100,000 write cycles. However, MLC is significantly more expensive. The less expensive type of flash, single level cell (SLC) has lower write endurance, typically 10,000 write cycles. Of course, the computer industry wants the lower price, and of course, the IT customers want the longer endurance and a long warranty. Putting all that noise aside, SSDs are getting bigger. It takes a long time to fill up a 100 GB SSD once; it takes a long, long time to fill it up 10,000 times; it takes a really long time to fill it up 100,000 times. When we get to 300 GB SSDs or 500 GB SSDs or 1TB SSDs . . . you get the point. All the reads and writes are constrained by the speed of the interface (SAS 6Gb/s, SATA 3Gb/s, FC 8Gb/s), we assume at least half the work load is read, so no more than half the work load is write (multiply the interface capacity by fifty percent), then calculate how long it will take to fill up the drive once, and then calculate the time it will take to fill up the drive 100,000 times. SSD's capacity solves the wear-out pboblem.

What happens when the wear-out limit is reached? From a business standpoint, higher capacity SSDs will last longer; even if they wear out early, they will have a useful life of two to four years, so planned replacement can be baked into the business or maintenance model. In three years, there will be a newer, bigger, faster device anyway, so replacing it for other reasons makes sense too.

Technically, when wear-out limit is reached, the SSD will stop writing. After the write cycle wear-out limit is reached, the data will continue to be readable; it's just that no additional writes are possible. The wear-out mode for SSDs is predictable and inconvenient, but certainly not catastrophic. Compare it to disk drive failure modes, when you're working one moment, then click, gone—it will not write or read. With backup, snapshots, replication, and RAID, the storage industry has done a truly amazing job engineering around the unfortunate failure characteristics of the HDD. One day, none of that will be needed—just use huge pools of redundant flash (or similar) and call it good.

14.4.3   Flash and RAM

SSDs are based on flash memory technology. Flash is capable of holding onto data even when powered down, a handy capability for situations where power is abruptly lost; the data is already saved and will be available when the power is restored. This is not the case with RAM, which will not retain data if the power is lost. Some enterprise-class SSD and SSS products get big performance numbers by caching data off the flash and onto on-board RAM. If that's the approach, the on-board RAM must be capable of protecting and storing the data in case of an unexpected power outage—either via a battery or a capacitor that will deliver enough power to write out the RAM data back onto flash memory. Most performance-optimized systems employ RAM somehow and somewhere. I advise you to be extremely diligent in determining failure modes with RAM. If there is a failure, and the data is in RAM (either RAM on the device, or RAM in the server), that data is lost.

Some (at least one) SSS products employ RAM in a less-than-thoroughly protected way. Part of the data is in flash, and certain metadata is in server RAM; if the server hangs unexpectedly or is ungracefully shut down, the metadata in system RAM is lost and the data in flash becomes inaccessible. This approach is fine for situations where the data can be pulled again from another server (e.g., credit card fraud, scientific simulations, content delivery). But this metadata in RAM is not fine for anything that involves writes.

Wrapping up the SSD section:

- The wear leveling problem is solved.
- Enterprise SSDs are financially responsible for situations in which hot data can be focused onto the SSD. SSDs are not financially responsible for situations where SSDs simply replace HDDs for both hot and cold data.
- Use SSD as a cache in front of hard disks, not as a replacement for hard disks. Caching delivers the desired result (speeding performance) without all the ugly by-products: big spending, wholesale replacement of HDDs, or big risk exposure for error modes.
- Put the SSD close to the server. Avoid the latency of the SAN.

Key Concept

Use SSDs for as a cache in front of hard disks.
Approaches in which SSDs replace 15K rpm drives in large scale are not yet viable.

This book is about applied storage, mostly focusing on business and intentionally avoiding discussions of future technologies. The reality is, all technology evolves and changes to better fit market needs. SSDs is evolving and changing faster than any other aspect of the storage business. It is reasonable to expect that SSDs will repeat much of the history we have seen in HDDs: SSDs will definitely drop in price; reliability will definitely improve; industry standards will form around SSDs (such as 6Gb/s SATA and 12 Gb/s SAS); SSDs will improve performance; SSDs will improve reliability; and SSDs will evolve (much as the HDDs did) to address specific storage submarkets—performance laptop, high performance read AND write for OLTP, high performance read for analytics, warehousing, and social media.

SSDs, right now, are at the same price point as 15K rpm "short stroked" drives. We advise getting a start on SSDs with a feasibility project, and the place to start is a wherever short stroked drives are used.

Chapter 15

Performance and Backup

Backup is an I/O workload that impacts limited resources.

The diagram in Figure 15.1 shows a typical server which is overprovisioned. In other words, the hardware is significantly bigger than the workload; you paid too much. The dotted line represents the I/O load; it shifts around a lot because, in this example, this is presumed to be a small server with only one or two workloads, dependent on a small list of users. Therefore, the workload fluctuates more than a bigger server or bigger storage array serving more applications and more users.

In Figure 15.1, we see a couple of backup tasks. Sometimes these backup tasks hit at low points and sometimes they hit at highpoints. And when they hit at high points, the performance impact is noticeable.

Even with an overprovisioned server with excess performance headroom, backup often does create a performance issue.

Servers attached to storage arrays that still employ server-based backup still encounter the same issue, because the I/O load related to the backup is still handled by the server.

In Figure 15.2, we assume a bigger server with lots of workloads, presumably virtual servers, and lots of users. With more workloads, presumably this creates a situation where the server is fully loaded most hours of the day, as depicted by the dotted line. In this case, the server is properly sized for the task at hand—until we add backup.

The solutions are:

- Move from incremental backups to snapshots. This reduces the load and has less system impact.
- Move backups from server based to array based, and let the array handle the I/O. Servers are built for computing and don't do I/O as well as storage arrays, which are built for I/O.

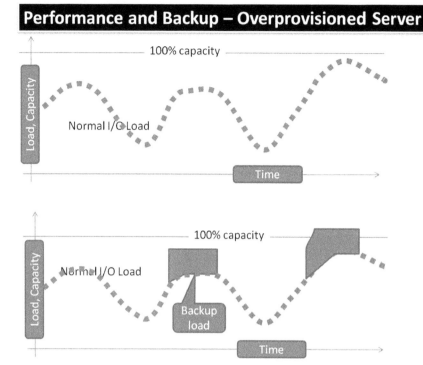

Figure 15.1   Performance, Backup, and Overprovisioned Server

- Reduce the load by moving stale data to Tier 2 storage. Back up the hot data frequently, back up the stale data much less frequently.

Find the root cause of your performance problems and make fact-based decisions. Ask the systems analysts for performance reports and I/O reports over a period of days or weeks to determine whether there is or is not a performance problem rooted in backup.

Let's get a clearer picture on how to put the hardware together, and why. Figure 15.3 shows the simplest of backup approaches: a server, some drives, and a tape device. Every so often, the administrator will create a tape. Almost every IT operation in the world has some installed base that looks like this. To use a metaphor, when we talk about cars, we talk about the performance sports car. But the minivan or sedan see all the daily use, all the miles, all the repairs, all the fuel, and all the tires. This is not glamorous, but it is in use, and it does consume money and staff-time, both of which are limited resources.

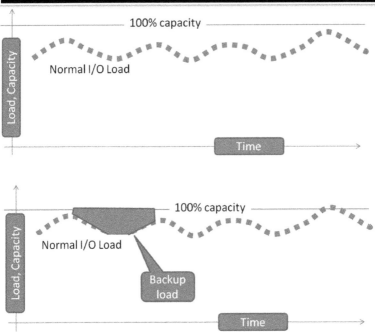

Figure 15.2   Performance, Backup, and a Right-Provisioned Server

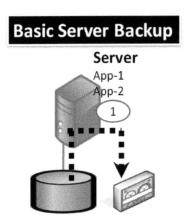

Figure 15.3   Basic Server Backup

The problems with this approach are numerous, but in this section we are focusing on performance. In this case, the datapath (1) dotted line indicates that the data is read from the disk(s), passed across the server memory bus, into system memory, then back across the memory bus.

Figure 15.4 shows what's happening behind the scenes.

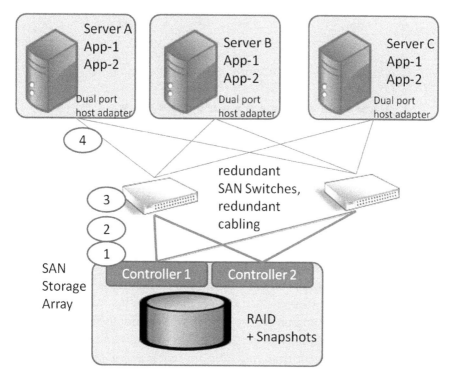

Figure 15.4   Basic Server Backup: Data Path, Too Much Time on the System Bus

Notice at point (1) that the data travels over the system bus *twice*, and notice at point (2) that the data travels over the memory bus *twice*. I ask you, is it any surprise that backup is a performance killer? The x86 architecture is a great architecture for calculation—after all, it is optimized around the CPU (central processing unit). But it is *not* optimized around the storage data movement. There's good news, though—storage arrays are organized to move data faster, more efficiently, and more reliably than servers.

Okay, so what about network backup—that's over the network, right? I am sorry to disappoint, but although network backup has the advantage of consolidating backup (and there is definitely value in consolidated backup), it has a major drawback to server-based network backup, as illustrated in Figure 15.5.

Because network backup still uses a data path that crosses the system bus (of Server A), writes the data into memory, then crosses the system bus

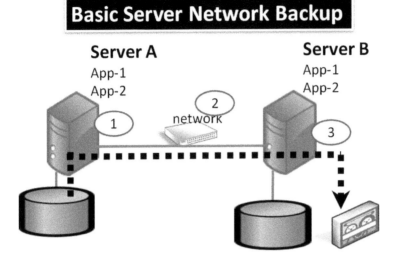

Figure 15.5   Basic Server Backup: Data Path, Too Much Time on the System Bus

again on the originating server (Server A) before moving across the network and competing for network bandwidth. Then ,as it moves onto the target backup server (Server B), it crosses the system bus yet again. If there are applications running on Server B, they will definitely be impacted, and the network will definitely be impacted. The workarounds are to run the backup during off-peak time, but this approach is not often practical in 24x7 operations. It's also limiting for RPO; sometimes, a four-hour RPO is required.

The application performance impact on Server B can be avoided by running the applications elsewhere, but in that case, you've overprovisioned Server B. Network backup is operationally more convenient than single server backup, but it has serious drawbacks.

Enter storage arrays and array-based backup. In Figure 15.6, we consolidate storage on array. Connect the servers to the storage array(s) with a fast SAN (e.g., FC, iSCSI, SAS). The SAN is low latency (remember, latency = waiting). SANs can be zoned, so the traffic created by the backup server (6) with the tape drive can be kept from interfering with the normal storage traffic for servers 1, 2, and 3.

Storage arrays improve server performance because they offload the backup task and traffic from the servers. This approach leaves the servers to do what they do best (calculation and data processing), and leave a the storage array to do what it does best (efficient, high-performance, reliable I/O).

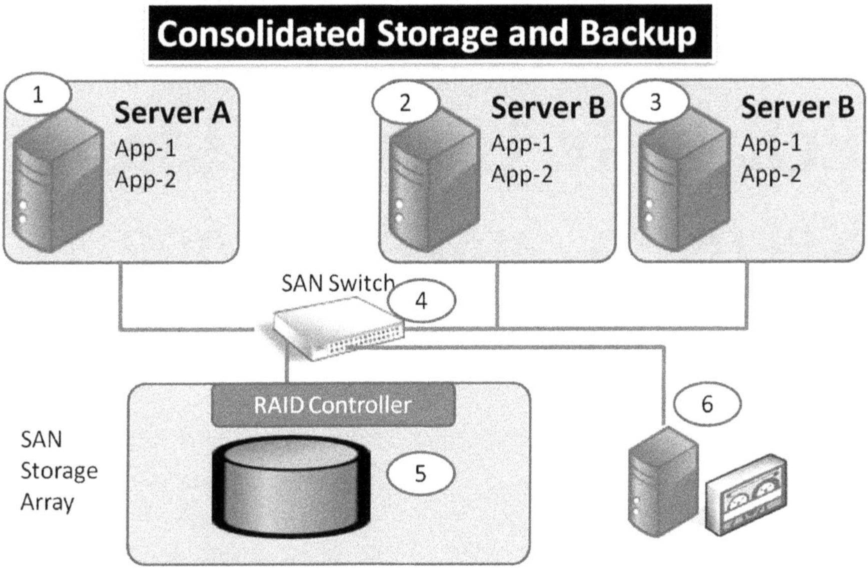

Figure 15.6   Array-Based Backup

Chapter 16

The Right Tools for Reliability, Uptime, Disaster Recovery, and Archiving

There is nothing like practice and preparation to remove stress, worry, or doubt.

When you're planning for the worst, how much insurance do you buy? Look for *high value* and *high likelihood* of risk. Spend to protect the high-value stuff, and avoid spending to protect the low-value stuff. Segment the problem by storage tier and SLA. Look for inexpensive, "good enough" solutions for the most commonly encountered problems, such as drive failure, cable failure, and server failure. And for the less likely stuff, like natural disasters, reserve spending for only the most important storage.

This chapter presents several examples to consider.

16.1 Server Problem (Direct Attached Storage)

Problem, Root Cause, Impact: A server problem that occurs in a server with direct attached storage (e.g., hardware failure, memory leak, problematic update, etc.). When servers have storage directly attached and servers fail, that data is offline until that server is recovered.

For Tier 3 and some Tier 2 storage, server direct-attached, when there is a problem, the impact is felt but is not catastrophic. In the worst case, recover the data from snapshot or from tape onto another server. Typically, the risk of a day of downtime is acceptable for Tier 2 and Tier 3. Tier 1 storage, by definition, is business-critical, and a day of downtime is an unacceptable risk.

Remedy: For Tier 2 and Tier 3, use shared external storage with multi-server access (nice-to-have) to reduce and manage risk, and practice restoration from tape or backup to prove you can have the system back up in some reasonable amount of time (a day).For Tier 1 storage (a must), install the data on a shared storage array set up for multiserver access. Include these values in your SLA.

16.2   Server Problem (External SAN Storage)

Problem, Root Cause, Impact: A server problem that occurs in a server that is accessing external storage (SAN storage). Server failure root causes include hardware failure, memory leak, problematic update, etc. The impact of this problem is that the data is unavailable until another server running the same application accesses the storage.

Remedy: Manually connect a new host to the shared storage. Practice the host mapping task so that when the problems arrive you can efficiently address them. Be sure to write down the instructions and leave them where they can be found when needed, such as in the sys_admin log book or knowledge base. For Tier 1 storage, the solution is to establish server failover so that when a failure happens, the remedy is automatic. Record these in your SLA.

16.3   Drive Failure

Problem, Root Cause, Impact: The problem of drive failure has a high probability: you can expect one or two percent of your installed drives to fail in a given year. When a drive fails, RAID logic takes over. If the RAID is mirroring, it simply runs on the other copy of the mirrored data with no performance impact—but it's like driving without a spare tire. If we're using some parity approach, such as RAID-5 or RAID-6, the system runs in "parity recovery mode" and there is a noticeable performance impact. Again, it's like driving a car without a spare tire; if you lose another drive, it's time to recover the last full backup. If normal production performance is barely adequate, then performance impact during rebuild will be, without question, a major problem.

Remedy: For Tier 1, Tier 2, and Tier 3, establish a RAID warm-spare, so that when a drive fails, a spare immediately takes its place, and RAID logic will rebuild the drive. The systems admin will need to replace the failed drive with a new warm spare. There is a bigger parity rebuild time for bigger volumes and high-capacity disk drives. The rebuild can take several hours to more than a day, depending on the size of the data, the performance of the controller, and competing workloads. For situations where parity rebuild performance penalties are unacceptable, consider mirroring to avoid this risk. For the rest, RAID-5 or RAID-6 is adequate. It is important to note that RAID is not backup; RAID cannot fix the problem of accidental deletion or virus. Practice the failed-drive scenario, measure performance prefailure under normal situations, measure performance during parity recovery mode (before the parity rebuild), and measure performance during parity rebuild mode; this will provide real-world insight and clear understanding of the performance impact.

16.4   Accidental Data Deletion or Modification, or Virus

Problem, Root Cause, Impact: Accidental data deletion or modification, or virus.

Remedy: A disk-to-disk backup or point-in-time snapshot can recover data captured predeletion or previrus. Incremental tape backup can also solve the problem, but it's expensive to maintain incremental tape backups on a large group of servers on a frequent (low RPO) basis. To practice the recovery, conduct a mock exercise by deleting a file or a mailbox folder and seeing how things unfold. Be sure to include the data recovery RPO/RTO in your SLA.

16.5   Storage Array Controller Failure

Problem, Root Cause, Impact: Storage controllers are designed not to fail; they are built on specially designed, specially tested firmware, and the test matrix is a very limited set of configurations (not every possible disk drive, HBA, software, shared library, browser, and plug-in in a many-to-many relationship). Tightly controlled configurations consistently demonstrated better reliability. The impact of a storage controller failure in a single controller environment is broad; the data is offline and inaccessible until the storage controller can resume normal operations. In the case of a dual controller, each storage array controller monitors the health of the partner controller; if one controller fails, the other controller senses it and takes over all host connections to all the respective volumes.

Remedy: Controllers rarely fail, and even single controller arrays are significantly lower risk than servers and direct attached storage. Single controller arrays are typically suitable for Tier 2. For Tier 1 storage, external storage with dual controllers is the typical configuration. Dual controllers typically include the ability to both read and write cache (to improve performance), and the cache is designed to protect against a controller failure (the cache is mirrored to the other controller) and to protect against loss of data in the case of a power failure (the cached data is written to local flash memory, and recovered into cache when the power is restored and system is back in operation). The difference in cost of single controller versus dual controller is insignificant compared to the entire cost of the external storage system, so having dual controllers is justifiable and is, by far, the most common solution.

16.6   Cable Failure

Problem, Root Cause, Impact: Cables fail; they can be accidentally disturbed while working on adjacent hardware or cabling or power. The connectors can fail. They can snag, get crimped, get tripped over or otherwise get unceremoniously dragged away.

Remedy: Neatness, wire wraps, labeling at both ends—these are good starts. It's usually not possible to initiate a project to label both ends of every wire or wire wrap. It is worthwhile to start a policy for all new/revised wiring going forward: Everything gets labels, everything gets wire wrapped. If you start this policy, soon enough you will see improvements such as shorter installation times and fewer interruptions.

The other obvious fix is redundant cabling from servers and redundant cabling for storage arrays and expansion cabinets. The redundancy does not guarantee that, if a cable is pulled, the storage path will automatically adjust and service will be maintained. Redundant cabling should be tested to ensure the redundancy behaves as expected.

16.7   SAN Switch Problem

Problem, Root Cause, Impact: If a SAN switch goes offline, servers do not communicate with storage. This problem has a big impact, but thankfully it is not high probability. Once SAN switching is in place, service is at low risk.

Remedy: Start with physical security; make sure all SAN equipment is behind a locked door and exposed to the fewest human beings possible.

Provide limited, standardized, thoroughly tested configurations with duplicated SAN ports. Every SAN port (FC, iSCSI, SAS) has an associated cost. The best and fastest ports cost more. SAN ports get less expensive with time. SAN usually means fibre channel (FC), but increasingly, IT has adopted iSCSI and is beginning to adopt SAS as a SAN. FC ports are the most expensive. iSCSI is less expensive, but much slower than FC ports. SAS is the least expensive, but does not have all the capabilities of FC, such as FC zoning and wide area network replication. SAS is the newcomer for storage area networks or, more clearly said, for connecting lots of servers to shared storage. Many external storage arrays have multiple SAS ports, which can be used to directly connect multiple servers to a single shared external storage array—no switch required. But there are also very low limits on the number of servers which can be connected. Increased server attachments can be achieved with SAS switches. Having a low-cost port means you can affordably employ duplicated SAN switches with redundant cabling; affordably, to more servers.

Once you arrive at a configuration that works, do everything possible to standardize on it and document the setup. That way, when your SAN expert or consultant is on vacation or changes employers or changes careers to become a professional historic war re-enactor (yes, that actually happened), you will know the SAN setup, passwords, SAN addresses, zoning, and the like.

Again, redundant FC or iSCSI or SAS switches and redundant cabling should be tested to ensure the system will behave as expected. Pull a SAN cable, see if access reroutes. Pull power on a SAN switch, see if the other SAN switch handles traffic. Calculate the cost of SAN-per-port and people, and reflect the costs in your SLA.

16.8   Data Center Power Problem

Problem, Root Cause, Impact: The root cause of a power outage is usually with the power company, so it is completely out of your control. Power outages are usually not commonplace, but obviously they have a high impact.

Remedy: Again, this is where the tiering approach helps you focus spending money where it's needed, and avoid spending where not warranted. Remedies include selective replication of data to another site or selective use of auxiliary generators backed by server-grade UPSs.

A server-grade uninterruptable power supply (UPS) provides continuous power to servers and storage for long enough either to gracefully shut down or for auxiliary generators to take over. Auxiliary generation is a well known, mature technology: Hospitals are required to have auxiliary power. In hospitals, auxiliary power does not provide power to every electrical load in the hospital. Hospitals have separate wiring and circuit breaker panels for "normal" loads and "emergency" loads, such as operating rooms, vital monitoring, intensive care floors, resuscitators, exit signs, and the like. Auxiliary power generators have a system to detect power outage; when that happens, the generators are started, and the UPS holds power for several minutes until the generators take over and provide power for hours or days. Data centers use this exact same stuff. Not every data center load is powered by auxiliary generation or covered by UPS; only selected and critical components are covered. A tiering approach will avoid every single load being assessed as "critical" and lead to a situation where the data center auxiliary generation system is overloaded and requiring an expensive improvement. The prevailing assumption by IT is that every load should be on auxiliary generation. It is risky to assume that financially mature decisions are automatic. Facilities people who run auxiliary generation systems do not know if any given piece of IT equipment is an important or unimportant load, they only know what they're told by the work order or by IT people putting new equipment into the data center. Tiering helps you focus your spending on Tier 1 equipment and avoid spending on Tier 3.

Alternatively, you can replicate to another site or take advantage of managed hosting services (covered later in this book). Taking the remote replication route accompanied by server failover and redundant remote networking relieves the need for auxiliary power.

So when someone comes to you with a big bill for auxiliary generation, you may consider sidestepping that altogether with complete remote replication (networks, servers, storage). Alternatively, if someone comes to you with a big bill for remote replication, you may consider consolidating to a single site, using local replication and auxiliary power. And in both these cases, be selective and avoid Tier 2 or Tier 3 loads wherever possible.

16.9   Data Center Air Conditioning Problem

Problem, Root Cause, Impact: If the A/C goes out, soon enough the equipment will overheat and fail, usually with data loss.

Remedy: Have a plan. Have a shutdown schedule to remove the noncritical heat loads. Identify critical equipment and have portable units, sized based on the heat load, available to deliver cooling to the sensitive equipment. Know that air conditioning units are composed of electrical delivery, chilling, air handling, control (thermostats). Separating the air conditioning into multiple chilling units, multiple air conditioning units with spare units, and spare capacity is a well-used approach to reduce risk. Spreading equipment through several computer rooms, each serviced by separate air conditioning equipment, is yet another means to reduce risk.

Remote replication to another site or managed hosting facility is an alternative approach to reduce risk. Tiering is an asset here, you can identify critical loads, invest in them, and have a plan to shutdown noncritical loads. Include the cost in your SLA.

16.10   Data Center Interior Problem (Sprinklers)

Problem, Root Cause, Impact: Some data centers are equipped with sprinklers, some are not. If your data center has them and the sprinklers are triggered, the equipment—and your data—will suffer. Water and computers mix as well as tequila and power tools.

Remedy: If your data center is equipped with sprinklers, check into the local building codes (your facilities folks or architect can help) and absolutely confirm that sprinklers are required. If sprinklers are not required, get them out of your data center, right away. If they are mandatory, look into a way to avoid accidental triggering; have them serviced; and have them installed with the least sensitive allowable heat sensors. Replace with some other fire retardant such as Halon. Get equipment away from the sprinklers by moving to another room—or another facility if necessary.

16.11   Data Center Act of Nature

Problem, root cause, impact: Sometimes, things happen that are beyond anyone's control—floods, fires, quakes, or acts of war.

Remedy: Remote replication to another site or managed hosting facility is the common approach. The plan must include complete redundancy with failover logic (network, servers, storage). Tiering is an asset here; you can identify critical loads, invest in them, and have a plan to do without non-critical loads. Include the costs in your SLA.

The examples given in this chapter are just a sample of commonly encountered problems, not an exhaustive list. The point is to improve organization and clarity on the various scenarios and protect against failure where it makes sense. It's not necessary to provide full disaster recovery for Tier 2 or Tier 3 storage; through this exercise, you will first catalog all the systems, think through the failure modes, and make conscious decisions on which systems to improve or harden and which to leave as acceptable risks.

It is realistic to go through the entire server-SAN-storage setup from end to end, identifying all the possible single points of failure (drives, controllers, SAN switches, servers, drives, power supplies, and so forth) and then simulate failure at every point to demonstrate no-single-point-of-failure as well as failure recovery. I guarantee that if you conduct this exercise, you will learn valuable lessons on how systems fail and how they recover.

Simulating failure at every point is straightforward: List all the points of failure (drives, controllers, SAN switches, servers, drives, power supplies, and the like), and then pull a drive to simulate a failure, check the performance and the RAID rebuild process, pull a controller, pull a cable, pull power from the SAN switch, and pull the power cord to simulate a power supply failure.

Also check operational stuff, such as recovery of a incremental backup, a snapshot, a full backup. Simulate all that when key people are on vacation or otherwise unavailable.

16.12 Spending Wisely on Reliability

Technologies fail; that's a fact. The only question is what to do about it. The level of investment in failure-proofing is proportional to the value of the uptime. Implementing failover and replication is like buying insurance; financial responsibility pushes us to analyze exactly what to insure and how much insurance to buy. It's likely that you will see pressure to buy more insurance than you need for things that do not merit coverage. And conversely, there are many situations where it's irresponsible to NOT hold insurance.

Risk management is the analysis of what problems (risk) might be encountered, the likelihood of the problem or risk actually happening, and the impact if the problem or risk does actually happen.

Risk--> Probability--> Impact

Let's have a little fun with examples to start the bounding process:

- Little kids like Reader Rabbit software, it's not such a high quality program and hangs up.
  - Risk: Reader Rabbit software hangs up
  - Probability: High, happens often
  - Impact: Low, restart Reader Rabbit
- Aeschylus, the father of the Greek tragedy, died when an eagle dropped a tortoise on his head.
  - Risk: Being hit by a dropped tortoise
  - Probability: Low, almost never happens
  - Impact: Death, very serious consequence

We take risks every day—acceptable risks. We get into our cars to go to work, we fly on airplanes, we eat foods without really knowing where the food came from or how it was prepared. These are acceptable risks, and yes, the consequences are may be fatal, but the probability of such a consequence occurring are pretty low if we take some basic precautions: drive safely and defensively, wear seatbelts, fly airplanes from commercially licensed carriers with trained pilots, eat food from establishments that have passed health inspections. These risks are mitigated, and therefore acceptable.

The disaster recovery/business continuity task starts by listing clearly defined risks and then prioritizing them with BOTH high probability and high impact. Developing disaster recovery scenarios around low probability problems is fruitless unless our mission is to build comet-proof installations.

Disaster recovery comes in different shapes and sizes—presented from affordable to costly:

- Server failover, also known as multipathing
- Near continuous data protection, also known as *asynchronous* replication
- Full continuous data protection (CDP), also known as *synchronous replication*

Servers fail and fail often. Complexity is the enemy of reliability, and the millions of lines of firmware, drivers, operating systems, applications, and patches rival the complexity of almost all things manmade. Server failure/reboot/servicing is the most frequently encountered source of downtime. Fortunately, server operating systems (almost without exception) have some sort of failover or multipathing capability; this means the servers can be configured so that if one server fails, another server can access the data and take over the network IP address (redirecting user traffic from the failed server to the backup server).

Let's start with servers and server failover in the next chapter.

Spending wisely on reliability requires you to get out of the details, come up for air, and think: "If I am buying insurance, where would I spend a limited budget?" Insurance is good, but it can go overboard. Hypothetically: Do you really need to spend large amounts of money to cover some household or auto event that is not only unlikely, but also low impact if the worst happens? Does it make sense to pay $20 on a service plan for a $60 electronics product? Definitely spend on reliability, but spend wisely.

Chapter 17

Reliability and Server Failover

We're going back to a central theme of the book: tiering.

- *Tier 3* storage typically does not require server failover, and never requires replicated storage.
- *Tier 2* storage may or may not merits server failover; it typically does not merit replicated local storage. Improving on existing direct attached storage . . . server failover is typically not an option. If you need more insurance and need server failover for selected applications, this justifies moving from direct attached storage to external SAN storage.
- *Tier 1* storage typically requires server failover and sometimes requires replicated storage, either local replication or remote replication.

A key capability to providing workable failover is having a server (or virtual server) set up and tested to be the server that takes the load in the case that the primary server fails.

Server failover deployment can be significantly improved with the employment of virtual servers and virtual storage. The configuration of the primary server can be captured and cloned for the secondary server. The term *server configuration cloning* is also referred to as *bare metal configuration*. Since the data is on the storage array (or replicated by a primary storage array to a target storage array), cloning configurations significantly improves confidence in rapid deployment of server failover and confidence that server failover will actually work when the time comes.

17.1 How Server Failover Works

- The secondary server monitors the heartbeat of the primary server (and vice-versa), typically over ethernet.

- If the secondary server senses no heartbeat, then the secondary server initiates failover.
- The secondary server accesses the storage volume.
- The secondary server takes over the ethernet IP address aliases. Client server addresses are redirected to the secondary server.
- The secondary server runs the same application (Oracle, SAP, SQLserver, or whatever).
- Basic failover, such as Linux Device Mapper (LVM) and Microsoft MSCS, simply involves server failover and assumes that they attach to the same storage array.
- Advanced failover can direct servers to failover to a separate (replicated) storage array.

The heartbeat and the shared storage are the weak links in the system. If the servers are in the same building, the ethernet heartbeat is reliable. If the servers are across the street or across the country, using the ethernet heartbeat can be problematic, because other ethernet traffic can keep the heartbeat from getting from one server to another; usually resulting in a erroneous failover. An erroneous failover inflicts a short-term disruption of service, poses a risk of loss of data (if a database write occurs at exactly the wrong moment, it's often a mystery whether the write did or did not complete). And an erroneous failover will always result in a failback, a restoration of service to the properly operating server. Failback inflicts another short interruption of service and is usually a cause of fear, uncertainty, and doubt with most people involved. The bottom line is that the heartbeat is critical, and it is important to use isolated network or multiple network paths to ensure the heartbeat arrives reliably.

Replication is a great way to protect data with a live copy. Failover is a great way to keep enterprise applications running and avoid downtime.

If you require server failover, the first step is dealing with the storage (see Figure 17.1).

- No consolidation, no failover advantages—simple, easy to maintain.
- No consolidation, no failover disadvantages—the clients (3) are forced to attach to either server (1) or (2), but not to both. If the chosen server fails, needs servicing, or something similar, then the application and the associated application data is unavailable.

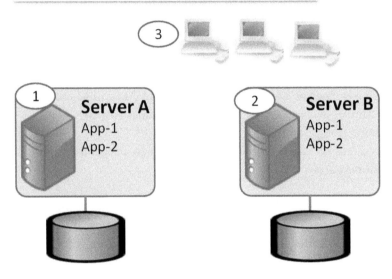

Figure 17.1   No Server Failover: Tier 3

For many applications, this is the financially responsible way to go. The expense of the extra hardware/software/care-and-feeding of servers capable of failover and arrays capable of failover is simply too large as compared to the cost and likelihood of downtime. This approach is suitable for applications that can tolerate the occasional hour or two of downtime and for which the risk of multihour downtime is acceptable . . . in other words, Tier 3.

Consolidated storage (Figure 17.2) offers an improved insurance plan. Here, if Server A fails, there are manual recovery options: Server B can be reconfigured manually, the IP aliases can be changed, and the application can be started. Usually, end users will need to exit and restart their applications. But the risk exposure is significantly lower than the nonconsolidated, direct attached storage approach.

Consolidation has significant benefits in reducing overprovisioning, and consolidating backup and recovery creates the opportunity for performance tiering. Consolidation can be a stepping stone into basic failover (where needed), and failover plus replication (where needed). Not every application merits these levels of spending, but no doubt some applications merit additional insurance.

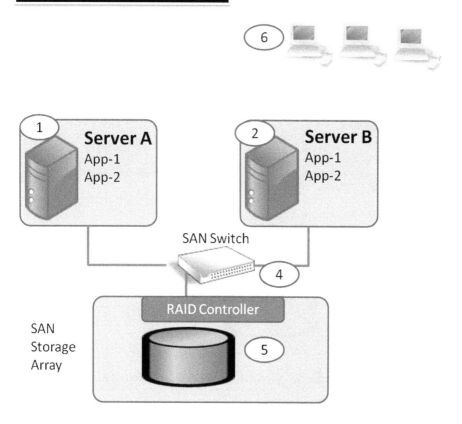

Figure 17.2   Consolidated but No Server Failover: Tier 2 or Tier 3

Basic failover without replication, also known as *shared everything*, requires maintaining two (or more servers) capable of failover. Data is protected through RAID and frequent snapshots or incremental backups. (See Figure 17.3.)

Basic failover without replication covers uptime for situations involving server crashes, application restarts, server reboots, and planned service outages. RAID and snapshots protect data. Server failover improves service uptime.

Basic failover without replication does NOT protect against situations that have an impact on the storage array: catastrophic hardware failure, flood, broken pipes, power problems, or network problems, for example. This approach is suitable for applications that cannot tolerate the occasional

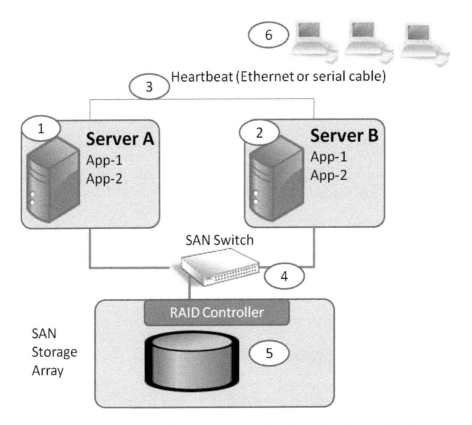

Figure 17.3   Basic Server Failover Without Replication, "Shared Everything": Tier 2

hour or two of down time but can tolerate risk associated with unlikely storage array catastrophic failure . . . in other words, Tier 2.

Basic failover with more redundancy (still no replication) is a no-single-point-of-failure approach illustrated in Figure 17.4 with dual storage array controllers (1) , redundant cabling (2) between the storage array and the switches, redundant switches (3), redundant cabling between switches and servers (4) to dual port host adapters, and more than two servers as backup. All these are optional; as with buying insurance, we spend incrementally to gain incrementally more redundancy. In this case, service will continue even if a disk drive fails, or if a storage array controller fails, or if a cable fails, or if a switch fails, or if a server fails; and in this example with (n+1) servers, if one server is off line, there are at least two others available for service. It's like having a flat tire and still having a usable spare tire in case of a second flat tire happens.

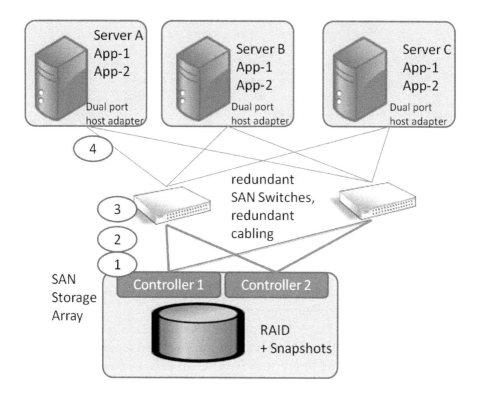

Figure 17.4   Basic Server Failover, More Redundancy, Without Replication, "Shared Everything" Tier 2

All failover with replication is not the same. There are two types of replication: server-based replication and storage array–based replication, as shown in Figure 17.5.

Failover with replication, also known as *shared nothing*, uses server-based replication software. Servers can be configured to process every write twice: once to local storage (2) and once to a secondary storage array (3). This approach requires maintaining two (or more) servers capable of failover as well as two (or more) storage arrays with duplicate information.

The upside of server-based replication is that it often can make use of excess server processing. The downside of server-based replication is it consumes server processing, consumes limited server I/O capacity, and forces I/O through a server architecture that was designed for calculation, not I/O. The other downside is that servers are the most complex and therefore least reliable component in the chain; if a server fails, it is likely the I/O will also fare poorly. The cost downside is that this configuration

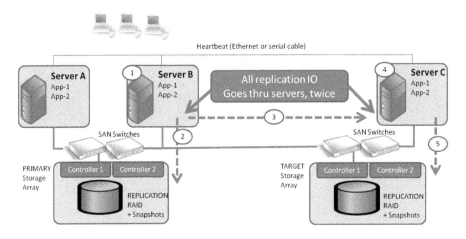

Figure 17.5   Failover and Server-Based Storage Replication, "Shared Nothing": Tier 2

costs more than twice the cost per GB in hardware and also requires a significantly higher cost of administration.

In this example Server B (1) receives a write request from the clients; the server writes to the primary storage array (2). Server B also creates a write command (3) and directs it to Server C (4) to be written to secondary/target storage (5). Server-based replication creates an inefficient I/O path. The I/O must go from Server B across a network to Server C, then through Server C's network stack and memory bus into RAM, back across the memory bus to the HBA driver, and from the HBA across the switch to the target storage array. The target storage array then issues a "write complete" message back across the SAN, to Server C, back to Server B. All this time, Server B has no confirmation that the write is completed. Server-based replication software must confirm the write is complete.

Additionally, replication is a substantial load which burdens both servers, increasing the likelihood of hang or memory leak when replication is performed by the server, the most failure-prone thing in the system. Regardless of cause, if either of those servers can fail or hang, the additional steps created by server-based replication open a large time window where if a failure happens, server based "write-complete" messaging is involved and puts the data at risk of being lost or in an unknown state. Server-based replication is not at all ideal, but workable in certain applications . . . such as those on Tier 2.

Failover with storage-array based replication (see Figure 17.6) employs storage array replication configured to process all writes and replicate them

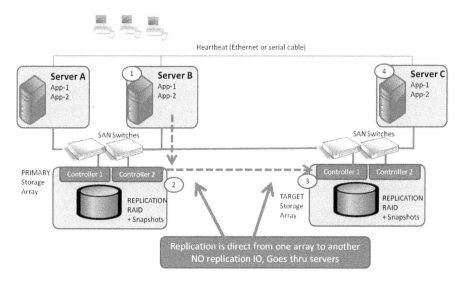

Figure 17.6   Failover and Storage Array–Based Storage Replication, "Shared Nothing": Tier 1 or Tier 2

to another storage array. The target storage array can be on the other side of the room or on the other side of the globe.

This approach requires maintaining two (or more) servers capable of failover and maintaining two (or more) storage arrays. For advanced storage situations involving multiple sites, *n*-way replication is possible with the right storage systems.

Storage arrays are designed with no single point of failure (dual controllers, dual path backplanes, dual port disk drives). Storage arrays do not have a huge and varied list of software applications, or accessory hardware or drivers loaded, just the core firmware (a controlled and consistent configuration), and therefore storage arrays demonstrate significantly higher levels of uptime than typical servers.

The upside of storage array–based replication includes significantly more reliable replication to local storage arrays or remote (WAN-accessed) arrays. An I/O command is received by a storage array designed with no single point of failure, with storage arrays that have an architecture optimized for I/O (not designed for compute), and with storage array–based replication does not consume limited server I/O resources on both ends of the wire.

The other huge upside of storage array–based replication is that the servers themselves are not burdened with the load of replication. Servers are really good at computing tasks, such as running a database, but server architectures are not optimized for storage tasks. When servers are used for a data movement tasks (replication, backup, snapshots), all the data typically is read from the original storage, then crosses the server south-bridge, to the server north-bridge, into server system RAM, then back to the server north-bridge, then to the server south-bridge and onto the destination storage. There are other ways to handle data movement (such as remote direct memory access, or RDMA), but these are exceptions and not the norm. This approach is inefficient at best; the real issue is contention over limited server bandwidth, CPU cycles, and limited server memory. Overloading an already fully loaded server can cause hangs, timeouts, and situations in which the main task of the server, as well as the task of replication, backup, and snapshots, all are poorly done or create a hang or reboot.

In high contrast, storage array–based replication is streamlined and efficient. The storage array firmware is designed to handle replication, backup, and snapshots alongside regular tasks such as servicing read and write requests, handling host connections, and handling errors. Storage arrays are very limited and closed; because storage arrays do not run applications, storage arrays do not have a long list of drivers or link libraries or other random software loads. Traditional IT best practices tell us that standard configurations, limited configurations, and simplified configurations deliver higher reliability. Storage arrays are more standard, more limited, and simpler than servers; therefore, they have higher uptime.

17.2   Load Balancing

Active-active failover (in the past) relied on one active controller and a passive controller that would become active in the case of a failover. Active-passive means there is no opportunity to balance the load (all I/O goes through one controller while the other controller is inactive). Wouldn't it be cool if both controllers were simultaneously active, and cooler still if I/O loads could load-balance traffic? The reality is that most failover systems can have active-active controllers, but if multiple servers have access to a single LUN (chunk of storage), there exists a high risk that two servers will open a single file or database page or similar and both write to that page without any consideration that the other server is also writing to the same file or database page.

As we consider the expenses relating to multipathing, fiscal responsibility requires us to selectively and intelligently use multipathing. If all your servers and storage use multipathing, it's a good indicator that your storage is overengineered and too expensive.

Redundant application software licenses mean twice the maintenance contract costs: additional people to administrate and to deal with support. You will need to be prepared for what happens when the application custom layer changes and what happens when the application undergoes a major revision or a service patch. Both servers must be simultaneously updated. And if the servers get out of sync on software, it's possible the failover will work, but it's also likely the misaligned revision levels will result in a significantly higher risk of failover problems. And let's not forget, failover also means failback, and that risk is magnified post-failover, during fail-back. See the failover scenarios presented in Table 17.1.

The majority of cluster problems (this from cluster support call data) are configuration problems including cabling mistakes, driver mismatches, inconsistent software/patches, and inconsistent settings. The remedy to cluster problems is to use standardized (and I do mean *highly standardized*) hardware configurations and virtual server configuration cloning to create the target failover server. Whenever the primary server is updated, a supporting process will capture the server configuration clone and then apply it to the target failover server. Whenever the primary server gets a hardware improvement, your processes will make it mandatory that the target failover server get a matching hardware change. It is highly inadvisable to cobble together some configurations based on whatever old hardware is lying about, or to allow the hardware or software configurations to get out of lockstep. This is failover, and therefore there is a driving business need to have servers up and running. It's a business, not a science project. If the business need is adequate, then spending on match-

Table 17.1   Failover Sequence

Failover Scenario	Comment
▪ Server A, running app version 1.1, fails; the failover goes to Server B app version 1.1 ▪ Server A is repaired and restarted ▪ Server B, running app version 1.1, fails back to Server A app version 1.1	Everything matches, this is the proper setup and should work without any problems

Table 17.1   Failover Sequence

▪ Server A, running app version 1.2, fails; the failover goes to Server B app version 1.1 ▪ Server A is repaired and restarted ▪ Server B, running app version 1.1, fails back to Server A app version 1.2	Not good. Frequently-updated applications extend the data structure, and previous revisions of the application cannot properly process the new data structures. Worst case, if the structures are too different, the Server B older revision may not run; in that case, the users will be down until Server A is back online. Less troublesome, read and write errors may be encountered on Server B. Assuming not too much read/write activity happened on Server B, once Server A is restored it's likely things will go back to normal.
▪ Server A, running app version 1.1. fails; the failover goes to Server B app version 1.2 ▪ Server A is repaired and restarted ▪ Server B, running app version 1.2, fails back to Server A app version 1.1	Not good. Frequently updated applications extend the data structure, and previous revisions of the application cannot properly process the new data structures. In this case, Server B running version 1.2 may introduce new data structures (new applications will invariably be capable of running against older data sets). But version 1.2 may introduce new data structure extensions, and the failover back to Server A may be unsuccessful—meaning you are stuck with Server B until Server A is updated.
Bottom Line: Multipathing requires constant love; the application updates for Server A must also be applied to Server B. That requires time, money, and discipline.	

ing configurations is fully justified. If the spending is not justified, then it is inadvisable to attempt server failover, because with mismatching configurations, it is not likely to properly failover. There are other ways to reduce the risk of server downtime.

Chapter 18

Reliability and Continuous Data Protection, Synchronous Replication

I'll jump to the conclusion: Synchronous replication is expensive, so use it only when the situation warrants. *Do not* use synchronous replication for everything.

The most basic form of synchronous replication is disk mirroring, in which a RAID controller writes every bit twice. The server waits for a response from the RAID controller that the write is complete (the writes to the primary drive(s) and the mirrored drive(s) are complete). Take that example and expand it to be between servers or between storage arrays. Every write to the primary storage is also written to the secondary (target), and the system waits on both "write complete" messages before signaling the server that the write has gone through. The server waits, and that's the key behavior of synchronous mirroring. For some applications (like banking transactions), that's the right thing to do. For other applications—*most* other applications—it's possibly overkill.

The "full monty" of continuous data replication is synchronous replication site to site. The key element in continuous data protection is a means to continuously connect to another site: dark fibre. Dark fibre is the pipe for synchronous replication. If you need continuous data replication, you are looking at two or more sites and leased fibre. It's very possible; organizations do this all the time. It's just expensive.

Chapter 19

Reliability and Near-Continuous Data Protection, Asynchronous Replication

Asynchronous replication establishes a remote mirror from one location (primary storage) to another (target or redundant system). Any time the primary system encounters a write, the replication kicks in and writes that same data to another system (e.g., the target or redundant system). The subtlety is that asynchronous replication allows the primary write operation to complete, and then allows the write to the target or redundant system a little later.

Asynchronous replication is ideal for applications such as medical records, where a sum-one-minute delay is acceptable. The typical failure mode is one server going down due to planned service, or operating hang, or application hang. In this case, the data can be accessed at the remote server. Once the primary server comes back online, the data can be replicated from the target system back onto the primary system.

The corner case (unusual) failure mode is if the primary write fails prior to replication on the target within that first minute. This corner case can be remedied by having paper backup of that information. There are applications, such as stock trading, where this is not an acceptable scenario, so that's the time to use synchronous replication (see the previous chapter). But for applications such as patient records, asynchronous mirroring is a workhorse.

Replication is only half the story. Having the data in two places is a means to an end, but doesn't help the doctor or nurse who needs to access that patient record to determine when they last had medicine.

Checklist of questions to resolve for replication:

- Asynchronous or synchronous?
- What should the asynchronous mirroring interval be? (Once per second? Once per minute? Once per hour?)

- What happens when the primary server comes back online? Automatic re-mirror? Scheduled re-mirror?
- What happens with alerting and alarming
- Will necessary operating systems be supported
- Server replication or storage array replication?

Chapter 20

Reliability and Data Integrity (T10-DIF or T10-PI)

There have been storage systems, not based on industry standards, that are capable of attaching additional data to each data package send to a disk drive. That data package serves to confirm and correct situations involving single-bit data errors. No surprise, these non-standards-based systems were typically high-priced (although they are becoming more affordable with time). T10-PI is an industry standard that solves a very real problem: end-to-end data protection. And T10-PI has the potential to solve that problem better, solve it more cheaply, and make end-to-end data protection much more widely spread.

T10-DIF (data integrity field), also known as T10-PI (protection information model), is a data-integrity extension to the existing information packets that spans servers and storage systems and disk drives. Basically, a server (or controller in a server) creates a write; it builds a SAS FIS (frame information structure, a data structure with a header, payload, and footer). In T10-DIF, the SAS FIS will contain additional data integrity information, basically a packet check-sum. This approach is new because the data integrity information is initiated at the host, then carried all the way through to be written to the disk drive media. The additional data integrity data, at a later time, is read off the drive and rechecked once the data gets to the requesting server. This approach, in which the data integrity information is kept with the actual data from start to finish, addresses a real problem of silent data corruption. Without this approach, data integrity wrappers are kept with the data every step of the way, but at each step along the way, the wrapper is added, data is transported, the wrapper is checked then stripped away; resulting in multiple instances where a data packet is stored without a check-sum or similar. Silent data corruption does not happen in a widespread, highly visible way, but it does happen. A Storage Networking Industry Association (SNIA) study (www.snia.org/images/tutorial_docs/Storage/RichardVanderbilt_Why_Data_Integrity_rev2.pdf) consistently indicates silent data corruption. There are many applications, including but not limited to anything financial, for which this is a legitimate concern.

Systems that support T10-DIF will begin to appear about the time this book gets published. I suggest you be selective on where and when you deploy T10-DIF. It would not be necessary for your e-mail or shared folders, but probably would be quite useful for your databases with financial transactions: banking, finance, stock, or big inventory.

Chapter 21

Virtualization Overview: Focus on the Business Benefits

According to news.cnet.com, Larry Ellison said, "the computer industry is more fashion-driven than women's fashion." He was referring to cloud computing, but his comment equally applies to virtualization. Virtualization has a definite business payoff, which we will identify. But virtualization is not the right fix for every problem, and there are many examples of virtualization with little or no business payoff.

Before server virtualization, the default approach was one server per application. The result was (still is) server sprawl and significant expenses for support and backup of data; physical expenses for power and floor space and overprovisioned servers; and lots of servers with wasted CPU cycles, wasted memory, and wasteful power consumption. Enter virtualization. Run one physical server, but run more than one application. You have fewer servers, they're easier and cheaper to manage, and you've reduced overprovisioning, improved backup and recovery, and provided better supportability.

In previrtualized servers (with the one-server-per-application approach), the operating systems, service packs, shared libraries, and drivers are isolated so that updating one application does not break the other application running on the same physical machine. When a server is used only for one application, things go pretty smoothly. If the application version needs to be updated, the server administrator looks at the operating system, patches, share link libraries, adjacent utilities (Java, and such), and brings them all up to the proper revision and everything is good to go.

Over the past decades, more and more server applications became necessary and having individual servers was not practical, so increasingly multiple applications were run on a single server. If one application required an update, the operating system, patches, share link libraries, adjacent utilities (Java, etc.) would be updated for one application and create unacceptable risk of breaking the other applications. So, one server-per-application is unworkable.

Enter VMware, HyperV, Citrix, and similar virtual machine applications. In concept, a virtual machine is simple: Typically, a virtual machine provides allocated memory address space and other protected resources, allowing an operating system, program, or process to operate in isolation, without interaction of other operating systems, programs, or processes. In other words, the applications can share the same hardware without stepping on each other (see Figure 21.1).

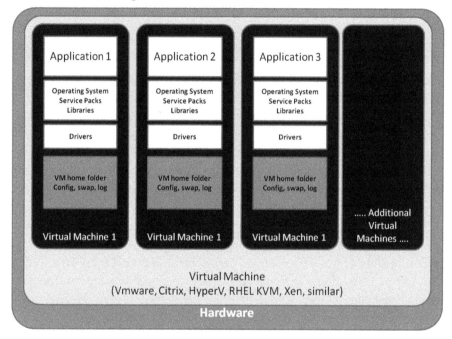

Figure 21.1   Server Virtualization

Moving from one server per application (nonvirtual) to virtual servers creates an opportunity to refresh the storage. The cost justification calculation for storage is really about consolidation, tiering, and operations. Calculating the business cost-benefit of storage for virtual servers is the same as for nonvirtual servers. For storage, this creates an opportunity to consolidate storage just like the consolidation of servers. For business thinking, virtual servers and storage go hand in hand.

Storage utilization improvement is the opportunity. Consolidated storage costs less in hardware, power, A/C, and maintenance.

Storage for virtual servers can be overengineered or underengineered. A bit of planning can find the correct balance and avoid issues:

- How much storage is provisioned with each virtual machine? How do we avoid overprovisioning?
- Will virtual machines deliver the desired performance? How should we avoid excessive load concentrated into a limited set of resources, and identify and resolve performance bottlenecks?
- How do we select the trade-offs between performance, capacity, cost, power, reliability in mapping storage SLAs over virtual machines?

21.1   Virtual Machine Sprawl

The value of server virtualization is to reduce server sprawl. Now VMs are so easy to create that there is an emerging VM sprawl problem.

And server virtualization succeeds in reducing server sprawl. Once hardware and VMware is set up, it's easy to create a virtual server—several clicks and you're done. The management challenge now moves from a physical sprawl (too many physical servers) to a virtual sprawl (too many virtual servers). Once a virtual machine (VM) is created, then what? When and why will that VM be retired?

Following the money:A leading server virtualization software company, VMware, announced pricing changes to bill-per-VM. The new pricing structure allows for a less expensive entry cost, but creates a big cost for lots and lots of VMs. IT departments now need to be responsible consumers of limited company money and control the consumption of VMs. Avoid VM sprawl and you'll save money that can be better applied elsewhere.

21.2   Aligned Server Virtualization and Storage

It's very simple:

The *starting point* when implementing server virtualization is having lots of physical servers. The *ending point* when implementing server virtualization is pooling of lots of server images (multiple VMs) that run on a few physical servers.

The *starting point* when implementing storage for server virtualization is that there will be lots of physical servers with unconsolidated direct attached storage or un-consolidated SAN storage. The *ending point* when implementing storage for server virtualization is pooling of lots of server images (multiple VMs) running on few physical servers with consolidated SAN storage.

We've covered this before, but in this context, it bears repeating: Storage for virtualized server environments will consolidate SAN storage to deliver the best return on investment to the company. Pooling reduces over-provisioning and enables quick provisioning of storage to support new servers. Setting up a Tier 1 for hot data and a Tier 2 for cool data helps improve performance, uptime, capacity, cost SLAs for Tier 1 and Tier 2, consolidated backup/snapshot, backup recovery SLAs for Tier 1 and Tier 2, and the ability to efficiently migrate aging data.

Chapter 22

Storage Virtualization

Virtualization has a similar meaning as *abstraction*. Storage virtualization disassociates (abstracts) the logical address of the data from the physical controller, RAID, or hard disk device. It's a highly useful concept when many servers attach to many storage arrays and when data is relocated as data ages or as older hardware is retired.

22.1 Virtualized Storage and Shared Storage for Virtualized Servers

For shared storage, database data (including Oracle, SQL server, MySQL, Sharepoint, Exchange, and many others) is specifically designed to safely allow multiple users to read and write to the same database without stepping on each others' writes. Write access control for databases, in principle, is easy: For any record open, the user has read-only access or read-modify-write access. In reality, distributed database is a difficult computer science problem if there are additional requirements for high performance and high levels of data integrity and error correction, but, that's someone else's problem. For database record write locking, the user with the record open is assigned a write lock, and no other user can write to that record until the write-lock is released.

The only tricky part of dealing with a database being accessed by multiple servers is the task of backing it up. To initiate a backup, the first step is to confirm there are no records open with pending writes (i.e., open with a read-modify-write lock). There are solutions (dependent on operating system), software utilities that run on the servers where the applications run. The utilities signal the application, "Hey, we are about to back up or snapshot, close or suspend all your pending writes until it's done." These utilities include:

- Microsoft Volume Shadow Copy Service (VSS)
- Storage Management Initiative—specification (SMI-s)
- Linux LVM

Many backup tools from Symnantec, CA, FalconStor, Quantum, and others call these utilities, which will suspend the pending writes, conduct the backup, then resume the pending writes.

These three tools are operating system–specific and allow the server to manage local mirrors, remote mirrors, clones, snapshots and a long list of other stuff, too, including commanding the database or file system to hold the pending writes until the backup or snapshot is complete.

Standard (nonclustered) file systems are designed with the assumption that only one operating system is reading/writing and therefore there is no need for sophisticated record locking for multiple computers.

Sharing storage with multiple servers is all about the setup and the access. Nonclustered file systems can be set up so only one server has write-access to a LUN.

What is the importance and relevance of all this in business terms? Server virtualization is about reducing server sprawl. Server virtualization allows multiple server images to be run on a single set of hardware. Storage virtualization is an industry buzz word with a range of definitions. Storage virtualization, in its simplest form, is the separation of logical storage from physical storage, providing flexibility to access storage without depending on hard-coded physical hardware addresses. Storage virtualization addressing abstraction is a major asset to server virtualization because it allows storage to be mapped to a pointer rather than to a physical hardware address.

One example (an expensive example) is IBM SVC. SVC is one or several appliances that abstract physical storage to something called a *VDisk*. The VDisk, or virtual disk, is a unit of storage presented to the host. The VDisk can be remapped by the virtual storage system (in this case SVC) to help with difficult tasks frequently encountered in large IT operations, such as migrating data and retiring aging hardware.

Basically, servers can be changed, retired, or added; storage can also be changed, retired, added, and moved transparently. Moving stuff around does not break the connections, thanks to SVC. One use-case for VDisks is with transactions like banking or point-of-sale; data will get stale with time. You could keep the most recent 90 days of data on fast storage, and migrate any data older than 90 days onto slower/bigger capacity optimized data. Using storage virtualization, it's straightforward to set up a VDisk called "Jan-2011", and then, after 90 days, migrate the physical data off the fast disk drives onto slower disk drives. The servers still mount to a VDisk called "Jan-2011", but they don't really care where it is. This is a useful idea, but there are also other manual methods to solve the same problem.

Many of the early virtual storage technologies and products were appliance based, sort of like a brain for the SAN switch. One significant criticism of the storage array appliance is the risk associated with storing all the metadata (data about data) on the storage appliance—if there is a problem with the appliance, what happens? Due to this risk and other related factors (which are well beyond the scope of this book), the appliance model for storage virtualization is gradually headed toward becoming embedded into the storage array itself.

Key Concept
■ *Server virtualization and storage virtualization are highly complementary.*
■ *Virtual servers must read data and write data, they must access storage somewhere.*
■ *Virtual storage provides that abstraction, providing great flexibility.*

Calculating the business value of virtualization is highly variable and subjective. Figure 22.1 displays one of many examples of the business case for virtualization.

David Floyer makes the case that the return on investment is based in reduced cost of storage, improved utilization of storage, reduced storage administration, and the like—many of the same improvements we have discussed earlier.

22.2   Thin Provisioning

The easy way to understand thin provisioning, is to start with a consolidated storage example:

- Server 1 has a LUN with 10 TB available, and 4 TB used
- Server 2 has a LUN with 10 TB available and 4 TB used
- Server 3 has a LUN with 10 TB available and 4 TB used

So, it's consolidated. We get easier backups, we get the option of server failover for improved uptime service. The problem is overprovisioning. In this simple example, 1.2 TB is consumed, but 3 TB is used. While some growth is to be expected, the likelihood that all three applications will all have maximum growth at once is highly unlikely. Thin provisioning was invented to address this overprovisioning problem.

Business Case for Storage Virtualization				
Project Summary				
IRR (Internal Rate of Return)	137%			
Net Present Value (7% Discount Rate)	$4.03million			
Payback Period	13 months			
Project Costs ($000)	Startup	Year 1	Year 2	Year 3
Additional Cost of Hardware & Hardware Maintenance	$500	$90	$90	$90
Storage Virtualization Software & Maintenance	$340	$75	$75	$75
Implementation Services	$84	$8	$8	$8
Net Project Cost	$924	$173	$173	$173
TCO Benefits ($000)				
Reduced Cost of Storage		$164	$273	$273
Reduced Cost of Storage Administration		$161	$268	$268
Reduced Cost of Storage Operations & Connectivity		$90	$150	$150
Reduced Cost of Storage Transmission		$50	$83	$83
TCO benefits of earlier enablement of Tiered Storage (6 months)			$1,900	
Total TCO Benefits		$465	$2,675	$775
Business Benefits ($000)				
Business Value of Availability		$15	$25	$25
Business Value of Performance		$0	$0	$0
Business Value of Flexibility		$300	$500	$500
Business Value of Security		$40	$67	$67
Business Impact of Delay on Projects		($200)	$0	$0
Business benefits of earlier enablement of Tiered Storage (6 months)			$800	
Total Business Benefits		$155	$1,391	$591
Financial Analysis ($000) - Total Business Case				
Net Value ($000)	($924)	$447	$3,893	$1,193
Cumulative Value ($00)	($924)	($477)	$3,416	$4,609
Net Present Value (7% Discount Rate $000)	$4,026			
Annual ROI	166%			
IRR (Internal Rate of Return)	137%			
Payback Period (months)	13			
Financial Analysis ($000) - TCO only				
Net Value IT Benefits (TCO $000)	($924)	$292	$2,502	$602
Cumulative Value IT Benefits (TCO $000)	($924)	($632)	$1,869	$2,471
Net Present Value (7% Discount Rate, TCO $000)	$2,123			
Annual ROI IT Benefits (TCO)	89%			
IRR (Internal Rate of Return) IT Benefits (TCO)	96%			
Payback Period (months) IT Benefits (TCO)	15			

Figure 22.1   Example Business Case for Storage Virtualization

Source: David Floyer, "Analyzing storage virtualization requirements," available via http://wikibon.org/wiki/v/Analyzing_storage_virtualization_requirements

Building on the previous example scenario, we deploy thin provisioning, we set up physical storage for 20 TB rather than the previously mentioned 30 TB. We set up three thin-provisioned volumes, each consuming 6 TB of physical storage, but we tell the servers they have access to three LUNs, each consuming 10 TB. The storage array is basically lying to the server, but it does save money. We can take that 10 TB of overprovisioned storage offline, or use it for some other purpose.

22.3   Storage Provisioning Before and After

Figure 22.2 and Table 22.1 illustrate the effects of thin provisioning and overprovisioning.

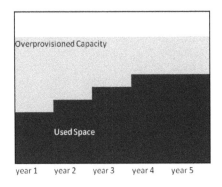 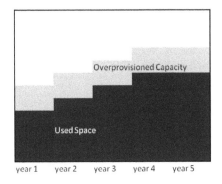

Figure 22.2   Thin Provisioning and Overprovisioning

Table 22.1   Thin Provisioning and Overprovisioning

	Without Thin Provisioning	**With Thin Provisioning**
Volume 1	4 TB used, 10 TB allocated	4 TB used, 6 TB allocated
Volume 2	4 TB used, 10 TB allocated	4 TB used, 6 TB allocated
Volume 3	4 TB used, 10 TB allocated	4 TB used, 6 TB allocated
TOTALs	12 TB used, 30 TB allocated	12 TB used, 18 TB allocated Save 12 TB
	No thin provisioning software required	Thin provisioning requires software licenses, renewals, and service
	Storage admin must purchase for growth based on raw capacity consumption.	Storage admin must put alarms in place and be ready to grow LUNs whenever a thin provisioned volume approaches physical capacity. Storage admin purchases based on consumed capacity. Accurate estimates pay off, padded estimates erase the value of TP

22.3.1   Thin Provisioning and Growth

As the three thin-provisioned LUNs grow, they will eventually outgrow the 6 TB allocated storage; at that point, human intervention is needed. The storage administrator allocates more storage to the virtual volume. If the 6 TB is fully consumed, the physical server or virtual machine will simply stop writing, produce an error message. The storage administration gets involved and allocates more storage (typically by growing a LUN and reallocating the thin-provisioned virtual volumes). A "must" feature for thin provisioning is alarming/alerting the storage admin for situations where the system is at risk of running out of storage. Another "must-have" are storage administrators who make the call on when to buy more hardware for growth capacity and how much hardware should be purchased in anticipation of growth.

Review the following criteria (money-saving opportunities) to determine whether thin provisioning makes sense for you:

- Is the storage expensive? Higher priced hardware, higher priced annual service expenses?
- Is there evidence of significant overprovisioning, especially over-provisioned mirrored or replicated Tier 1 storage (double the financial impact)
- Is the IT operation staffed with experienced, trained storage administrators capable of predicting storage growth, tracking that growth, and tightly managing the purchase cycle of new hardware to save money?
- Is the IT operation staffed with experienced storage administrators capable of reliably setting up alarming/alerting on every storage array involved? Is the IT staff capable of consistently and quickly responding to alarms by growing LUNs? What happens on off-hours?

If the answers to the questions above are "yes," then thin provisioning makes good sense. The analysis should determine how much overprovisioning can be eliminated with TP and associate a price tag with the changes. Make sure to recognize the costs associated with administrating, managing growth planning purchases, and maintaining IT staff to deal with alarms/alerts when a thin-provisioned LUN is outgrown.

The math does *not* always point to implementation of thin provisioning. Typically, thin provisioning has a low pay-off in Tier 2 storage, where the storage is less expensive and the growth is less predictable. Thin provisioning also has a low pay-off for smaller IT shops short on skills and/or staffing. And there are other ways to solve the overprovisioning problem, mostly involving managing stale data and tiered storage approaches.

It's worth mentioning thin provisioning and business unit bill-back: If the business unit says "I need 10 TB," the IT department can define a thin provision capacity of 10 TB that consumes only 6 TB of physical capacity. Then we have an interesting bill-back to the business unit. IT can charge the business unit for 10 TB, for 6 TB, or for something in between.

Chapter 23

Virtualization, Storage Tiers, and Manual Data Movement

The main problem with unstructured data growth is rooted in the difficulty in managing the data lifecycle. Data begins life "hot" and frequently accessed, but as data ages, at some point it should be moved to a lower tier. But moving data to a lower tier breaks the links, as shown in Figure 23.1.

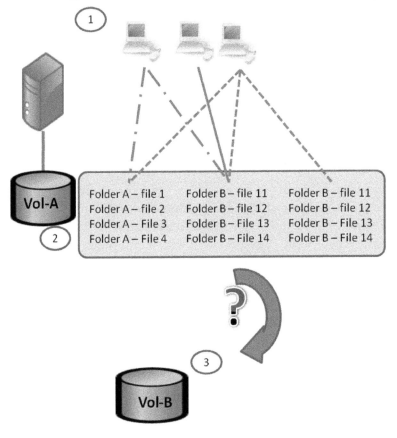

Figure 23.1   The Challenge of Migrating Unstructured NAS Data

In Figure 23.1, Vol-A (2) is filling up, and aging data needs to be moved to Vol-B (3). Physically copying the data is no big deal, but the problem is that every link breaks. When the servers (1) look for data, they look on Vol-A, where it once was, but the data is now on Vol-B and the servers cannot find it. Yuck. The path of least resistance is to simply expand Vol-A, and since RAID groups must consist of the same consistent drive type (e.g., RAID group consists of fifteen 600 GB 15K drives), expanding that RAID group means adding more 600 GB 15K drives; there's no option to expand with capacity-optimized drives.

The alternative is a virtual file approach that uses file stubs and pointers. The client sees the stub; the virtualization software accesses a lookup table that identifies the stub and the location of the real data. The big advantage is that the stubs (also known as pointers) can remain in place, therefore not disrupting client access to files, but the files themselves can be migrated as they age. This translates to less expensive storage, less power, less data center floor space, less backup on the old data, and more backup on the new and changing data.

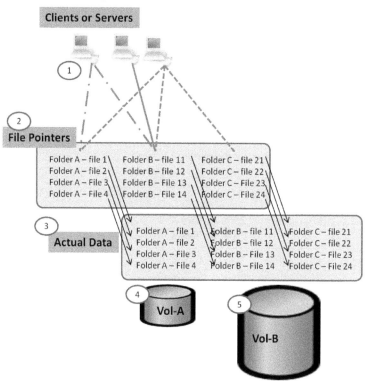

Figure 23.2   File Virtualization and Migration using a Pointer System

In Figure 23.2, clients have pointers (1) to NAS data. The virtualization system provides file pointers (2), which allow clients to find the actual data (3). The beauty of this system is that if the storage administrator chooses to move some portion of the data from Tier 1 storage (Vol-A, 4) to Tier 2 storage (Vol-B, 5). the files can be moved from Vol-A to Vol-B and the pointers (2), will be updated to point to Vol-B. And it's all good: the data is migrated, no server or client reconfiguration is required, there is no need for no unstoppable growth for expensive storage. And it all still works. That's the manual version, where humans are involved in data movement.

There is a more advanced version, in which a system with some fast storage and some slower/bigger storage can figure out what data to put where using a similar pointer system, without human intervention. As wild as that sounds, this computer science problem has been solved many, many times: Servers and PCs have RAM, and the operating system manages what data is stored in RAM and what data is stored on hard disk drive(s). Even better, many servers have good-better-best cache—L0, L2 and L3 caching systems.

We saw this table earlier in this book regarding migration. Migration is a manual process for moving data from an old hardware platform to a newer, better hardware platform (retiring old hardware saves money and improves the consistency/manageability/supportability of IT hardware).

This is similar, but rather than retiring hardware, we keep the hardware and move the data as it goes through its lifecycle. Virtualization is the tool that enables data movement from Tier 1 to Tier 2 to archive. The important function is to keep Tier 1 clear of stale data and make room for new incoming hot data. See Table 23.1 for an example.

Table 23.1   Tiering, Before and After

	100% on Tier 1	**25% on Tier 1 74% on Tier 2**	**Comment**
Performance	30,000 IOPS peak 5 MB/s peak	Tier 1: 20,000 IOPS peak Tier 2: 10,000 IOPS peak Tier 1: 2MB/s peak Tier 2: 3MB/s peak	Notice Tier 1 is heavier random I/O (higher IOPS) and Tier 2 is heavier sequential I/O (higher MB/s), due to the different workload. The hardware can be selected and configured for each.

Table 23.1   Tiering, Before and After (continued)

	100% on Tier 1	25% on Tier 1 74% on Tier 2	Comment
Data Growth	20 TB total growing at 2 TB/yr	Tier 1: 10 TB growing at 0 TB/yr Tier 2: 15 TB growing at 2 TB/year	Notice the Tier 1 has zero growth. The growth is in the less expensive Tier 2 storage. Adding Tier 2 capacity costs 10–20% of the cost of adding Tier 1 capacity.
Power	20 TB on 7-watt 300 G drives is 84 HDD. 588 watts unburdened, 1470 watts burdened	10 TB on 7-watt 300 G drives is 84 HDD. 294 watts unburdened, 740 watts burdened. 10TB on 8-watt 2TB drives is 6 drives. 48 watts unburdened, 120 watts burdened. 860 watts total	After migration, consumes around half the power.
Backup/ Recovery Cost	20 TB incremental backup every 12 hours is $4000 per month in staff time and $2000 per month for tape and tape management: $6000 per month total	10 TB incremental backup every 12 hours, and 10 TB incremental backup every 24 hours $4500 per month total	

23.1   Information Lifecycle Management (ILM or HSM)

Information lifecycle management (ILM) and hierarchical storage management (HSM) have both been around for years; they attack the same problems as migration and tiered data movement. Some IT shops find these tools invaluable; others have found another way to manage aging data (usually involving scripts). In 2004, I interviewed a data center manager for a bank. His bank had a process of keeping recent banking records (less than 32 days old) on Tier 1 storage and moving any records older than thirty-two days to high-capacity storage using SATA drives. Any data older than a year was archived. I asked what portion of the data was in Tier 1 and what portion of the data was in Tier 2; he replied that ten percent was in Tier 1 and ninethy percent in Tier 2. He used capabilities in the banking database to select and extract older data, moving it from Tier 1 storage to Tier 2. He used processes and scripting—homegrown automation—rather than ILM or HSM to manage the bank's tiering. He had the advantage of dealing with highly structured relational database data, and was able to take advantage of the database tools.

The point is, managing data migration and storage tiering will save money. My banking friend managed the aging data and saved his employer big money. The alternative would have been to keep growing the Tier 1 storage.

Chapter 24

Virtual Desktop Infrastructure (VDI)

Earlier in the book we covered converged SAN and NAS; these provide the infrastructure for virtual desktops. For virtual desktop infrastructures, converged SAN and NAS are preferred but optional.

Here is a brief but highly relevant refresher on snapshot technology: Snapshots start with a *time-zero copy.* This is a data baseline; the system then separately captures only the changed blocks in a separate *point-in-time* volume. For server storage, a point-in-time snapshot is used to recover the data back to a point in time (PIT) in order to recover data from an accidental deletion or from virus infection. The snapshot process will set a point-in-time snapshot that will remain unchanged, but the changes to data will be kept separately. In this way, the system will only "see" the most current version of the data (the most recent point-in-time snapshot plus the changes made since the snapshot). But the administrator can roll back changes to see the earlier point in time.

24.1   Why VDI?

Which is easier and cheaper: Managing *one* desktop, or managing *one hundred* desktops? Figure 24.1 helps illustrate the answer.

Figure 24.1 shows the *server* use case; the virtual desktop use case is a very different use case. It uses the same technologies, stores point-in-time snapshots, but these technologies are applied to solve a very different problem than the server point-in-time problem. A "golden" PC image can be constructed, including the operating system, applications, IT tools, etc. When multiple PCs decide to boot, they boot from the main volume (a single copy serves numerous PCs) ; then changes to their specific image (user data, scratch, swap, etc.) are held in the snapshot (one per PC).

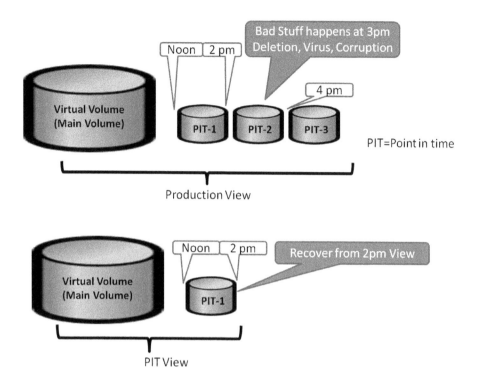

Figure 24.1   Server Use Case for Snapshots

24.2   Implementing Virtual Desktops

24.2.1   Option 1: The Clone Approach

Set up a partition per PC. Make one copy of the operating system and applications on each partition, then use thin-diskless. PCs can diskless boot; you have now mastered VDI! This approach has a big drawback, involving a static partition per PC (usually overprovisioned) and a separate copy of the operating system per PC, resulting in numerous separate images to manage.

Need to apply a patch or deploy a new application? This approach means you get to do that 100 times. Workable, but not cheap, and not easy to manage. There is a better way . . .

24.2.2   Option 2: The Snapshot Approach

Set up a "golden" image of the operating system. Set up a operating system snapshot per client. The clients do a diskless boot off the golden image; then, as each client uses the system, the snapshot capability will handle the

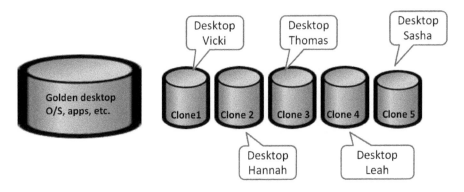

Figure 24.2   VDI, the Clone Approach

unique data for each desktop (individual scratch, swap, user data, etc.) as illustrated in Figure 24.3.

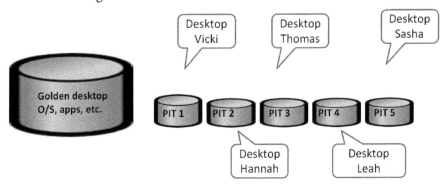

Figure 24.3   VDI Use Case for Snapshots

Set up a golden image of the operating system. Use a point-in-time snapshot for each desktop. This approach minimizes storage requirements and, most importantly, minimizes desktop management difficulty. If you need to patch, do a volume copy of the golden desktop and test the patch. When you are satisfied that it will work, apply it to the golden desktop image and tell your users to reboot at a convenient time. Done and done. Have a problem? Just reinstate the previous golden image, have your users reboot, and disaster is avoided.

With virtual desktops, we have additional capabilities relating to thin provisioning and de-duplication. Consolidated storage is easier to manage, and it is also easier to avoid overprovisioning. And with virtual desktops, all the usual other data management applies. All of the server storage array benefits of consolidated storage for databases and e-mail still apply.

24.3   Common Mistakes to Avoid

Consider I/O workload, both peak and average. If all your users boot at precisely 8:00 A.M. Eastern Daylight Savings Time, you can expect poor boot times (even with the golden desktop in cache). This risk can be mitigated:

- Spread out the time of day when heavy loads (like booting) occur
- Avoid the heavy loads; who says you need to shut down and reboot on some robotic time scale?
- Split up the simultaneous loads over several different systems

Before deployment, it is advisable to first do the math on processors, memory, and I/O (IOPS per PC). Ubuntu takes about 500 M RAM and a thin 1Ghz core to run well. Microsoft's Windows Vista takes triple that. I am optimistic that Windows 7 will be less demanding on resources.

24.4   Data Security

Data security is one of those topics that merit its own book, but it's useful to cover the basics. We just covered the virtual desktop infrastructure (VDI), which has a big data security payoff: a highly controlled application space that disallows installation of random applications or plug-ins that might be harmful. VDI allows the best possible enforcement of strong passwords and frequent password change. VDI offers the best possible application space update or reconfiguration/reinstallation of application space. Because of these characteristics, VDI environments are typically not cluttered, like normal PCs and laptops, with personal content and applications.

All security approaches start by reducing the numbers of people exposed to risk: People with access to sensitive information or potentially tempting situations such as intellectual property, key business secrets, personnel info, patient records, banking records, investment records and the like. There is risk any time big money may or may not change hands, as in supplier selection. There is risk.

To reduce the risk, reduce the humans exposed to the risk: physically secure sensitive hardware, electronically secure access to sensitive data, and add a buddy system oversight in supplier transactions. Physical security is a great start; Keeping production hardware and spare parts inventory behind locked doors reduces exposure and reduces temptation. Controlling physical access to backup tape is another fundamental improvement. Limiting electronic access to sensitive information is accomplished with Access Control Lists (ACLs).

Once you've gone through the process of reducing the numbers of humans exposed to a risk, it's appropriate to review the humans who are still exposed to risk and screen for financial issues and for drug abuse. Just a thought: If you do surface something through screening—and unfortunately, that is likely—consider simply reassigning that person so that he or she is not exposed to the risk. Just because someone has credit card debt does not immediately confirm criminal intent. But bad stuff happens. I witnessed a situation where a smart guy, with a good track record at a good company, was selling spare hardware on eBay because he became financially strapped by unfortunate decisions related to day-trading. I witnessed a situation involving extraordinary travel and expense abuse and an "unusual" employment situation. In a separate situation, I witnessed supplier-customer relationships that were, let us just say, less than professional and definitely a conflict of interest with the employer.

Humans are flawed, and if we are presented with enough opportunity, sooner or later someone will do something to benefit themselves and not the employer. You must manage the risk.

Data security checklist:

- *Physically secure production hardware and backup data.* For very sensitive areas, install key-card access and video surveillance. Support with audit.
- *Electronically secure sensitive data.* Support with audit.
- *Financially secure supplier relations with a buddy system.* Support with audit.
- *List the humans exposed to significant risk.* Reduce the number of humans exposed to risk. For humans still exposed to risk, conduct a drug screening, financial checks, and background checks. Reassign to further reduce risk.

Chapter 25

Converged NAS and SAN

One of the new buzzwords in the storage industry is "converged NAS and SAN." There are situations where this makes good financial sense, but there are other situations where this is a waste of money.

NAS stands for network attached storage, also known as file storage. The Z: drive on your workplace PC uses CIFS to access a storage (a directory) on some remote server via the network. Network attached storage presents files to the server (files and folders, not devices). The server or the NAS array runs a file system (system software that maps disk sectors into files and folders). NAS is great for use with applications that produce multiple files (e.g., Word, Excel, PowerPoint, photo editing, video editing, engineering design, and software design). When you hear the phrase "file-level access," it means NAS where the storage is running a file system.

SAN stands for storage area network, also known as block storage. The storage network presents devices (disk drives, not files) to the server. The SAN does not present files or directories to the server. SAN is great for applications designed for multiple simultaneous users, such as Oracle, MySQL, SQL Server, Exchange, SharePoint, and similar applications. When you hear the phrase "block-level access," it means SAN—typically, Fibre Channel (FC), iSCSI, or SAS.

Both NAS and SAN have disks and controllers. Both NAS and SAN require administration: capacity management/provisioning, backup/restore, performance monitoring, and balancing/zoning of SAN and network traffic. And therefore, more than a few NAS and SAN administrators have asked for management with the same management interface. Table 25.1 compares the two.

Table 25.1   NAS and SAN Consolidation Strengths and Weaknesses

	Separate NAS and SAN	Consolidated NAS and SAN
Infrastructure	Weakness.0	Strength. (Huge, with 10 Gb/s ethernet) As 10 Gb/s ethernet becomes more widely adopted, iSCSI over 10 Gb/s ethernet can provide block access. NAS (NFS or CIFS) protocols over the same 10 Gb/s ethernet infrastructure provides file access.
Consolidation	Weakness. Separated NAS and SAN impose a barrier to storage pooling, potentially increase wasteful over provisioning, and potentially create additional work on backup and snapshot	Strength. Consolidation effectively pools storage, reduces wasteful overprovisioning, and reduces time/effort/expense associated with backup and snapshot
Performance	Strength. Separated NAS and SAN allow separate partitioning of network/SAN traffic and specific tuning.	Weakness. SANs are designed to be individually tuned for block sizes, for specific FC zones. Putting NAS and SAN together reduces the ability to performance tune and isolate traffic
Backup/Snap	Weakness (minor). Separate backup and snapshot processes cost more for administration. But tiering advantages compensate for that (if you provide more backup for top tier and less backup for lower tier).	Strength (minor). A consolidated backup and snapshot process costs less. Tiering approaches can be applied (more backup for top tier and less backup for lower tier), but tiering is rarely applied in these situations.

Table 25.1   NAS and SAN Consolidation Strengths and Weaknesses (continued)

	Separate NAS and SAN	Consolidated NAS and SAN
Tiering	Strength. NAS applications are very different than SAN applications.	Weakness (minor). It is possible to set up SAN storage with some high-performance drives and some high-capacity drives and segment accordingly. But it is usually difficult to individually performance tune, segment network traffic, or implement tiering.
Console Administrative ROI	Weakness (slightly). Not much value or upside to the company to automate a very short list of storage administrators. Attach a number—how much do the storage admins cost? Multiply that by some percentage of improvement. Is the payroll going to be reduced to pay for the NAS and SAN software and maintenance? Will significantly better quality of service result? Can we have that in writing?	Strength (slightly). It is simpler and easier to administer from a "single pane of glass" a single console. But there is very little upside unless this is a very large shop using many storage admins.
Cost	If you can live with separate NAS and SAN, that gives you greater vendor choice (very few offer consolidated NAS and SAN).	If your operation really merits consolidated NAS and SAN, if there are reduction in expenses for consolidated backup, reductions in expenses for backup, and reductions in administrative expenses, consolidated NAS and SAN makes sense.

Table 25.1   NAS and SAN Consolidation Strengths and Weaknesses (continued)

	Separate NAS and SAN	Consolidated NAS and SAN
Take-away	Separated NAS and SAN makes sense for situations involving smaller operations, where storage is distributed across several locations and where applications naturally lend themselves to either Tier 1 or Tier 2. iSCSI (block access) today is usually limited to 1 Gb/s, which is usually a performance bottleneck. It's pretty good for moving data from primary storage to secondary storage at another site, but performance of 1 Gb/s keeps iSCSI from real adoption.	Consolidated NAS and SAN make sense for situations involving larger operations, where storage is concentrated in single locations, and where applications are very similar (consistently Tier 1). With 10 Gb/s ethernet infrastructure, consolidating NAS and SAN is a huge cost savings in infrastructure, and it makes iSCSI (block) and NAS (file) highly feasible.

Key Concept

Consolidated NAS and SAN has solid Return on Investment in bigger shops, with a heavier storage administration load, lots of storage, frequently repurposed storage.

Consolidated NAS and SAN becomes feasible with 10 Gb/s ethernet.

Chapter 26

Storage for Nontraditional IT Applications

Nontraditional applications means video content, audio, images, and similar—basically, *not* databases, e-mail, content management, or similar (these are traditional IT applications). We use computers (and therefore we use storage) for all manner of data that is not databases, numbers, or text—voice, voicemail, and videos, for example. Blurring the lines are flash, images, publications, and PowerPoint presentations.

Increasingly, e-mail systems are used for the inbox for more than just e-mail. E-mail is being used for voicemail, and this is for good reason: storage for e-mail is a fraction of the cost of storage for voicemail. E-mail, specifically Microsoft Outlook, includes a unified messaging capability: e-mail as well as voice, fax, auto-attendant, and Outlook voice-access. But that's just one example; here are a few more:

- Surveillance cameras are increasingly IP (ethernet)-based and connect to computers.
- Voice Over IP Protocol (VOIP) phone systems are computers that have handsets, voicemail and network interfaces.
- Smart cellular telephones interface with voice systems, voicemail systems, e-mail systems, and Web systems.
- E-mail easily handles attachments, including audio voicemail, scanned images, and faxes.
- E-mail is translatable text; voice can be converted to text and translated
- Surveillance video is time-stamped, point-of-sale transactions are time-stamped
- Mapping, global positioning, phone communications, text communications, e-mail communications, and delivery point-of-sale transactions are increasingly becoming merged.

Network convergence is the efficient coexistence of telephone, video and data communication within a single network. The use of multiple communication modes in a single network offers convenience and flexibility not possible with separate infrastructures. Network convergence is also called media convergence.

Source: *searchnetworkingchannel.techtarget.com*

The bottom line is that network convergence and media convergence need storage.

Storage and network convergence is happening and has been happening for a long while, just with different fancy marketing labels. If applications share the same network, that presents an opportunity to make multiple applications work together to provide greater capabilities for less money that if the applications worked separately.

Here's a retail point-of-sale example: Point-of-sale cash registers are connected to servers. These servers process all cash register events against a set of rules, such as "no checks above $50.00," "no cash drawer between the hours of midnight and 8:00 A.M.," that sort of thing.

Here's the convergence part: a security camera oversees the cash register. A point-of-sale+surveillance application allows managers to review rule excursions, one by one. The review shows the cash register point-of-sale text information stored in the database on the POS server, and shows corresponding time-stamped security surveillance video for each transaction. The manager selects an event on the list and the associated time-stamped video shows what happened at the cash register at the time of the excursion.

The new challenge is that the application now involves both POS database and surveillance data. The surveillance data needs to be stored somewhere accessible by the application, and all the usual storage issues apply. One thing that is certain about surveillance, the data just keeps coming, 24×7. And sooner or later that data needs to be archived.

26.1   Video Surveillance

For good reason, we see a convergence between IT and surveillance. In case you were wondering, close to one hundred percent of surveillance data is digital and recorded onto disk drives. Surveillance cameras are proliferating at a remarkable rate; the surveillance camera market is $9 billion for cameras alone, with annual growth rates approaching thirty percent. Those cameras all record onto disk drives, and the resulting data has some value, needs protection of some sort, and needs archival of some sort, so we'll need to get ahead of that rather than just react.

For video surveillance, everything is about the disk drive. The drive industry has created enterprise-class capacity-optimized drives that work very well for video surveillance.

- Look for the highest capacity drive and the best cost per TB array (either SATA or SAS interface).
- Look for strong support after the sale and strong customer satisfaction.
- Look for either 7200 rpm or 5400 rpm (any drive spinning faster will not have the necessary capacity).
- Look for 1.2 million hours mean time between failure (MTBF) or higher. This differentiates the surveillance drives from lower reliability desktop drives.
- Require a strong warranty and some service level agreement (what happens when things break or need upgrading?).

The warranty should include replacement of hardware—full credit (not less than one hundred percent) advanced hardware replacement. Advanced replacement means you can call the system vendor support desk and say "a drive failed," and the system vendor will ask for a serial number; if the part is still under warranty, the systems vendor should ship the replacement next business day. Your tech department receives the replacement part, your tech department puts the failed part in the packing and returns the failed item to the manufacturer or representative. No partial credit, no requirement for the failed hardware to be sent back first. Anything less interferes with your business operation.

With that understood, what should we do with that data? How can we reduce spending and increase the value of the data itself? The first step is to understand the existing baseline of performance and ensure that even when the activity is the highest, the system performance will stand up. Going back to the point-of sale example above, the worst case is during the end of the month in peak buying season (in the United States, this is December). Video surveillance hardware is smart enough to avoid retransmitting unchanging bits. So if the video surveillance is of a doorway, and no one is using that doorway, the data traffic is minimal. If there are people using the doorway, the bits change and the data traffic increases; also, the analytics increase, with facial recognition and pattern matching creating an additional load on the storage. In addition, the data load increases: The cash register is (hopefully) ringing, the call center is receiving calls (product orders, transaction questions, etc.), Web traffic is increasing with people shopping, wanting information, wanting to place orders, wanting to track orders. These things, coupled with operational things like backup, end-of-the-month accounting, and end-of-the-month full archiving for both the video data and the cash register data, result in generally heavier network traffic. Acceptable performance in this situation can be estimated.

26.2   Audio (Call Center)

The call center is a classic convergence of data and audio. Call center storage volumes are a straight line calculation of the number of call center active lines, multiplied by minutes, multiplied by KB/minute. Account for growth, then determine how much storage will stay on active storage before going to archive. The point of a call center is to map the phone support to the financial transaction, or insurance quote, or benefits call, and database records. The phone call recordings are timestamped and the database transactions are timestamped.

Presumably, you'd use Tier 2 storage for audio files and Tier 1 storage for database files. This begs the question whether snapshot consistency groups are in order, since the audio file is basically written once and timestamped, and does not change. The database snapshots can be run frequently, and don't need to be consistent with snapshots, which are run less frequently against the audio data.

26.3   Web Marketing, Web Content, and Converged Communications

Simply putting some Web site out there and hoping for the best most likely will not result in anything significant.

The alternate approach is to design the system based on business expectations. If the expectation is to secure new customers, then make sure there is some good way to interact with the customer—typically text chat and voice chat capability on the Web site. If a user goes onto the site, a pop-up will ask, "Can I answer questions for you?"

If the expectation of the site is to drive e-commerce business, then it will need a shopping cart application, a database to record credit card transactions, a link into UPS or FedEx shipping services, and a way to return materials if they are not what was wanted.

If the expectation is knowledge transfer and training, it is advisable to think through the quantity of content, type of content (text/low-def video, high-def video, audio, test-ware) the numbers of users, and storage related to testing.

If the expectation is brand improvement, awareness, and demand improvement, it's appropriate to design the site with an emphasis on fast content load and zero empty-buffer situations based on the volume of content and the volume of users. In the interest of affordability, it may be best to assemble a modestly configured system and lay plans to expand. The beauty of Web content is it is readily scalable—usually, it's as simple as adding adjacent server and storage systems with a bit of network load-balancing software.

The bottom line: Look for specific storage-related needs—recorded voice, video served simultaneously to a large number of users, a database for credit card transactions. Set up your performance monitoring tools to line up with business goals. If your business goal is to have fast loads and have people stay on your site, then monitor page load times and page traffic, and monitor unique versus returning visitors. If your total volume of returning visitors is not growing, something is wrong. If your business goal is to have video loads and banner revenues, the monitor video load times, especially at peak load times, and monitor visitors dropping off early. Sometimes the content is uninteresting, but a trend might indicate they leave in search of another site with acceptable load times. Generally, however, you should see indications that your return users are growing in numbers. Try it for yourself, be a secret shopper.

Don't compare yourself to yourself; that does not result in anything compelling or different for your target audience. It is better to compare yourself to other sites, and (through the eyes of your target audience) determine what makes that audience come to your site, what makes that audience leave your site and go to another, and what makes your site better and different than the alternative sites. So much of Web marketing and content is about delivery and response time as experienced by the end user. A rule of thumb is if content takes longer than four seconds to load, users will get impatient and go elsewhere.

For performance or related problems, be sure to take an evenhanded diagnosis if there are problems. It might be network speed, it might be slow servers, it might be slow storage, and it might just be an uninteresting site with uninteresting content. But view it all through from the end users' perspective.

26.4   Storage Approaches for Converged Applications

What does this mean about storage? What does this mean to me? All the usual questions:

- How do you establish storage infrastructure (Tier 1, Tier 2, Tier 3, or some variation)? Still true: all data including digital media has hot and cold data. So fortunately, the approaches to aging data covered in this book are applicable.
- How do you establish a performance infrastructure with the right data protection and data recovery system?
- And how do you accomplish both of the above items without overengineering or overspending on hardware, software, facilities infrastructure, or people.
- How will you affordably establish supporting storage? How much capacity do you need?
- What is an acceptable uptime? How can you deliver good-enough uptime, without overengineering?
- What are acceptable performance levels? How do you establish acceptable performance without overengineering?
- How do you establish support? What happens when something breaks?
- Can this be on server-direct-attached-storage? If so, what happens when servers must be serviced? What happens when storage capacity is outgrown and must be expanded?
- What type of backup will you use?
- What type of archiving will you use?

Establish SLAs for uptime, performance, provisioning, backup, and archiving.

Chapter 27

Part II Wrap-Up: Projects Within Reach

- *Improvement 0*. Every proposal to spend on expanding Tier 1 storage hardware must be accompanied by a proposal to migrate/archive data off Tier 1.
- *Improvement 1*. Initiate migration projects to retire old hardware and archive aging data.
- *Improvement 2*. Establish performance profiles for key storage systems; establish a performance SLA.
- *Improvement 3*. Establish a knowledge-base to debug/resolve storage performance issues quickly without guessing or wasteful spending.
- *Improvement 4*. Pilot SSDs.
- *Improvement 5*. Use a storage array–based snapshot/backup (rather than server-based backup). Measure performance improvements.
- *Improvement 6*. Review your servers and catalog where you use failover and where you do not use failover. Eliminate failover for nonessential server applications. Implement server failover for essential applications. Spend wisely on reliability.
- *Improvement 7*. Create e-mail quotas, PC mail folders, and PC network backup.
- *Improvement 8*. Use content management (Alfresco or SharePoint). Completely replace and decommission shared folders to secure the financial benefits.
- *Improvement 9*. Use manual storage tiers, and move aging data from Tier 1 to Tier 2.
- *Improvement 10*. Pilot automated storage tiers.
- *Improvement 11*. Use a Virtual Desktop Infrastructure (VDI).
- *Improvement 12*. Establish IT Infrastructure Standardization.

27.1   Improvement 0. Every Proposal to Spend on Expanding Tier 1 Storage Hardware Must Include a Proposal to Migrate/Archive Data off Tier 1.

Consider Tier 1 storage to be like living on a sailboat: every time you bring something on board, you need to be disciplined and take something off the boat. I'm suggesting you concentrate in curtailing your Tier 1 growth; Tier 2 growth is expected.

It's dangerous to generalize, because there are a large number of storage administrators out there who already embrace the concepts in this book. They think of adding Tier 2 storage *before* they think of adding Tier 1 storage. But there are other storage administrators who only think in single-tier—everything is Tier 1 to them. For those administrators, a bit of discipline is in order. To break that "everything is Tier 1, all data is hot data" thinking, require all proposals for expansion of Tier 1 to also include a proposal to move data off Tier 1.

27.2   Improvement 1. Initiate Migration Projects to Retire Old Hardware and Archive Aging Data.

Retiring old hardware will help you in so many ways: You'll use less energy, improve server performance, improve storage performance, and use hardware retirement to drive consolidation. Any time old hardware is retired, it's an opportunity to archive stale data and to standardize on simpler, more manageable hardware and configurations.

Retiring old hardware has other benefits, too. It creates power and AC headroom in overfull data centers, and it also serves to retire/archive old data.

27.3   Improvement 2. Establish Performance Profiles for Key Storage Systems, and Establish a Performance SLA.

Start with baselining your current storage performance. Keep it simple and meaningful. All additional improvements are measurable above the baseline. Find that key metric which says how much performance is enough. Rely on tiering to help avoid spending in areas that don't need high performance and to concentrate spending on areas that do need high performance.

Service level agreements serve to attach a price tag to storage. SLAs help you make the case for accepting Tier 2 storage for many (most) applications. Setting SLAs establishes a metrics-based discussion for storage performance, identifying how much performance is good enough. SLAs also establish a metrics-based discussion for backup, recovery, RPO, and RTO, again establishing how much is good enough. SLAs establish a metrics-based discussion for tiering and reliability.

27.4   Improvement 3. Establish a Knowledge-Base to Debug/Resolve Storage Performance Issues Quickly

Establishing a performance SLA and a knowledge base will generally help the organization understand storage performance and will show incremental improvements across all systems—without guessing and without wasteful spending. The idea is to demystify and spend wisely on storage performance. If storage performance really needs significant spending, you will have assurances that all other remedies have been pursued, that you know root causes of performance problems and you have high confidence that the spending will deliver needed improvement. Take the first step, just get started, insist on consistency and closure (which includes adding to the knowledge base), and acknowledge and reward the right behavior. Bring it up at every meeting; this is a positive habit that everyone needs to adopt.

27.5   Improvement 4. Pilot SSDs.

In the right situation, SSDs are a viable and financially responsible alternative to 15K rpm HDDs. In the wrong use case, SSDs are a waste of money. Use a pilot program to get familiar with SSDs and use them when they are the right tool for the job. SSD adoption is best digested a little at a time. Find a pilot project and deploy; let SSD develop its own track record in your shop. Those facts, based on experience, will help you make the bigger decisions as SSDs get more mainstream.

27.6   Improvement 5. Use a Storage Array–Based Snapshot/Backup.

Rather than server-based backup, run an array based snapshot/backup. Measure the performance before and after. This approach is a biggie if your servers suffer performance problems or if your network slows unacceptably during network based backups. Storage array–based snapshot or backup serves to offload those other bottlenecked resources. Pilot a storage array snapshot and compare it to tape. The difference in time/effort/efficiency/money is really big; snapshot is not just for large systems anymore.

27.7   Improvement 6. Use Server Failover and Spend Wisely on Storage Reliability.

In the right situation, server failover is a financially responsible approach; in the wrong situation, server failover is a waste. Review your servers and catalog where you use failover and where you do not use failover. Eliminate failover for nonessential server applications. Implement server failover for essential applications.

Any of the three approaches are fine: *shared everything failover*, where two or more servers are attached to a shared storage array; *shared nothing with server replication*, where the servers handle the replication; or *shared nothing with array-to-array–based replication*. Server failover with array-based replication is a highly efficient approach. Also, it provides an opportunity to take advantage of storage array benefits. If you are using a SAN storage array, you can use server failover. Spend wisely on reliability.

27.8   Improvement 7. Create E-Mail Quotas, PC Mail Folders, and PC Network Backup.

This improvement is also a biggie. E-mail can grow uncontrollably without quotas and some motivation for each person to manage their own mailboxes. The approach is to establish e-mail quotas and coach users to use personal folders and implement PC backup. The alternative is to implement Web-based e-mail for some or all of your users. E-mail is expensive, and it keeps on growing. Implementing e-mail quotas can contain growth.

Of course, when you enact quotas, you can expect complaints. Handle those complaints with instructions to use personal folders and implement PC backup to keep those personal folders protected. This is just another form of tiering, in its own weird way, but it will have a huge payoff.

27.9   Improvement 8. Replace Shared Folders with a Content Management System.

Somewhere in your company, someone is using lots of shared folders. Help them get those transitioned over to SharePoint or Alfresco. The users will be pleased, and you'll be pleased when you can safely retire/archive old data without guessing.

Content management systems (CMSs), such as Microsoft SharePoint or Linux Alfresco, provide a better alternative than shared folders. They offer better user interface, advanced features such as dashboards, and RSS feeds to help users stay on top of new data. But most importantly, CMSs offer structure in a world of unstructured data growth. Unstructured data in shared folders is growing at a ridiculous rate, and the root cause is a combination of high volumes of incoming data, bigger files, and no real way to clean it up as it ages. Content management systems hold critical metadata that captures the date/time of last reads and last modify. Content management can select aging data and archive it, solving the problem of what to do with aging data.

27.10   Improvement 9. Using Manual Storage Tiers, Move Aging Data from Tier 1 to Tier 2.

Tiering makes your top tier storage work better. It removes the load and reduces the backup. Tiering also sets you up to take advantage of the cloud and managed hosting described in the next part of this book.

Storage tiering can be as simple as assigning one application to Tier 1 and assigning other applications to Tier 2. A superior method, but more challenging to implement, is to move data, as it ages from one tier to another. For structured data like banking records this is straightforward; for unstructured data it's harder, but the payoff is bigger.

27.11   Improvement 10. Pilot Automated Storage Tiers.

The manual storage tiering improvement described in Improvement 9 paves the way for automated storage tiering. If you can do a repetitive task manually, then having a computer automate that repetitive task is pretty straightforward. Doing repetitive tasks is what computers are for!

Automated tiering is challenging, so do a pilot first. Make sure the data can be automatically located after it's automatically migrated. And make sure the automated tiering tool can be removed from the mix when things go wrong. Troubleshooting a system with automated tiering active might be challenging.

27.12   Improvement 11. Use a Virtual Desktop Infrastructure.

The beauty of virtual desktop and shared storage is the ability to manage just one desktop, which everyone uses. It is easier to manage one desktop than one hundred or one thousand desktops.

27.13   Improvement 12. Establish IT Infrastructure Standardization.

Pick that Tier 1 storage configuration and pick that Tier 2 storage configuration and stick to it. Retire that old weird stuff. Yes, there is work to move the data or archive the data; and yes, there is risk when you move data—*however*, you will save the company lots of time and money.

Part II Conclusions

Part II built on the approaches covered in Part I, where we moved from direct storage to shared storage and consolidated backup and introduced service level agreements and bill-back. Part 2 offered guidance on how to deliver better SLAs while controlling/reducing spending on really big ticket items, such as e-mail, shared folders, performance, and reliability.

Part III will build on the first two parts, offering a further path to save additional money by taking advantage of managed hosting.

Part III
Managed Hosting and Cloud

Part I and Part II have value as stand-alone IT improvements, but Part I and Part II are part of a bigger picture with significant long-term benefits to your operation. In fact, it is not an overstatement to say your company is either applying the approaches reviewed in Part III and experiencing a competitive advantage, or your company has competitors applying approaches reviewed in Part III, and *they* have a significant competitive advantage.

Part III applies the storage tiering and storage SLAs in the context of managed hosting.

Chapter 28

Managed Hosting and Cloud Computing

This book is not about futures. This book is about intelligently applying storage technologies to affordably deliver the best service levels. It's hard to accomplish that with yet-to-be-delivered technologies. However, there are important trends in managed hosting and cloud computing in use today. This section is not about future, undelivered technologies; instead, this section provides a stepping-stone approach with your people, processes, and technologies today that will prepare you to take advantage of soon-to-be-mainstream technologies.

Remember the Darwin diagram (shown in Figure 28.1)? .

Figure 28.1   Darwin's Evolution (courtesy wpclipart.com). IT Storage is Evolving, Too.

More than half the world's enterprise storage is (still) directly attached to servers (Figure 28.2), and that is appalling.

The expensive parts are the people, the backup (and lack of protection), and overprovisioning. If your organization is past this, congratulations, you're more evolved. But it's in your interest to double-check and uncover

Mostly DAS

Figure 28.2   Mostly DAS

the "below the radar" servers that most companies have. In the first sections of Part III, we discuss this evolution.

In Figure 28.3, we've been able to evolve from *Mostly DAS* (1) to *Mostly SAN* (2), to *Mostly SAN, Tiered SAN* (3). The result is considerable savings in backup and people, as well as a reduction in overprovisioning. Other expensive stuff remains, though: people may be reduced, thus reducing staff expenses (although they are still expensive), but floor space, power, and air conditioning (A/C) are still expensive.

The next step in the evolution is to shift more and more to managed hosting.

Figure 28.4 demonstrates the shift from (3) *Mostly SAN Tiered SAN* to (4) *Combined Tiered SAN with Managed Hosting*. You gain all the same big savings in backup, saving in people, and considerably reduced overprovisioning—*and* you gain additional flexibility with the managed hosting

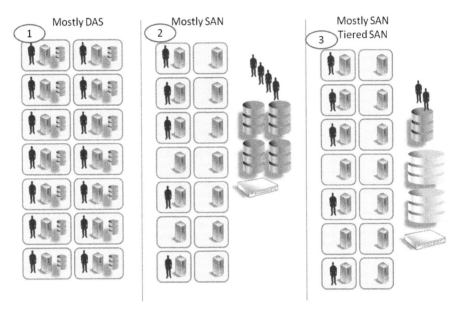

Figure 28.3   Evolution from Mostly DAS to Mostly SAN to Mostly SAN, Tiered SAN

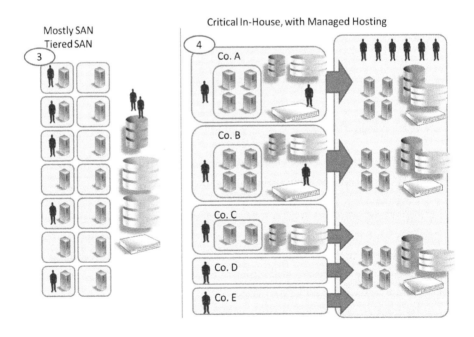

Figure 28.4   Evolution from Mostly SAN, Tiered SAN to Managed Hosting

option as a way to avoid overfull data centers, not to mention the reduction in costs gained via economies of scale with managed hosting.

Without exaggerating, I can say that managed hosting is the future of IT. Managed hosting is significantly more efficient than in-house IT, to the extent that there are now situations where companies using managed hosting rather than in-house IT are experiencing significant advantage in cost structures. Not only is staffing reduced, but higher-skilled staff is accessible, saving resources and budget that can be reapplied to more effectively compete in the market place.

Leveraging Economies of Scale:
- One big facility is cheaper to operate than lots of little facilities.
- A facility in suburban Texas is not as expensive as a facility in downtown Chicago. Purchasing a "dead mall" in suburban Texas and recycling that floor space, power system, and A/C system for a data center is considerably less expensive than running a data facility in downtown Chicago. People in suburban Texas to do tech support, phone support, sales, physical security, networking, management . . . and everything is cheaper: floor space, trainable and skilled labor, low-turn-over labor, taxation, fuel, and power. I keep mentioning Texas because of the highly concentrated managed hosting industry growth in Austin, Dallas, San Antonio. It's not "silicon valley," it's "silicon prairie" (Hook 'em Horns!).
- Managed hosting teams scale better. Managed hosting can specialize (help desk, problem diagnosis/resolution, networking, server O/S, database, e-mail, Web hosting, security, SAN storage, data protection, data migration) and they are in an environment where processes are used, are continuously improved, and become highly beneficial. Thereby, they get more done with fewer people as compared to typical in-house IT operations.
- There are numerous opportunities to use managed hosting with lower risk applications and keep the critical/high risk applications in-house.
- Tech support is available 24×7×365. Most in-house IT operations find it challenging to find people who can be trained and are willing to do shift work, weekend work, and holiday work. Most IT operations settle for a call center without deep content training. This approach leads to longer average problem resolution times and more frequent escalation of problems to Service Level 2 or 3 support. With managed hosting, economies of scale come into play and the investments necessary to provide trained staffing 24×7×365 are spread across a much larger IT operation.

Numerous big companies are outsourcing large components of their IT operation to managed hosting. The skills, services, and prices between managed hosting providers are *highly* variable, from little "wannabe" hosting providers, to specialists, to managed hosting for the largest and most complex SAP and database systems in the world. We will cover selection and vetting in this section.

This section will cover the business driving cloud and managed hosting and help you understand and engage where it makes the best sense for your business. We'll also review how to select and vet a managed service provider. And of course, the book all along has been getting you ready to take advantage of the cloud and managed hosting: consolidation, unified backup, service level agreements, tiering, performance, virtualization, reliability . . . all these things are setting up for the adoption of managed hosting and cloud storage. Actually, the whole point of the book is to set you up to take advantage of managed hosting.

Chapter 29

The Business Driving Managed Hosting: What It Means to You

Key Concept

Managed hosting providers live in a very different world from in-house IT. No doubt, in-house IT encounters pressure to deliver and perform; managed hosting providers operate in an environment where customers vote with their dollars and their feet—and where weekly, CEOs and CIOs review spending, earning, and account wins and losses.

Managed hosting providers survive (and sometimes thrive) in an intensely competitive business environment where managed hosting providers compete aggressively to win customers, retain customers, grow business within existing customers. To compete, managed hosting providers must operate at the lowest possible cost to offer the customer the lowest possible price and still deliver performance, capacity, and high service levels, backed by Service Level Agreements and guarantees.

Hosting comes in all shapes and sizes. At the highest levels, you have the top-tier massive worldwide hosting of Daimler's SAP system (yes, Daimler), which is outsourced to T-Systems; if the SAP system stops, then Daimler's factories stop. And there are various levels of service, all the way down to entry-level $5-per-month host-your-Web-site.

This is an environment and scale unknown to in-house IT. Hosting providers come in a variety of sizes and specialties; the tough questions for you will be arriving at clarity for your short-term and long-term goals, picking what application and data to host, and picking the best hosting provider for your needs and pocketbook.

These companies compete, and compete hard, with each other, and the managed hosting business is evolving quickly, for good reason: traditional IT data centers are being rapidly outgrown. During the 1990s and in the early 2000s, data center facilities (floor space, structural, A/C, etc.) were typically designed for a ten-year useful life with planned growth of (usually) twenty percent per year.

These data centers encountered a different reality. Annual growth rates were often thirty-five to forty-five percent, instead of the predicted twenty percent. Rapidly, data centers are becoming overfull and outgrown. And IT managers and CIOs must respond.

Let's look at the basics of a data center designed for a ten-year lifespan, assuming twenty percent annual growth per year. It starts with an initial load (power, cooling, floor space, aux generation, etc.); the load at Year 1 is twenty percent higher than at the beginning, the load at Year 2 is twenty percent higher than at Year 1, and so forth. In ten years, you are looking at a load that is *620 percent* of your starting point.

If the data center growth encountered is greater than twenty percent per year, then the data center is outgrown well ahead of its planned ten-year lifespan based on a twenty-percent-per-year growth assumption.

- With a twenty percent growth rate, the data center has a planned and useful lifespan of ten years.
- With a twenty-five percent growth rate, the data center is outgrown in eight years.
- With a thirty percent growth rate, the data center is outgrown in seven years.
- With a thirty-five percent growth rate, the data center is outgrown in six years.
- With a forty percent growth rate, the data center is outgrown in five and a half years.
- With a forty-five percent growth rate, the data center is outgrown in five years.
- With a fifty percent growth rate, the data center is outgrown in four and a half years.

Growth rates vary, but data center growth exceeding planned rates is constantly encountered. Data center growth rates below planned growth rates are almost never encountered.

Industry data points at a situation where data centers are becoming rapidly outgrown. If you are a CIO with a data center that has been outgrown, you are faced with one of three options:

1. Revise or refurbish your existing data center (expensive, risky and disruptive)

2. Build a new data center (also expensive, risky and disruptive)

3. Push selected applications to managed hosting

These are tough choices, but pushing into managed hosting is obviously the lowest cost, least disruptive, and lowest risk option, and this phenomenon is driving the growth in managed hosting.

Terms in This Section

- *Cloud* refers to a shared resource, such as search engines, ad-sponsored mail, or ad-sponsored applications. Examples include Gmail, Facebook, YouTube, Yahoo, eBay, Digg, Amazon, Priceline, and so on. The things being bought (or bartered for seeing advertising) are e-mail, search, personalized news, a social media account, entertaining content, searchable shopping/deals/coupons.

- *Co-location* refers to facilities capacity, redundant high speed network drops, floorspace, A/C with backup, and power with redundant source. The things being bought are floor space, redundant power, redundant A/C, network access, and physical security.

- *Managed hosting* refers to dedicated or shared hardware running some software (e.g., e-mail or financial software) specifically used to conduct company business. The thing being bought is a Service Level Agreement (SLA) for application delivery, usually including uptime, capacity, bandwidth, data protection, and some sort of backup/recovery. Managed hosting can be shared hardware, but typically consists of dedicated servers and storage allocated to a specific company.

- *Web hosting* refers to a service that runs other companyies' Web sites, including external company sites as well sa internal company portals for employees, customers, partners, and suppliers. Typically this includes HTTP, HTTPS, and eCommerce. The things being bought are the Web site(s), e-mail, etc., limited on bandwidth and storage space. Typically, the economies of scale revolve around a specific software stack and specific operating system, such as LAMP (Linux, Apache Webserver, MySQL database, and PHP for scripting and Web development).

Today all of these categories are growing significantly faster than traditional IT. Now, it is true that traditional IT is, at the moment, a larger market than cloud, web hosting and managed hosting combined. To put some numbers to it: the Internet infrastructure market has approximately $30 billion in annual revenue growing at around twenty percent annually (my guess is that twenty-five to thirty-five percent of that total IT market number is specifically storage—around $10 billion). This amount covers infrastructure only; it does not include all the money for Internet services, advertising, or content. For traditional IT, the total storage infrastructure market (including hardware, software, and services) is higher than $60 billion in annual revenues, but is growing at five to eight percent annually.

My point is that the Internet infrastructure is large, and it is growing larger at a rate significantly faster than that of traditional IT. That takes money and real usable solutions to costly painful IT problems.

29.1   Why Managed Hosting?

Outgrowing a data center is a problem that cannot and will not be ignored. When you reach the limits of floor space, power, and cooling in five years instead of ten, leaving no capacity for power, air conditioning, aux generation, and/or rack space to add storage or servers; that means there will be no more space to add data.

As long as there have been computers, there has been managed hosting. While cloud is relatively new, ad-sponsored business is basically the off-spring of Google; managed hosting has been around as long as we've had computers. Managed hosting has seen a resurgence in business because of a "perfect storm" situation: expanded use of computing throughout all levels of businesses big and small, the need to reduce costs related to floor space and salaries, the need for redundant power and data center A/C, and the availability of affordable, reliable, high-speed, secure global networking.

We will build on previous sections: single-tier and two-tier; adding managed hosting and cloud storage strategy; and planning and implementation for the different storage classes: database, e-mail, Web, file, streaming media. We will compare the return-on-investment of single-tier, multi-tier, and cloud. We also offer insights on the impact of faster communications, desktop virtualization, standards, open source, and social computing on the data center, particularly as these bleed into mainstream IT; and we'll help you plan to stay competitive with these new forces in play.

29.2   Data Center Definition(s) According to TIA-942

Managed hosting providers have an industry standard good-better-best data center classification they rely on: the TIA-942 standard (Telecommunications Industry Association). (Source: ADC, via http://www.adc.com/us/en/Library/Literature/102264AE.pdf).

Traditional Tier 1 (Basic Computer Room: 99.671% Availability)
- Susceptible to disruptions from both planned and unplanned activity
- Single path for power and cooling distribution, no redundant components (N)
- May or may not have raised floor, UPS, or generator
- Takes three months to implement
- Actual downtime of 28.8 hours
- Must be shut down completely to perform preventative maintenance

Tier 2 (Redundant Components: 99.741% Availability)
- Less susceptible to disruption from both planned and unplanned activity
- Single path for power and cooling disruption, includes redundant components (N+1)
- Includes raised floor, UPS, and generator
- Takes three to six months to implement
- Annual downtime of 22 hours
- Maintenance of power path and other parts of the infrastructure require processing shutdown

Tier 3 (Concurrently Maintainable: 99.982% Availability)
- Enables planned activity without distribution paths but with one path active, includes redundant components (N+1)
- Takes fifteen to twenty months to implement
- Annual downtime of 1.6 hours
- Includes raised floor and sufficient capacity and distribution to carry load on one path while performing maintenance on the other.

Tier 4 (Fault Tolerant: 99.995% Availability)

- Planned activity does not disrupt critical load and data center can sustain at least one worst-case unplanned event with no critical event
- Multiple active power and cooling distribution paths, includes redundant components (2 (n+1), i.e., 2 UPSs, each with n+1 redundancy).
- Takes fifteen to twenty months to implement
- Annual down time of 0.4 hours

Sometimes the expense for TIA 942 Tier 4 data center is warranted, but often this is overkill and irresponsible use of company money. So very much of our business world and our personal world is driven by expectation. There is a giant gap in expectation between the quality and reliability of the software for the space shuttle and that of the PC software for Reader Rabbit; it's all about the task at hand.

The whole point of this book is to understand that one tool does not fit every job, and to be conscious of humans with expectations and emotions (often subconscious, unspoken expectations) We're all keenly aware that this is a book focused on data center storage, not computer facility design or industry standards. Each of these data center levels has an expense and therefore has a price tag. There are some (few) applications that merit the TIA-942 Tier 4 price tag, definitely. But most of your applications simply do not have enough of an impact on your business to merit that big TIA-942 Tier 4 expense.

Also, please consider that the people who wrote these industry standards were most likely products of the old world of AT&T, where (literally) money did not matter. The entire AT&T culture evolved from a pre-Bell breakup, cost-plus financial model. It did not matter how much was spent by AT&T, they were a federally sanctioned monopoly, allowed to generate costs without constraint, then pass the costs plus a markup on to their customers (anyone with a phone).

That's a harsh but frequently encountered example that often applies to IT and especially often to storage. The entire data storage culture, for many years, grew from a mindset of "it doesn't matter how much it costs; just don't be offline and don't lose data!" Expect screaming and tears if that happens; a very emotional and unhappy day if problems occur; and no reward for saving money.

As a result, unfortunately storage managers often used that "no matter what the cost" mindset in every storage situation, regardless of whether the application was critical, or important, or not-so important; or whether the data had not be seen by human eyes in months or years. People get busy and other urgent stuff happens; if there is no reward for cleaning up and no penalty for not cleaning up, it's human nature not to clean up. So not only is it expensive and overdesigned, it's overfull with often stale data.

The tools needed to break the logjam: consolidation, tiering, stale data management, SLAs, and managed hosting.

29.3   Working Around the Overfull Data Center

Key Concept

- *The big gains . . .Reduce stale data on expensive Tier 1 storage*
- *Use tiering as a tool to send less used data to less expensive storage*
- *Focus protection and performance spending on the important data*
- *Spend more on data protection for hot (Tier 1) data*
- *Spend less on data protection for cooler data*

Table 29.1   Tiering Quadrant

Current data for critical applications	Stale data for critical applications
Current data for noncritical applications	Stale data for noncritical applications

Easy question: Look at Table 29.1, and identify which quadrant(s) should be on Tier 1, and which should be on Tier 2? It's your task to identify and execute on the tasks to reduce stale data and implement tiering as a tool to reduce spending, and thereby sort out which applications are really critical and which are less than critical.

Managed hosting give you an opportunity to selectively push data into managed hosting.

Bottom line with managed hosting:

- Start a managed hosting pilot program. Establish program objectives at the start of the project—measure service levels (both the good and the bad), save money over in-house, set a clearly understood time limit.

- Identify one or more noncritical applications. First, migrate the noncritical application's aging data (old projects, old e-mail, old business documents, old database data) onto the cloud.
- Migrate the noncritical application in its entirety to managed hosting.
- Migrate critical application data that is aging/stale/older onto managed hosting.
- Establish a baseline (the cost of the application today, storage, people, facilities, performance, up time, RPO/RTO, costs of backup)
- Measure results, especially the costs. But also, measure the uptime, the RPO and the RTO. Organize a mock data-loss data-recovery event to capture that information.
- Set up an acknowledgement or some reward for saving money (catch them doing something right).
- Put teeth into the managed hosting SLA so the managed hosting providers (and not your people) experience the anger and tears if their service goes wrong.

Hold a project review once the managed hosting project timeline is complete. Evaluate the results in costs and service. It's a little over the top to expect one hundred percent uptime; it's realistic to expect some small amount of downtime. During the project review, cover the money saved, and balance that against the real impacts of the downtime (or lost data, or other malady). During the project review, it is not a bad idea to drill into the comparison of downsides versus cost savings: "We had downtime, what was the impact? What money did we save? Are we net ahead?"

29.4   The Dynamic Data Center and Cash Flow

The concept of the dynamic data center will have major financial appeal to your CIO and CFO.

Managed hosting business operations are built around scale and return on capital investment. Simply put, that means the managed hosting operations folks are motivated to keep every piece of the hardware they buy earning for them 24×7. The pessimists among us will think, "That means we use older hardware." The business people among us will think, "This is about service delivery supported by SLA and costs. If the hardware works reliably and performs reliably, where is the drawback?"

Managed hosting operations can make good use of hand-me-down hardware. Managed hosting has scale that in-house IT operations do not.

Managed hosting operations have a stream of incoming customers asking for capacity and service, week in and week out; it is easy for a managed hosting provider to repurpose servers or storage arrays and thereby keep costs down while still delivering service. And the managed hosting business environment dictates they compete for business at market prices and deliver solid service. In contrast, only the very largest of IT organizations has the luxury of candidate customers to host on used servers and storage.

Managed hosting offers a real, long-term advantage for IT: managed hosting providers can scale. They can add more floor space, more compute of all classes, more storage of all classes. Managed hosting providers—not individual companies' IT departments—assume the risk of outgrowing the facility, as well as the risk and liability of generating the return on investment for purchased hardware and often purchased software, too. Wasted spending on stuff IT doesn't use or doesn't need is cut close to zero through managed hosting. Managed hosting offers a very predictable (budgetable) cash flow. If the IT department needs more capacity or a software upgrade, those costs are spread across the lifecycle, thus avoiding situations in which millions are spent for major hardware and software updates.

29.5   Is Managed Hosting Proven and Viable?

I'll jump to the punchline: YES, it's ready—but choose your hosting provider with care. Underspending and falling short of service levels is possible, and the results are not satisfying. Overspending by selecting a super Tier 1 provider for your Tier 2 needs is possible, and even likely. And double-spending in the form of continued spending on your existing in-house while also spending on managed hosting is perhaps the most significant risk.

Pick your applications based on ROI; pick your managed hosting provider based on ROI and service level agreements.

Today, companies like Royal Dutch Shell and Daimler outsource the systems that run entire factories and complex supply lines using Internet-based applications and storage, and they achieve a big cost savings. This is a clear indicator that cloud storage is practical and proven.

Royal Dutch Shell and Daimler's SAP systems are outsourced to T-Systems. T-Systems provides outsourced IT, specializing in hosted SAP. T-Systems offers reduced costs ("at least 30% cost savings", states T-Systems' Dr. Stefan Bucher on cloud.netapp.com) as well as high reliability and agility (i.e., bringing on capacity quickly and avoiding a lot of future capacity planning).

What this leaves us to review is how to pick the right application(s) from your shop, how to select the right cloud or hosting partner, how to financially justify the change, how to manage risk, how to migrate, and how to manage on an ongoing basis.

The cloud or managed hosting business model is, at its simplest, about economies of scale for an expensive thing. By consolidating the data centers, network head-ends, servers, storage, power/AC, and (most importantly) the processes and expertise, T-Systems and similar companies have proved to be viable alternatives to in-house data management. As an additional advantage, cloud hosting can choose locations and offices in areas where expenses are lower: cheaper floor space, cheaper network service, cheaper people.

Once great example is a managed hosting company that has taken over a defunct shopping mall in central Texas as a data center. It's in a city with low tax structure, low cost of living, a good university system, and other tech employers to supply a technical and business talent pool. This managed hosting business in the shopping mall enjoys inexpensive floor space, more than adequate network capacity, and abundant, affordable power and AC.

Put yourself in the shoes of Daimler or any other big operation with a complex supply chain with worldwide factories. A proven company like T-Systems, which offers application management, hardware management, one hundred percent reliable snapshot/restore, and the ability to quickly provide new capacity without the need for lots of future capacity planning, all supported with a strong SLA, appears to be a really good alternative compared to doing it in-house.

If we paw through all the IT end-user surveys, the key concern over cloud adoption appears to be security. The use of managed hosting and dedicated hardware considerably reduces security risk, compared to a Gmail. And comparing security for managed hosting compared to IT hosted in-house e-mail, there may be differences, but I'm not seeing them. I'd argue it's highly possible that security risk at managed hosting providers is lower than security risk in many (not all) in-house IT e-mail systems.

It is an expected practice that personnel at managed hosting with access to systems are highly screened. If you do go to managed hosting, it's in your best interest to inquire about the people involved as part of the managed hosting vetting process.

Chapter 30

Managed Hosting Vetting Process

If you tell a salesperson (any salesperson) you want to write a check, it's a sure bet they'll try to earn your business and get you to write that check to them. The same is true in managed hosting, but managed hosting providers come in a surprisingly large spectrum of managed hosting business models, and part of the vetting process is to sort out the managed hosting providers that will best fit your use-case and your pocketbook.

Managed hosting is well worth considering, because it's often to your advantage to consolidate all your hosting into one provider. When you consolidate your business in this way, you get better business terms and better treatment when you interact with your hosting provider. However, hosting providers come in many shapes and sizes. If your needs are highly varied, such as some combination of delivery of video footage to promote your product, e-commerce and Web site hosting, and dedicated server and storage hosting, then you may opt to go with several different hosting providers, based on your needs and their strengths, support, SLA and pricing.

30.1 Hosting Provider Categories

Sort through the hosting provider categories and determine which type of hosting provider you need.

30.1.1 Services-Centric Hosting

Services-centric hosting includes both managed hosting and content delivery. Ask yourself whether your project or long-term need involves digital content (video, audio, images). Companies like Akamai have made a healthy business in delivering "info-tainment" content (my term, not theirs) for media, business services, hotel and travel, manufacturing, and automotive companies. If your operation is a cruise line or anything else that depends on rich content for business or demand creation, services-centric hosting is what you are seeking.

30.1.2   Dedicated or Shared Hosting

Dedicated hosting companies offer per-month charges for your very own server (no one else sharing) and your very own storage, with humans to manage the platform hardware, operating system, patches, platform environment (PHP, secure sockets), network, applications such as database, e-mail, Web server, and security. Ask yourself: Does the situation merit dedicated (unshared) hardware? Does the situation merit the help/involvement/services of people at managed hosting providers to service and support the dedicated hardware you are on? If so, then managed hosting with dedicated hardware is probably a good fit.

Is shared hardware is acceptable? You get the same services as above, just delivered on a virtual server or storage LUN on hardware where others are also hosted. And in a large number of cases, shared hardware is acceptable, evidenced by the very large numbers of managed hosting shared servers and storage in use today. It's advisable to fully understand shared resources capabilities, including quality of services, isolation of resources and data, and price-tag. For specific uses, shared hosting gets the job done and at an affordable price. Shared hosting is about affordability.

30.1.3   Facility-Centric Hosting (Includes Interconnection and Co-Location)

CoLo or co-location includes floor space, rack space, network, power, air conditioning, and aux power, but typically not much more. You own or lease the equipment and software, so you get to pay for the hardware and software and service contracts. And you get to handle ALL the serviceability issues of the system, including the expense of the service contract. Co-Lo is appropriate for situations where you have existing hardware that you need to move out of your data center. And Co-Lo is appropriate in situations where data is sensitive and there are legal or security reasons to only have it accessed by your screened employees with access.

30.1.4   RFQ, Selection, SLA and Risk Management

Draft a Request for Quote (RFQ) that includes the following:

- Request the hosting company's financial fundamentals: revenues, gross margins, years in business, number of servers/storage, numbers of employees, locations, employee average time employed. You're looking for evidence of stability, performance, and low risk of the hosting company failing to perform or failing to stay in business.

- Who owns the hardware? Who employs the people? Establish whether you are dealing directly with the managed hosting company who owns the hardware and directly employ the technical people. The person presenting you with the contract may simply be a intermediary or middle-man. If there are problems, you want your contract directly with the hosting company; a contract with an intermediary holds an unnecessary risk.

- What happens when the hardware needs an upgrade/update, either initiated by you or initiated by the managed hosting provider? Where is the hardware located? Is it new, if so, what's the install schedule? Is it used, if so, is it recent and non-obsolete hardware? You're looking for evidence that you will get what you pay for, and not get stuck with hardware that falls short of the task at hand.

- Has there been an independent site audit? What were the results? You're looking for third-party confirmation that the facility and service are what they say they are.

- Has there been a financial audit? Ask whether the company is going out of business or investing in high risk. You're looking to avoid the risk of the hosting provider going out of business due to financial problems or overextension.

- What physical hardware protection does the company have? Security, fire, flood, earthquake, storm? Disaster insurance or other coverage? You're looking to avoid risk in case something bad happens; you want to confirm that the company will have the means to restore service and to survive financially.

- What happens if the hosting company shuts down? Are there terms and staffing to allow you to migrate to another hosting company? You're setting yourself up for a successful migration if the situation requires it.

- Who manages the hardware? Whom are they employed by? (Does the hosting company outsource their 24×7 support?) There is additional risk if the staff is employed by someone else. What happens if that other employer has financial problems, or simply sees a better business opportunity for that staff?

- Does the managed hosting company have a staffing audit, training, security screens, background checks, drug testing? You are confirming the employer is using well-trained, well-qualified, low-risk people. If an employee has a financial problem, drug problem, or some other behavioral problem, it creates a risk of bad stuff happening to the equipment or to your data.
- Is there a support staff on call 24×7×365? What are the training levels? There may be very qualified people in play, but only for first shift. You're confirming qualified people are also available second and third shift.
- Who provides system support, and how? What happens in the case of a networking problem? A system software problem? An application software problem? A hardware problem? What is the time period required to replace failed hardware? Are there spare systems or spare parts stored locally?
- Review the staffing rotation plan. What human beings, with what supervision and with what training, provide tech support? What happens on December 24, 25, and 31? What happens on international holidays such as October 2 (Mahatma Gandhi's birthday), or Chinese New Year? Who will answer the phones? Will they be trained and solve problems? Make sure your provider can cover all the holidays, including the international holidays.
- Review call rates, call hold times (average and maximum), rates for problem closure on the first call, statistics of call severity, and time to close issue. Ask for the raw data, don't settle for single numbers, averages, or best cases.
- Check the quality assurance for the call center; ask for information on the types of calls, volumes of calls, and continuous improvements in problem areas. Request a Pareto chart of problem types, how the top trouble areas are remedied (training, processes, tools), and what quantifiable quality improvement results have been made over time. Also, check the quality process. Is there a quality review? Review defects, root cause analysis, and closed loop corrective action. Check to see if the company has ISO 9000 registration or certification. Here you are looking for evidence of continuous improvement (the alternative is making the same mistakes again and again).
- Are call center calls recorded? Are auditing, coaching, and training provided based on recorded calls? Here you are looking for evidence that the hosting provider can keep a clean staff. If there are

one or two underperformers, there is a method to know and resolve through coaching or through replacement.

- How is the data protected? What are the SLAs for recovery from hardware failure and from accidental deletion? Is the backup periodically exercised to ensure it will operate when needed? Backup and recovery are needed in managed hosting centers for the very same reasons they are needed in IT data centers: to recover from operator error, accidental deletion, virus, and so on.

- Is there adequate storage bandwidth? How big are the pipes, what's the other load? Here you are ensuring that there is adequate network bandwidth to deliver adequate service. If there is a concern, ask for the network overview and ask for raw data on the network load; if they cannot find the data, that's an indicator of inadequate network management or something worse.

- When using tape, what is the security process for tape? What steps are taken to ensure that the data on tape is available when needed? What steps are taken to ensure the tape does not go missing or get into the wrong hands? What happens to tape backups when the contract is terminated?

- What happens with initial migration, when you bring your data and application to their site for the first time? What happens with subsequent migrations, when you migrate to a different, bigger platform still under their management? What is the migration process, full backup, and so forth? Are there charges? Here you are confirming that your data arrives intact without data loss.

- What are the managed hosting company's password management protocols? How do they know that unauthorized people are not in possession of systems passwords? Do they require each admin to have unique username/password, and is there a system (usually involving LDAP password management) that requires password rotations? In a managed hosting environment with hundreds of systems, using an unchanging common admin username and password creates a risk of the wrong people accessing data.

- What are physical management protocols? Magnetic badges and locks? Auditing? Video security?

- What happens to aging hardware? How is aging hardware disposed? What happens to disk drives? How is new hardware adopted? Is the data on retired drives completely erased and irretrievable? Ensure that your accessible data is not left at risk in a Dumpster.

- Ask for reference accounts in businesses similar to yours. Trust and verify—call these reference accounts, ask them for other reference accounts, and pry out any less-than-satisfactory experiences to guard against a repeat performance. Ask about the SLA and whether the reference company has the visibility to determine whether the SLA is met and whether there is a gap in SLA delivery that the company made good in a meaningful way.
- Try it for yourself—ask for the tech support number and an account number. Call them with a problem and see how they do. Call them several different times during the day/month.

30.2   Implementing SLAs

The drive to use a private cloud is to avoid sharing resources with others, thereby avoiding a risk situation where those sharing the resources will have some workload peak and overuse the resources, resulting in a less-than-acceptable quality of service for you. Perhaps a solid quality of service agreement with your cloud provider is more important than dedicated resources, however.

Quality of service boils down to simple concepts:
- 24×7 call center support
- Network uptime, system uptime, application uptime, alarming, and alerting
- Performance threshold (maximum response time)
- Data protection, recover point objective/recover time objective (RPO/RTO)
- Change control: applying OS patches, security patches, and application patches specific to you, without the problems generated by patches for your neighbors that are not needed by you.
- Support, consulting, and access to experts with the necessary experience and answers
- Audit
- Cost (price protection)
- Adding or reducing capacity (CPU, memory, storage capacity, services)

Here's a quote from a typical SLA from a cloud provider:

We refund the Customer 5% of the Customer's monthly service fees for each 30 minutes of downtime (up to 50% of Customer's monthly service fees for the affected server).

So, this wimpy guarantee provides modest motivation. Assuming you pay $5,000 per month, that's a penalty of $250 for each 30 minutes of downtime, capped at $2,500 per month. It's better than nothing, but lacks substance. Ask for more; perhaps you can get it. The worst they can say is "no." Look for managed hosting providers who are willing to put real consequential penalties and real means to measure into their SLAs.

To determine whether the SLA is delivered, the cloud provider should provide some sort of monitoring to confirm that SLAs are being met. It's a good idea to exercise that tool: Create a mock event and show the monitoring will properly register time and magnitude.

30.3   Managing the Risk

Risk management is about identifying risk and organizing ways to proactively avoid it. When risk must be embraced, risk management is used to anticipate problems and become aware of problems in time to recover with minimal (or acceptable) negative consequences.

Hardware failures

Take a "no single point of failure" approach. In the RFQ, ask what happens when the network fails, when server hardware fails, when server operating systems or applications fail, when an adapter fails, when a cable fails, when a storage array fails, when a power supply fails, when a storage adapter fails, when a disk drive fails . . .

Operational failures

What happens when a snapshot fails? Is there snapshot integrity checking? Are there periodic mock recoveries? Is there an alarm to say the snap did not occur?

What happens when a snapshot/recover attempt fails? Are several previous snapshots available?

What happens for updates, service packs or patches (is there downtime?) What about operating systems updates (service packs), application updates, storage firmware updates?

- What happens in the case of viruses, Trojans, and the like?
- New technology fails more often that older technology with more runtime hours.

Every cloud service company is in control of some things, but not in control of other things. The vetting process should *identify exactly what is and what is not controlled by the service providers*. Some "services" are just middlemen. Other services have full-on 24×7 network operating centers.

Key questions:
- What happens if your network feed is disrupted? Are there redundant network feeds from different sources?
- What happens if your network operating center (NOC) loses power? Are there alternate power sources or alternate locations? Does the alternate power source have adequate capacity for powering the entire facility, or is the capacity applied to some smaller portion of the entire facility?
- What happens if your NOC loses cooling? Are there alternate means of cooling? Does the alternate cooling source have adequate capacity to cool the entire facility, or is the capacity applied to some smaller portion of the entire facility?
- Do you own your network facility?
- Do you have a list of references I can contact? Do you have outstanding lawsuits against you?
- What is your track record for delivering Service Levels? (Here, the healthy response is for your cloud service provider to review specific failures, root causes, and corrective actions).
- Is there an account representative assigned to my account? What other accounts does that representative look after? Do we have any say in assigned representatives (can we keep or lose our rep?)
- How is the data center air conditioned? Air handling should be $n+1$ redundancy. Chilling capacity should be $2n$ capacity.

In summary, as you complete your managed hosting decision, make sure there is alignment between your needs and their core business. Make sure they are not "selling you up" and having you pay for a specialty service you may not need—simply ask them to take it off the bill, and you'll discuss adding it when you need it.

30.4   Hosted Management Migration Project Planning and Execution

The big advantage of managed hosting providers is they have experience: experience running systems efficiently, experience in migrating data, experience in protecting data. You'll put this experience to work for you. You can rightfully expect managed hosting providers to confirm with you what exactly you want to happen and when. But, as Ronald Reagan said, "Trust, but verify."

- Key contacts for their team and your team, with points of escalation on both sides
- Periodic project reviews.
- Applications, operating systems, and users
- Server, storage, network hardware, configurationApplications, add-ins, utilities (and the like), and catalog data that will be migrated
- Security audit
- Performance audit
- User accounts
- Administrator accounts
- Administrator training
- Acceptance test criteria
- SLA review, quality process review, dashboard and trouble tracking
- Provisioning, service, and upgrades—Sooner or later you'll want to add more capacity. What is the SLA? What happens when we need to add hardware or upgrade software?
- Data protection review—How is data protected? How is it recovered? What are RPO/RTO?
- Archival—Sooner or later, data ages and needs to be archived. What are the archival services, where is it stored?
- High availability review, load balancing, failover, disaster recovery review, business continuity review
- Contract review, billing review
- Test migration and test application exercise
- Test backup and recovery
- Timeline with cut-over schedule

30.5   Managed Hosting Simple Cost Analysis: Before and After

Co-location and managed hosting are significantly different from cloud--and not merely in price, as shown in Table 30.1; some differences are outlined in Table 30.2.

Co-location means locating equipment your IT operation owns in someone else's building. They provide physical security, power, air conditioning and wide area network connection; you provide the equipment and the people to manage it.

Table 30.1   Managed Hosting Simple Cost Analysis

	Scenario 1 Internal Hosting	Scenario 2 External Hosting
Cost of hardware depreciation (per year)	$30,000	$0
Cost of power and floor space	$10,000	$0
Cost to administrate business	$10,000	$10,000/year
Cost of technical support	$25,000	$15,000/year
Cost to manage backup	$20,000	$0
Cost to manage archival	$10,000	$0
Cloud server Hosting		$1,000 per month
Cloud storage hosting cost per TB per month		$1,000 per month
Cost to manage active data		
Costs and risk of data security leaks		
Totals (per year)	$105,000 per year	$49,000 per year

Managed hosting means you run your applications and store your data on equipment owned by someone else and housed in their facility. They provide physical security, power, air conditioning, and WAN; they also provide the equipment, the operating system(s), and the people to manage them. You provide the applications and IT application support. The big benefit of this model is that if you need more servers or storage, they can be up and running in hours or days; the cost is predictable; and you have technical help if anything goes wrong.

Cloud means a lot of things to a lot of people; but to keep it simple, we'll define cloud for the purposes of this discussion as "an application platform." The hardware infrastructure is not presented to the IT consumer, but the application/service infrastructure is presented (e-mail, database, backup, Web server, e-commerce server, CRM, etc.).

The common component is the physical infrastructure; they all offer floor space, power, A/C, security, and network. The big difference is the computer and storage infrastructure: With co-location, it's compute and storage owned and operated by the IT department. With managed hosting, there is a menu of compute and storage owned and operating by managed

Table 30.2   Keeping the Definitions Straight

	Co-location	**Managed Hosting**	**Cloud**
Floor space	Provided at CoLo	Provided at hosting data center (efficient)	Provided at cloud data center (highly efficient)
Physical security	Provided at CoLo	Provided at hosting data center (efficient)	Provided at cloud data center (highly efficient)
Power (and backup power)	Provided at CoLo	Provided at hosting data center (efficient)	Provided at cloud data center (highly efficient)
Air conditioning (and backup A/C)	Provided at CoLo	Provided at hosting data center (efficient)	Provided at cloud data center (highly efficient)
Network (wide area connectivity)	Provided at CoLo	Provided at hosting data center (efficient)	Provided at cloud data center (highly efficient)
Server hardware and operating systems	Provide by IT dept.	Provided at hosting data center (efficient)	Provided at cloud data center (highly efficient)

Table 30.2   Keeping the Definitions Straight (continued)

	Co-location	Managed Hosting	Cloud
Server hardware and OS maintenance	Provide by IT dept.	Provided at hosting data center (efficient)	Provided at cloud data center (highly efficient)
Storage hardware	Provide by IT dept.	Provided at hosting data center (efficient)	Provided at cloud data center (highly efficient)
Storage systems maintenance	Provide by IT dept.	Provided at hosting data center (efficient)	Provided at cloud data center (highly efficient)
IT customer choice of hardware, OS, apps	IT chooses, no limits	Hosting data center offers a menu of hardware, OS and applications	Cloud does not present hardware or OS or applications. Cloud presents an e-mail platform, Web server, content delivery, e-commerce, backup, database, or CRM
Basic applications: e-mail, collaboration, basic database	Provide by IT dept.	Varies widely	Varies widely

hosting companies. With cloud, there is no menu of compute or storage, there is only a menu of capabilities, such as e-mail platform, Web servers, content delivery, e-commerce, backup, database, or CRM.

Chapter 31

Why Cloud is Relevant

Larry Ellison says (paraphrased), "The cloud is all the stuff we are already doing", and from Mr. Ellison's technology-centered point of view, I agree with him. It's the same applications-operating systems- servers-storage-networks, with a few differences. What's different is consolidation and scale. How many IT departments deal with more than 100,000 customers, with more than 100,000 servers, with relentless pressure on operational and capital expenses, with a weekly CEO/CIO level report of new customers and lost customers? Hosting and cloud businesses do go out of business. The strong survive, the weak are acquired.

And there's no question that IT departments are under pressure. Entire IT departments don't often go out of business, but there are examples of entire IT operations being outsourced (e.g., Eastman Kodak outsourced IT to IBM in the 1980s).

In our quest to deliver data center storage to exceed business unit needs, the hypercompetition at play in the cloud can be applied to mainstream IT, selectively.

You may remember the "dot-bomb" era—the tech-stock bubble burst around 2000. In my observation, the situation leading to the bubble burst was a combination of real user value coupled with a lack of infrastructure to deliver that value.

There were (and still are) lots of companies motivated to run Internet-based businesses. Alas, around 2000, the infrastructure to deliver was inadequate (network complexity, browser immaturity, security concerns, immature e-commerce capability). Now, ten years later, the promise of e-commerce and social networking has been realized; we're past the chasm between early adopters and mainstream adopters (Go! Team! Go!).

The promise, the value, the disruptive technology was there . . but the infrastructure was not. For cloud storage, the similarities are profound. The promise, the value, and the disruptive technology for cloud storage are in use today. Most of the infrastructure issues are resolved, a few infrastructure issues remain and can be avoided. So, it's our task to start the process for your IT organization to take advantage of cloud storage and to take advantage of the capabilities and the cost points offered by cloud computing, while managing risk through selective deployment, audits, and informed decision-making based on firsthand experience and facts rather than secondhand information, marketing spin, or opinion.

31.1   Origins and Blueprint of Cloud Computing

The blueprint of cloud computing came from Google. Rumor has it that in the early days of Google, they created large server farms with inexpensive PC motherboards, power-supply, one or two disk drives, all attached with Velcro straps into plastic trays sitting in bakers' racks. The hardware was cheap. The complexity was low. Every server ran the same image. The magic was in the file system, the indexing, and the search capabilities. The cloud server architecture did not rely on RAID; instead, it relied on replication.

That's the perception we're dealing with, the cloud is just a repurposed Google architecture made of open source, commodity servers, direct-attached commodity disk drives, and replication. Let's acknowledge that this search-engine-optimized architecture *was* the origin of cloud computing—but let's also acknowledge that the Google "front-office" search-engine architecture is not the only cloud architecture. In every cloud system, there is a "back-end or back-office" function that collects/stores/manages the transactions such as ad-click revenues or e-commerce credit card transactions. Cloud computing has come a long way since Google established that search-engine blueprint.

Let's also realize how disruptive that thinking was, and the implications for mainstream IT. The overall cloud approach to computing is based on the balance of scale and total cost of ownership. Traditional IT DNA was (often still is) based on avoidance of data-loss and avoidance of downtime as the only thing that matters; cost is no object. Therefore, we overengineer data centers, and especially overengineer storage for Tier 2 and Tier 3.

31.2   Cloud and the CIO

There are some concerns with the cloud, voiced by various CIOs. Here are the top five:

1.   Security

2.   Availability

3.   Performance

4.   Cost

5.   Standards

Source: IDC September 2009 CIO Survey

"The [CIO] customer is never wrong." These are no doubt concerns, but based on this data, it feels like both the survey makers and the CIOs are thinking in the one-tier-for-everything mindset. The survey asked the wrong questions, and the CIOs answered the wrong questions. Risks can be avoided, mitigated, or managed by selectively deploying less sensitive (Tier 2 and Tier 3) applications and storage in the cloud while keeping the more sensitive (Tier 1) applications in-house.

Let's address these concerns one at a time.

31.2.1 Security

The level of spending on security depends on the nature of the data in use. Let's start with data-in-flight and the reality that millions of messages containing sensitive information, such as confidential e-mail and credit card transactions, EDS business transactions, and the like, are safely transmitted over the Internet daily. This risk can be addressed with proven security practices and technologies (HTTPS and VPN) to mitigate the risks associated with data in flight.

Regarding security for data-at-rest, the recommendation is more of the same. Keep your most sensitive information in-house. Task your cloud provider with a security audit of cloud applications and storage, include both security metrics (how may excursions), security processes (password management, old account cleanup), and physical security (access to computer rooms, surveillance, transport of tape, handling old hardware). It's not always about technology. Do an internal review of the audit; probe for weaknesses in the system and either resolve them or agree that they are acceptable risks. The internal review will get your team on the same page, improve your RFQ, and improve buy-in. We've trained our IT staff to be risk-avoiding worry-warts, so it is no surprise when they demonstrate this same worry-wart behavior for a cloud deployment. The review will at least give them an opportunity to voice their worries and get the response "We know it's a risk, but it's an acceptable risk."

During the review you will encounter objections and push-back. The response is, "How are we doing it in-house? Is there any reason that approach cannot be applied in a hosted situation?" (If you're using dedicated hosting, the answer will approach YES one hundred percent of the time). The review process will defuse the objectives and avoid a situation with negative spin on the project.

The bottom line? Recognize that there is no additional risk above the currently accepted risks inherent in sending information over the Internet. Select applications and data with reduced security-sensitivity to move to the cloud. Have the provider produce an audit, and do an internal review (more to get your team into agreement than anything else). Avoid the assumption that "everything" is going to the cloud, and avoid the one-tier-for-every-thing thinking. Be selective.

31.2.2   Availability

The availability requirements are tightly tied to the application. Tier 1 is higher uptime; Tiers 2 and 3 can tolerate lower uptime. I'll be brief: audit the hosting provider, compare their performance to your internal uptime, pick a Tier 2 application to pilot, and track the resulting uptime.

31.2.3   Performance

The competitive environment faced by cloud and managed hosting providers is not faced by in-house IT. Cloud and managed hosting providers compete aggressively with other cloud and managed hosting providers on delivering performance and capacity at the lowest possible cost and best service levels. The big performance metachange in recent years is the availability of high-speed Internet; in many cases, Internet service into branch offices or home offices is better than network service inside the office. I'm using 21 Mb/s Internet service right now. If we can assume the network is no longer the performance bottleneck, we can task the cloud provider to demonstrate performance for servers and storage (in many cases, cloud providers are more skilled than in-house IT people in delivering best optimal balance between performance and cost). Select a Tier 2 application to pilot (it's best to stay away from Tier 1), collect information about existing system and performance, the number of users, amount of I/O requests, and the amount of bandwidth. Ask the hosting provider for feedback. Run a pilot, collect actual results.

31.2.4   Cost

Really? CIOs think cloud will cost more than in-house IT? *Really?*

To illustrate the hypercompetitive environment, consider that there is a top-rated Web hosting company called iPage that advertises unlimited disk space and unlimited bandwidth for $3.50 per month with a money-back guarantee. That's their entry price; they offer a wide variety of products, services, and applications, including Microsoft Exchange hosting. They've been in business for fifteen years and host more than 1 million Web sites. Oh, this service includes multiple fiber-optic connections, BGP4 gateway routing protocol to improve multiple connections between unrelated routing domains, NetApp snapshot backups, UPS backup power, and diesel backup generation and wind-power to offset energy consumption. Wow, what IT department operates at that scale and offers service at that cost? iPage is just one example.

Lastly, I find fault with the survey itself. To say "Are you concerned about cost?" is not useful at all—*every* business person is concerned about cost. The real question is what cost points get CIOs motivated to fund a cloud project. And the reality is that cost-point depends on which tier; the cloud industry is most often considerably below the cost points where a CIO will be motivated.

31.2.5   Standards

This is a head scratcher; what standards are missing? TCP-IP, HTTPS, DNS, PHP, Perl, Python, Flash, Javascript, Ruby, BGP4, SQL, SAS, FC and the mother of all standards—open source.

The purpose :

1.   Industry standards create an ecosystem of interoperable systems (e.g., a disk drive is compatible with many different servers and storage types).

2.   Industry standards create choice, create competition, and avoid predatory pricing. I have the highest possible confidence in saying "mission accomplished." There is a big ecosystem, interoperability has been firmly established, and hypercompetition is

driving pricing so low that CIOs have difficulty believing the managed hosting and cloud claims. What critical, meaningful standards are missing? I'm not seeing anything missing; perhaps IDC knows (I'm guessing not).

31.2.6   Refining the Answers

Back to the survey, though. Perhaps the relevance of the survey results could be improved with this line of questions:

- For Tier 1 applications, what are your biggest concerns?
  In rank order: Security, Availability, Performance, Cost, Standards
- For Tier 1 applications, what service levels do you require?
  Up-time, Performance,
- For Tier 1 application cost, what price per TB per year will cause you to fund a cloud project?
- Ask the same questions for Tier 2 and for Tier 3.

This approach adds the dimension of cost and the dimension of application Tiers 1, 2, and 3. It's my belief that if the questions are framed in terms of Tier 1, the CIOs' response would be the same, but if the questions are framed for Tier 2 or Tier 3, you'd get much less push-back and risk-avoidance behaviors from the CIOs. It's also likely at least some of these surveyed CIOs see their budgets getting slashed wholesale and people laid off. The reality is a better planned, manageable shift, not a big high-risk "move everything" situation.

31.3   Traditional IT versus Cloud Approaches

Everything about traditional IT dictates a "not a bit lost" approach. Computers were conceived as a means to stack up punch-cards, run a mathematical operation (a program) against those cards, and spit out an answer in the form of a printed report. Back in the 1960s, early computers were bought with the expectation that the math would be without error; this was the original value proposition of the computer. Tallying the accounts ledger and compiling the inventory listing without human error was the main event. This unstated expectation is the basis of today's unspoken foundation of traditional IT: no bits lost, ever.

Traditional IT systems are optimized for one hundred percent bit integrity. The very soul of computers is rooted in banking. Early computers sorted and tallied data imprinted on cards. Since then, the data was moved from cards to magnetic tape, and then to magnetic drives, and then to storage arrays, and then to networked storage. Along the way, the modern computer was built around the fundamental premise that no bit should be lost or flipped. Therefore, computers for traditional IT focus first on bit-for-bit integrity and, as a distant second, focus on performance, simplicity, cost, and scalability.

In great contrast, public cloud systems are not optimized for one hundred percent bit integrity. It's not banking or accounting, it's free e-mail, social networking, content (video-on-demand movies), and search. In the early days of the search engine, there was Yahoo, Alta Vista, Webcrawler, on and on. These search engines took thirty to sixty seconds to display a page. Then along came Google, with a search engine concept that delivered results in less than one second; the world beat a path to their door. In 2009, Google netted $23.6 billion.

To deliver this sub-1-second search, Google founders Sergey Brin and Larry Page used arrays of commodity motherboards to provide the fastest search (arguably, this was the first real cloud architecture).

My point is that the cloud architecture was optimized for performance, scalability, and low cost. It was not optimized for bit-for-bit integrity.

Typical public cloud systems are built with fifty to one hundred CPUs, directly attached disk drives, and data replication, rather than RAID; this is one example of many. If a server fails, there is a load-balancing component that skips the failed server and goes to the next healthy server. The failed server is repaired and full operations are restored. Ingenious, is it not?

None of this is with a bit-for-bit data integrity approach. In the example above, if the server failed and there was data sitting in system RAM, that data would be lost. That prospect is utterly unacceptable for banking, accounting, or inventory applications—but for search, free e-mail, social networking, or video content, this public cloud fail-repair model is perfectly acceptable.

Chapter 32

Implementing Cloud Storage in Your Operation

Paving the way to take advantage of cloud

1. Start with a small application at Service Level 3 or 2, for trial deployment; definitely not Service Level 1.
   Establish pass/fail criteria for (typically) uptime, performance, and cost. Establish a timeline and track problems and resolutions.

2. Set up a process to protect data (snapshots and restores), include a restore-testing SLA, an uptime SLA, and an average performance SLA.

3. Set up processes to migrate data onto the cloud storage, and processes to migrate data off the cloud storage. You need to migrate data from Tier 1 to Tier 2 to Tier 3 anyway, so why not migrate to cloud storage

4. Plan deployment for next applications and report the savings.

The key success factor to the cloud process is whether the end users can access and use their data. Make search tools a priority.

- Perform initial migration of data to cloud
- Provide an access method (SharePoint, e-mail, shared folder)
- Provide a process to grant and revoke user account access
- Educate/train users
- Deal with support calls, providing e-mail and phone support
- Provide support diagnosis tools
- Subsequently, migrate to the cloud, and move data to archival media

32.1   Cloud-Based E-Mail

Increasingly, it is workable and acceptable to push e-mail services into the cloud (Gmail or similar). It's relatively simple to map your domain ("yourcompany.com") to Google applications (e-mail, calendar, apps, sites, Blogspot). Setting up e-mail accounts (you@yourcompany.com) involves simply filling in a list of account names. Accessing those e-mail accounts using a Web browser is trivial, and setting up laptop clients involves configuring the Outlook client.

E-mail is a storage hog. No one wants to delete anything. And when e-mail becomes unavailable, it's not unlike having a phone outage: communications stop, business stops, there are tears and anger. There are techniques to reduce in-house e-mail expenses: limiting mail box sizes, pushing archives to local PCs, and automating local PC backup is one tried-and-true method. The alternative is to move from on-premise e-mail to cloud e-mail (see Table 32.1 for a cost comparison).

In 2012, industry analysts expect that more than ten percent of corporate mailboxes will be using cloud.

All this begs the question, "What specific actions should I take on this?". The objective is to provide the service and save the company money, recognizing the volume of data, the data growth, and all the control spending on all the ancillary expenses.

1. *Demo/Test.* Set up a handful of accounts and use them for some period of time. Test specific capabilities (client functionality, search, mock failure-recovery, mock help desk events, SLA metrics review, etc.). Set a timeline, review the metrics and move on to the next phase.

2. *Trial.* Have a number of end users (more than ten, fewer than fifty) use the system. Configure the accounts to also automatically forward to another regular account in case there's an unforeseen problem. Set a timeline, review the metrics, and move on to the next phase.

3. *Limited Deploy.* Select a list of end users (some significant portion of the total company) based on e-mail being used but not so important in their work. Based on security concerns, avoid selecting/including people who handle HR data, patient data, financial data, or strategic planning data; do those folks later (or never).

4. *Full Deploy*

Table 32.1   Quantify the Costs of Internal Hosted E-mail versus Cloud E-mail

Simplified Managed Hosting Cost Comparison	Scenario 1 Internal Hosting	Scenario 2 External Hosting
Cost of hardware depreciation (per year)	$50,000	$0
Cost of power and floor space	$20,000	$0
Cost to administrate business	$10,000	$10,000/year
Cost of technical support	$65,000	$5,000/year
Cost to manage backup	$20,000	$0
Cost to manage archival	$10,000	$0
Cloud e-mail per user per month cost		2000 users × $5/month × 12 = $120,000 per year
Cloud server hosting		$0
Cloud storage hosting cost per TB per month		$0
Cost to manage active data		
Costs and risk of data security leaks		
Totals (per year)	$155,000 per year	$135,000 per year

32.2   Cloud-Based Content Management and Collaboration

Shareable content, shared folders, SharePoint, and similar content management are much the same as e-mail in regards to unfettered data growth. The incoming data arrives at a high rate, the arrival rate is increasing at an alarming rate, and once the data arrives it never seems to go away. Shared folders and files are especially troublesome to retire, as there is no insight on the need for the aging data; lacking practical means to retire aging data, the data simply piles up. The resolution to out-of-control growth of files and folders is content management systems, such as Microsoft SharePoint.

If you like SharePoint as a collaboration tool for your company, there is every reason for you to like hosted SharePoint, or hosted Graffiti, or Hyper Office, or Alfresco, or Google Sites. There are tools to migrate existing SharePoint to Google Sites.

Just like the cloud e-mail above, all of this begs the question, "What specific actions should I take on this?" The objective is to provide the service and save the company money, recognizing the volume of data, the data growth, and all the ancillary functions like backup, recovery, user support and the consumption of limited and valuable data center space.

1. *Demo/Test.* Set up a handful of accounts and use for some period of time. Test specific capabilities (client functionality, search, mock failure-recovery, mock help desk events, SLA metrics review, etc.). Set a timeline, review the metrics, and move on to the next phase.

2. *Trial.* Have a number of end-users (more than ten, fewer than fifty) use the system. Configure the accounts to also automatically forward to another regular account in case there's an unforeseen problem. Set a timeline, review the metrics, and move on to the next phase.

3. *Limited Deploy.* Select a list of end-users (some significant portion of the total company) based on e-mail being used but not so important in their work. Based on security concerns, avoid selecting/including people who handle HR data, patient data, financial data, or strategic planning data; do those folks later (or never).

4. *Full Deploy*

See Table 32.2 for an example of quantifying the costs of content management versus cloud content management. The objective is to deliver the service, then save the company money.

Outsourcing your e-mail and/or your content management system may not appear to be a giant silver bullet to solve all your problems, but it may be like the household who overspends just a little every month; it's huge relief to make modest changes that bring the household cash flow to underspending rather than overspending. That approach can make the difference between spending 102 percent of the available money every month to spending 98 percent of the available money every month. Make sense?

Table 32.2   Quantify the Costs of In-Sourced versus Outsourced Content Management Systems

Simplified Managed Hosting Cost Comparison	Scenario 1 Internal Hosting	Scenario 2 External Hosting
Cost of hardware depreciation (per year)	$30,000	$0
Cost of power and floor space	$10,000	$0
Cost to administrate business	$10,000	$10,000/year
Cost of technical support	$25,000	$15,000/year
Cost to manage backup	$20,000	$0
Cost to manage archival	$10,000	$0
Cloud server hosting		$1,000 per month
Cloud storage hosting cost per TB per month		$1,000 per month
Cost to manage active data		
Costs and risk of data security leaks		
Totals (per year)	$105,000 per year	$49,000 per year

Chapter 33

Hybrid Cloud

I'm cutting to the chase: Cloud changes the thinking about enterprise storage. Hybrid cloud storage is an approach that enables you to store seldom-accessed data on the cloud and frequently accessed data locally on your site; it also enables you to manage the migration of aging data out to cloud storage without creating access problems.

Cloud storage systems exist that accomplish this while still complying with data retention regulations. Take care, however, to be sure that the system can be easily removed without loss of data and that data access (presumably manual or with some work-around) can happen with the hybrid cloud tool out of the path.

Establish an SLA for both recovery and security; test recovery periodically; and test security periodically. Set yourself up for a future second step (hybrid cloud) by replacing shared folders with content management systems (CMSs), an approach that sets you up for a CMS future where hot CMS data can be held on your corporate site and cooler CMS data can be pushed to the cloud, including document storage mandated by legal and regulatory agencies. The organization offered by CMS makes it possible and easy to automate the selective push of cool data to cloud storage.

33.1   Steps to Prepare for Cloud Technologies

Structure DataAdd structure and intelligence to data, and reduce unstructured data. Know when data (files/directories) is created, when it was edited, when it was read, who created it, and whether there are legal associations to the data. Databases are already structured; they just aren't too portable or migratable. E-mail is already structured, just not too migratable. Your tactics should include the use of a CMS such as Microsoft SharePoint, Linux Alfresco, IBM LotusNotes, MindTouch, ProjectSpaces, Hyperoffice, or FirstClass. Make sure your CMS has a data migration feature so data can be selected by folder or by date and shipped off somewhere cheaper (power, people, hardware).

33.1.1   Be Selective on Cloud Migration

This is elaborating on the obvious. There is no need to attempt to move the entire operation onto the cloud all at once. Run low-risk trials first. Then transition low-risk applications into production and migrate data that is seldom accessed. Think geographically: Do you have a remote office, international office, or work-from-home people who can benefit easily from cloud-based operations?

33.1.2   Have Data Management Retention Policies

Data management retention policies, such as limits on e-mail inbox sizes, file/folder aging retention policies, archival, and retrieval policies will make the transition of selective applications to cloud easier to implement.

33.1.3   Have a Migration Process

Start with an in-house migration project: Identify aging hardware in need of retirement, preferably running low-impact or low-risk content. Migrate that information and associated application off old hardware onto shiny new servers and storage. Document the steps very thoroughly, add step-by-step checking to confirm each step is successfully completed, and add a checklist for final acceptance and cut-over. This in-house process can be revised and used for in-house to cloud migration. This list is not intended as an exhaustive checklist, just something to get you thinking about your specific situation, capture this stuff for planning, and your implementation will be better off. Table 33.1 breaks it down by phases.

Table 33.1   IT Cloud Hypothetical Roadmap and Roadmap Phasing

Phase 1	Phase 2	Phase 3
Reduce e-mail backup Set personal e-mail quota Require laptop backup to cloud Develop a migration process	Develop cloud processes: SLA, restore testing, security audit	Business continuity on cloud storage
Selected application using snapshots (in-house) rather than backup	Selected application snapshot on cloud storage	Additional applications using snapshot on cloud storage

Key Concept

Because cloud storage can significantly offload your IT department workload and IT infrastructure, is a responsible move is to store infrequently accessed data in cloud storage.

Cloud is not the right tool for jobs involving high access, so the responsible approach also involves keeping high risk applications in-house. With time, push selected low-risk apps to cloud storage in the future.

- *Start with seldom-accessed data—backups, etc.—and insist on a Service Level Agreement with real consequences*
- *Set up for a future of hybrid cloud—replace shared folders with a content management system.*
- *Internet hybrid cloud offers affordable, workable alternatives for specific tasks. Plan deployment of hybrid cloud services in Phase 1, Phase 2, and Phase 3.*

33.2   Examining Key Norms of Traditional IT versus Cloud Approaches

Traditional IT has a performance expectation of "a little delay won't hurt." For example, consider a bank teller, or a cash register, or a gas pump with a credit card authorization. Waiting for five to ten seconds is no big deal.

Do you remember search sites before the days of Google? We had search engines, but they were slooooowwww. In the days before Google, a search from Webcrawler, Ask, Dogpile, Yahoo, and all the other search engines took thirty to forty seconds to return a page, and another thirty to forty seconds for the next page. And that was in the days when the list of indexed Web sites was much, much shorter. Then Google came along with a one-second search, and that made Google the default search engine, created the entire pay-per-click ad-word market and created a Google business that earned $26 billion last year

But it's important to note that the improvement was in *performance*, not bit-for-bit accuracy. It did not matter if a search was less than one hundred percent accurate. It is not a big concern if the occasional click-through was not properly recorded.

Figure 33.1 illuminates a typical "traditional IT" approach. Performance concern stands out; the folks concerned with performance assume performance-sensitive applications are deployed in the cloud. What if, at first, cloud deployment was targeted at applications that are insensitive to

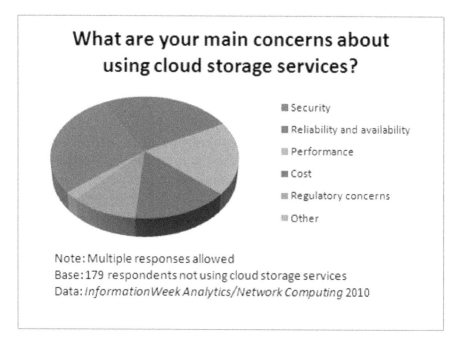

Figure 33.1   The CEO and the Cloud, an Opinion Survey

(Source: http://www .networkcomputing.com/ser vers-storage/cloud-storage-lags-behind-the-hype-study-finds.php)

performance—stuff like archived documents, inactive projects, reference libraries, or older business records?

Our task is to efficiently and economically deliver storage matching service levels:

Service Level 1—Optimized for highest performance and highest uptime. Suboptimized for capacity.
Service Level 2—Optimized for affordable capacity, good enough performance, good enough uptime.
Service Level 3—Optimized for affordable capacity, good enough sequential performance. Suboptimized for random performance and uptime.

Let's match cloud strengths: capacity, good enough performance, good enough performance. The best-fit applications for cloud are SL2 and SL3 applications:

- Not performance critical
- Not up-time critical
- High capacity
- Affordable capacity

33.3   Cloud Performance

The table below is a reasonable, if simplified, picture of cloud performance. No doubt, your mileage will vary on a long list of factors, not the least of which is the speed of your network and the outside Internet. Often, these network bridges between the internal IT network and the outside Internet are small capacity, overburdened with traffic, and burdened with overhead such as firewalls, filters, and the like.

Table 33.2   Overview of Cloud Performance

	LAN	**Cloud (quicker)**	**Cloud (slower)**
Action/Approximate Latency	LAN (<10 ms)	Cloud (~100 ms)	Cloud (~200 ms)
Upload 3 MB	26.74 seconds	88.54 seconds	109.03 seconds
Download 3 MB	10 seconds	38 seconds	40 seconds

Chapter 34

Cloud Spectrum of Options

Network, compute, and storage are the three legs of the stool that make computers useful. And because of advancements in networking, security, and storage networking, compute (servers), clients, and storage are no longer constrained to reside in one physical location; separation is feasible. As a result, a spectrum of services has emerged to meet various IT needs, presenting an opportunity to selectively transition your IT shop from one hundred percent in-house IT to some mix of in-house and cloud-based. Using an incremental approach, you can start small, keep risks low, gain experience, measure payback, resolve the problems related to growing pains, and keep on growing in the best financial interest of your business.

- *Co-location* provides a building, floor-space, rack-space, physical security, air conditioning, power and network access.
- *Managed hosting* adds servers, either shared or dedicated. Either you add the software or the hosting company adds common software and storage capacity. Managed hosting offers an increasing spectrum of optional things to buy, including applications like Exchange or SharePoint, various compute capabilities, and storage options from direct attached storage all the way to dedicated SAN storage. In addition, managed hosting provides a call center with SLAs to support it all.
- *Web hosting* adds a URL (DNS), public access to your Web site(s) and a Web programming platform (HTML, XML, Perl, Ruby, etc.).
- *Software-as-a-service* comprises a huge list of options, including SAP outsourcing.
- *Application-as-a-service* does what it says—it offers applications as a managed service. The notable example is Salesforce.com. The big upside is that you need not purchase the software application or the maintenance contract, or have any of your staff assigned/

trained/on-call to support it. Probably the biggest challenge here is moving off legacy applications and migrating/transitioning the application data.

34.1   Handling Objections and Resistance to Change

The point is, cloud is not an all-or-nothing proposition. I recently heard an IT person criticize Google mail as being unacceptable; the comment was, "Would you put your CEO on Google mail and hope none of his data got lost or accessed?"

My response to that pointed question and others like it would be, "Not if your CEO handles government or military high security information; otherwise, yes, I would put the CEO on an e-mail service from Google and others. If they have proven up-time, proven security supported by SLAs, adequate security, adequate uptime, and provide all this at a significantly lower cost to the company, it makes sense. And in these commercial e-mail services, data ownership is retained, unlike free services. You know, in-house e-mail has its own set of issues too; does it make sense to write the check for full-time security experts and network experts supported by well-trained entry-level people? Setting these issues aside, no one is suggesting Gmail and no one is suggesting an all-or-nothing cut over. We do a pilot, and assuming the pilot is successful, we transition low-risk accounts, and then transition the rest."

34.2   Trends in Public Cloud that Will Materialize in IT and Private Cloud

As I write this, I'm listening to Internet radio, specifically on-demand Pandora radio. This on-demand system shows capabilities that, without a doubt, will eventually materialize in traditional IT.

Pandora (and many others: Hulu, Netflix online) are on a path to replace cable TV and dish TV. Pandora allows you to build your own radio station; just type a type of music ("traditional jazz") or an artist ("Diana Krall") and a station starts playing music that matches the "type" you've given. You can provide input on if you do or don't like it by giving a song "thumbs-up" or "thumbs-down." As a result, the station will plays stuff more to your taste. Pandora, Netflix, and others are capable of connecting to living-room devices like home audio and Blu-ray systems. These are different from regular radio, because each user session selects or rejects, starts and stops unique audio content. The interaction places application and I/O burden on the data center. Behind the scenes, there is a Pandora datacenter with storage arrays holding a ton of digital media (indexed songs) and a database that holds my login information, my list of stations, and my list of likes/dislikes for each station.

Also, there is the business side. The Pandora application sends targeted advertising based on my demographics and preferences, and the application keeps track of advertisement banners I have viewed and banners I have clicked. At the end of the month, the good people at Pandora are paid by advertising sponsors based on how many eyeballs viewed their banners and how many humans clicked through. The number of humans clicking through is directly related to both the volume of humans and the targeting (how relevant the banners are to the individuals in the audience).

The business results are tracked on a daily basis by the executives at Pandora. They review trends on how many listeners they have, demographics about those listeners, what content they listened to, what they voted "thumbs-up," and what they voted "thumbs-down." If users are attracted to Pandora by good content and good quality of service, then Pandora will bill more advertising, and the Pandora bottom-line financials are happy.

This model magnifies the impact of user experience and user-perceived quality of service (performance). In the Pandora model (as well as at Google, Netflix, Comcast, Facebook, Youtube, Amazon, Ebay, and others), performance matters. In the Internet world, users will simply find another site that gives them a better experience (good content, quick loads, no jitter). Also, scalability and costs matter. This model magnifies the impact of expense: hardware, people, power. The inescapable business truth is that there is a huge difference in generating profits that equal 110 percent of your expenses and generating profits that equal 90 percent of your expenses.

Executives have immediate visibility to both income and expense, and they have the insight and ability to make course corrections. In this model, the strong survive. Google, with its one-second return of search results thrived; its competitors, who returned information in one minute, struggled, and many were acquired or have gone out of business. The final metric of success: in 2008, Google earned roughly $20 billion in revenues, mostly from search -elated advertising. No other company, including the mighty Microsoft, is even close.

There's big-time money at stake. If end user searches (or social site, or content, etc.) do not load fast, users will naturally migrate to a different Web site. The Web-search industry was reshaped because Google was so much faster than Yahoo; end users switched by the millions. Because of that, cloud computing and cloud storage are optimized for end-user quality of service (not for bit-for-bit data integrity). Cloud computing relies on replication rather than RAID.

"Cloud" and "hybrid-cloud" are buzzwords that mean different things to different people. We're still using CPUs, memory, storage, network connectivity, application software, and systems software. The one and only key difference between cloud storage and traditional IT storage is that cloud storage typically applies replication in place of RAID data protection, and because of that approach, cloud storage is simply not the right tool for applications with high levels of I/O, high performance, and bit-for-bit data integrity requirements. Perhaps it's best to prioritize that mission-critical database application onto the cloud in a later stage. But *do* offload your IT operation by pushing large quantities of your cooler data to the cloud: laptop backup, stale e-mail backup, Tier 2 or 3 server backup, file shares, and content management system stale data, including regulatory records retention.

In terms of private cloud evolving to hybrid cloud, private clouds are an unshared compute/net/storage resource; hybrid clouds use traditional in-house IT for hot data and managed hosting for cooler data. Natural application divisions allow targeting of low-volume/low-access data to be pushed to the cloud. Since backup data is almost never accessed, that's a logical candidate for cloud, with the qualifier that backups need to be tested and service providers need to offer a Service Level Agreement that has real consequences if the SLA is not met, including real recovery situations as well as recovery testing situations.

You can expect to be approached by people trying to sell you on moving high transaction or key applications onto the cloud. Don't. It's best to concentrate initially on low-risk, low-value, but relatively expensive applications first. In Phase 2 (later), the higher-risk, higher-value applications can be migrated to the cloud, or private cloud, or hybrid cloud.

Chapter 35

End Game and Hardware Roadmap to Leverage the Cloud

This book is for those who are motivated to apply financial responsibility when spending on data center storage. It provides alternatives that exceed business needs and are clear, quantifiable, and understandable by the CIO and the CFO, allowing communication, understanding, agreement, and execution.

Earlier in the book, we hit some big-value updates. We covered:

- How to move data from inefficient drives to efficient drives (capacity-optimized, performance-optimized, and solid state). Consolidation of lots of independent servers onto consolidated shared storage.
- Cost-effective data protection using a Tier 1, Tier 2, Tier 3 approach: replication, local mirroring, and snapshots.
- Improvements to high-growth areas: e-mail and unstructured data growth.
- Data aging and data migration from an expensive performance tier to a less expensive capacity tier. Increasing the pace of archival, using search and reducing costly tape.
- Employing cloud or managed hosting as a means to deliver the performance, capacity, uptime, and rapid turnaround for additional storage.
- So, this is all very interesting, but how do we make it pay off for your organization? How do we deliver more and spend less?Consolidate; get rid of DAS, migrate old 10K to capacity-optimized storage, and reduce tape
- Establish Tier 1 and Tier 2—static—based on application and SLA
- Migrate hot data to Tier 1 and migrate cooler data to Tier 2; reduce the amount of data on Tier 1 and reduce tape

- Spend money to improve performance and disaster recovery of hot data, with matching SLA and matching price tag, for Tier 1
- Match the SLAs to the price tags for Tier 2, as well
- Migrate to managed hosting and cloud, selected applications
- Establish tiering—dynamic and SSD; move data as it ages and use SSD to increase performance without increasing the footprint of 15K rpm drives

These steps create the opportunity to standardize on hardware (see Figure 35.1).

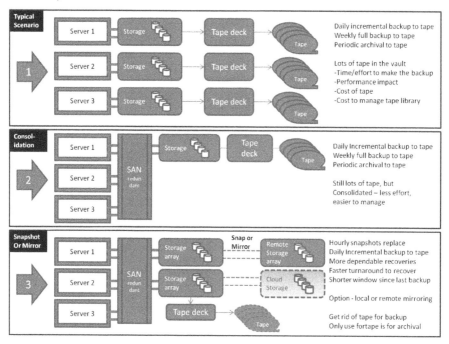

Figure 35.1   Creating the Opportunity for Standard Hardware.

Step 1   Retire old servers and old drives; replace them with a combination of new performance drives and new capacity drives. Consolidate that storage onto shared SAN or iSCSI storage arrays.

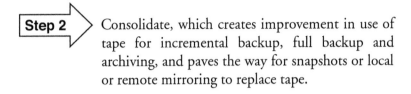

Step 2 Consolidate, which creates improvement in use of tape for incremental backup, full backup and archiving, and paves the way for snapshots or local or remote mirroring to replace tape.

Step 3 Replace daily incremental tape backups with hourly snapshots. Get rid of tape for backup; tape is used only for archiving, not for incremental backup of live data.

Figure 35.2 is the ideal picture to improve in the areas of data aging and tiered storage:

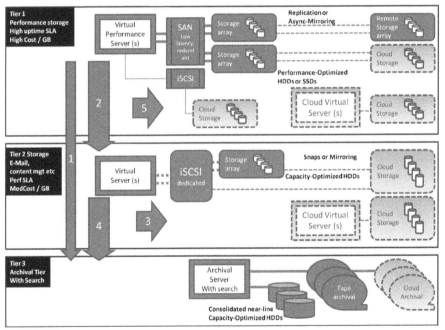

Figure 35.2   Architecture to Affordably Handle Aging Data.

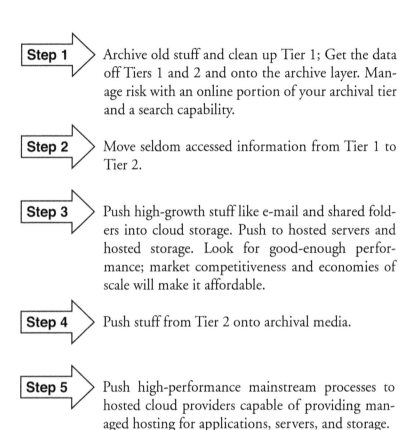

Step 1 Archive old stuff and clean up Tier 1; Get the data off Tiers 1 and 2 and onto the archive layer. Manage risk with an online portion of your archival tier and a search capability.

Step 2 Move seldom accessed information from Tier 1 to Tier 2.

Step 3 Push high-growth stuff like e-mail and shared folders into cloud storage. Push to hosted servers and hosted storage. Look for good-enough performance; market competitiveness and economies of scale will make it affordable.

Step 4 Push stuff from Tier 2 onto archival media.

Step 5 Push high-performance mainstream processes to hosted cloud providers capable of providing managed hosting for applications, servers, and storage.

Chapter 36

Strategy and Execution

Yes, it takes time and effort to build a storage roadmap and Zero-Based Budgeting (ZBB). It takes even more time and effort to socialize the road-map with your management, your customers, your staff, your peers . . . why? Fundamentally, "no roadmap" is a literal phrase. It means you have no direction, will keep repeating the same behaviors, and will keep getting the same substandard results.

Execution takes discipline and planning:

- Identify and prioritize high priority/high value projects (show the business upside)Estimate costs and risks (business expense)Identify the strategic upside for the business as well as the downside of inaction (show strategic value)
- Review the resources available; *review* means to free up existing resources allocated to lower value tasks. It also means that some spending on lower value tasks will need to be discontinued and redirected to higher value tasks.

At its core, ZBB is a prioritization process. ZBB grabs the budget, grabs all the various ways to spend that budget, and sorts those based on business value and risk. The ZBB process provides discipline and clarity. It requires grouping all spending into spending packages and rank-ordering those packages based on cost and value. Then you compare the rank-order list to available money, go down the list and draw the line where the money runs out. Lower priority packages that did not merit spending are referred to as "below the line" and are not funded, at least not funded in this time period. It's okay to have a roadmap showing "below-the-line" packages farther out in time. Obviously, only "above-the-line" packages should appear on the short-term roadmap and receive staffing/funding. The ZBB process can be used as a tool to look at the entire budget and create an opportunity to reduce spending in one area and therefore free up resources to be spent on some higher value package.

But ZBB is often challenging; it's messy and unclear to put together spending packages because of all the variables. It would be nice if the ZBB process was science, but really it's more art than science.

Technology adoption is an art, a balancing act.
- Balance the tactical with the strategic
- Balance between the short term and the long term
- Balance the easy with the hard
- Balance the simple low value with the more complex high value
- Balance finite resources/funds with demand
- Align with customer need and competitive environment
- Balance the needs of the existing customers with the needs of the business to expand into new markets and new customers (and customer needs change)
- Deliver more, spend less

A roadmap and ZBB serve to focus resources on high-priority/high-value projects. Executing without some form of roadmap and ZBB leads to indulgence, distractions, pet projects, and generally a situation where the "urgent" unimportant stuff gets in the way of the important stuff that really needs doing. Attempting too many things simultaneously (also known as "boiling the ocean") without proper resources almost always leads to poor execution.

Roadmap construction causes us to think in terms of phases over time to create a longer-term stepping-stone plan in which each project builds upon the last to deliver a sustainable competitive advantage. Roadmap construction also offers a way to analyze and reduce risk, giving the business the means to identify a risk or thread in time to do something about it. Roadmaps are designed to serve as a framework for course corrections and change of plan.

Most importantly, roadmaps communicate what is NOT budgeted (below the ZBB line) as a clear list of what will be done in the future, which serves to eliminate the vacuum that draws an endless stream of unrelated requests, suggestions, and mandates without rhyme, reason, priority, or clarity as to business value/expense/risk.

So, how to construct and more importantly, how to manage a roadmap? Start with the ZBB; an example is included Table 36.1.

Table 36.1   Zero Balanced Budget

ZBB	Business Up-Side	Cost, Risk, Timeline
DAS consolidation Phase 1, 2 (2)	Migrate DAS storage off servers 1 through 16 to SAN. Save $50,000 in backup; free up space in computer data center; free up people	$30,000 in HW $30,000 in people/time
Tier 1, Tier 2 Phase 1 (4) Tape reduction Phase 1 (5)	Migrate data into either SAN Tier 1 or Tier 2 servers 1 through 16. Improve SLA for Tier 1, reduce tape, and save $30,000 in backup; free up space in computer data center; free up people.	$50,000 in people/time
DAS consolidation Phase 2,3 (3)	Migrate DAS storage off servers 17 through 40 to SAN. Save $70,000 in backup; free up space in computer data center; free up people	$40,000 in HW $30,000 in people/time
Tier 1, Tier 2 Phase 2 (6) Tape reduction Phase 2	Migrate data into either SAN Tier 1 or Tier 2 servers 17 through 40. Improve SLA for Tier 1, reduce tape and save $40,000 in backup; free up space in computer data center; free up people	$30,000 in people/time
Tiered SLA (7)	Strategically improves transparency with business units. Creates option for shift to managed hosting and then to cloud	$3,000 in people/time
"the line"	Above the line is funded for Year 1 Below the line waits for Year 2	

Table 36.1   Zero Balanced Budget (continued)

ZBB	Business Up-Side	Cost, Risk, Timeline
Clean Tier 1 storage, migrate stale data to Tier 2 (7)	Tier 1 storage for "Order Entry" servers 22-24-25-26. Data more than 12 months old will be moved to Tier 2, and a process will be set in place for ongoing movement of aging data. Tier 1 data reduction allows more frequent snapshots, improves RPO/RTO. Leads to improvements in affordable disaster recovery with bare metal recovery, failover, affordable local mirroring, and affordable remote mirroring. Less stale data will improve performance.	$60,000 in hardware (CAPX) $55,000 in people (OPX)
Local server failover (8)	Set up servers 22-23-24-25-26 for failover (Multipath IO) Improves overall uptime. Servers can be maintained/upgraded with near-zero service downtime. Server failures handled with failover.	Production server hardware already exists Need loaner servers to test, train, document $25,000 in people
Local mirroring Tier 1 Remote mirroring (9)	Mirror primary SAN storage to local SAN storage Improves disaster recovery	$30,000 in hardware for local (just Tier 1 storage) $30,000 in hardware for remote (just Tier 1 storage)
Remote server failover Tier 1 (10)	Once remote SAN mirroring is in place, Remote server failover can be implemented Improves disaster recovery	Add server remote capacity: $25,000 $15,000 in people

Table 36.1   Zero Balanced Budget (continued)

ZBB	Business Up-Side	Cost, Risk, Timeline
Bare metal server recovery (Tier 1) (11)	SAN feature to completely image the server setup (just system data, not application data) Allows new server hardware to be deployed quickly (60–90 minutes) without lengthy setup Respond to business unit requests and recover from hardware failure quickly	$15,000 in people
"the line" (second)	Above the line is funded for Year 2 Below the line waits for Year 3	
Data center 12 (12)	Once the changes to storage (especially the Tier 1/Tier 2) have been finished, improve cold air delivery directly to the load and control with thermostat per load, rather than one thermostat per room or zone. Free up data center capacity in 12, and reduce power bill	$7,000
Data Center 8 (13)	Once the changes to storage (especially the Tier 1/Tier 2) have been finished, improve cold air delivery directly to the load and control with thermostat per load, rather than one thermostat per room or zone. Free up data center capacity in 8, and reduce power bill	$7,000

The ZBB process helps you prioritize the high-value stuff and deprioritize the low value. The roadmap communicates the ZBB as a series of separate but related projects, and adds clarity on timing.

Chapter 37

Constructing a Roadmap

The point of a roadmap is to show a progression of multiple, manageable, low-risk, affordable projects, each of which builds on the previous ones. A roadmap is built to be adjusted over time, but without a roadmap, your organization is stuck either attempting to change very little, or attempting to change everything at the same time. The beauty of a series of small projects is that a particular component can be pushed and have a landing zone in the next stepping stone. This is the roadmap of the concepts we've reviewed in the book (and reflects the Zero Balance Budget (ZBB) discussed in the last chapter.)

Add the timeline, think through the time required to execute with the people and money available, and develop a stepping-stone approach in which one project builds on the next, as shown in Figure 37.1.

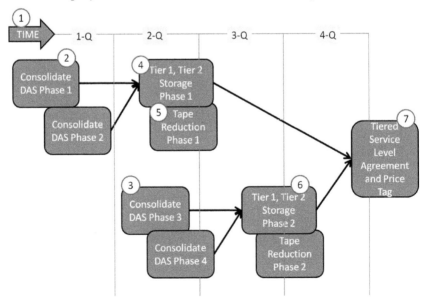

Figure 37.1   Roadmap Single Tier Storage Improvements

1. *Time.* The timeline is a critical element of any roadmap. A time-line matches the resource/staffing plan. A timeline establishes expectations, communicates there is a reasonable limit to the time to implement based on real analysis, and creates a sense of urgency.

2. *Consolidate DAS.* Establish SAN storage to replace a bunch of independent servers with direct attached storage, consolidate onto a SAN, and retire old hardware. (The financial improve-ments for consolidated storage are covered in Part I.) Break your approach into phases: a test phase, phase 1(or the pilot phase), phase 2, phase 3, and phase 4. Phasing sets reasonable goals and gives a sense of accomplishment when a project completes. A phased approach sets the expectation that the work will land on the IT team in manageable incremental loads. Phasing is a good technique to deal with a situation where there are not enough resources available to bite off the entire project all at once. Phas-ing breaks a large problem in to smaller more manageable prob-lems for limited resources to execute over time. Be sure to retire old DAS gear, otherwise you will pay twice and not save money.

3. *Consolidate DAS phases 3 and 4.* Time it out to accommodate existing resources.

4. *Tier 1 and Tier 2.* Building on the SAN storage established in DAS consolidation project, now we have the opportunity to establish separate performance-optimized virtual volumes and capacity-optimized virtual volumes (i.e., Tier 1 and Tier 2). Insti-tute a policy that all proposals for spending on Tier 1 also include a plan to migrate selected data to Tier 2. Be sure to retire old hardware, otherwise you're paying twice and not saving money.

5. *Improve backup and snapshots.* With Tier 1 and Tier 2 established, we have the opportunity to improve the backup/snapshot situa-tion. Tier 1 (low capacity) gets frequent backups or snaps; Tier 2 (much larger capacity, but cooler data) gets less frequent backup and snap, thereby reducing tape. Be sure to adjust the backup/recovery for Tier 1 (improve SLA) and adjust the backup/recov-ery for Tier 2 (less often to save money).

6. *Phase 2 tiering.* Focus resources on one thing at a time for execu-tion, learning, and quality improvement.

7. *Share with business units.* The SLA to the business units is critical to show the business units that IT is being responsible to reduce spending and increase service levels, but only in storage where high service levels are warranted.

The ZBB approach will help you live within your means. ZBB also helps avoid spending on stale stuff just because you spent on it in the past. Let's tackle the next big roadmap, as shown in Figure 37.2.

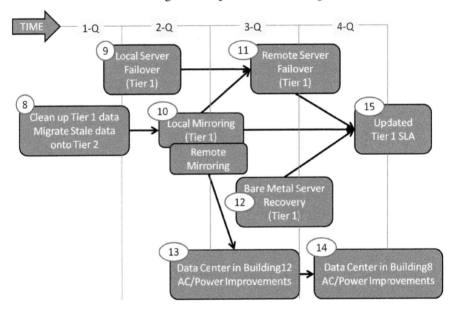

Figure 37.2   Roadmap: Tier 1 Improvements

8. *Tier 1 focus.* This is the data most important to the company. The first step is to protect it affordably by reducing the clutter. Get stale data off Tier 1 and onto Tier 2. This migration serves to reduce the overall quantity of Tier 1 data; as a result, that data can be affordably protected with local mirroring and failover and remote mirroring. It all becomes affordable if we clear out stale data and focus spending on the key hot data.

9. *Server failover.* Server failover is very proven and feasible, but should be used in Tier 1. It is not feasible or manageable with DAS environments.

10. *Mirroring.* Local and remote mirroring of Tier 1 data is a proven method to protect the business in the case of a disaster. It's afford-

able if we focus replication resources only on scrubbed Tier 1 data (i.e., the stale data has been migrated to Tier 2).

11. *Remote server failover.* With local server failover in place, local mirroring, and remote mirroring in place, remote server failover becomes feasible for business continuity.

12. *Bare metal server recovery.* For shops that frequently bring on server capacity (or server provisioning), especially many servers with the same config, bare metal server provisioning is possible once the SAN is in place. The SAN can provide diskless boot and then install a preconfigured server image. This keeps IT off the critical path of business units and enables the performance of repetitive IT tasks more efficiently.

13,14. *Data center facilities improvements (buildings 12 and 8).* Intentionally stage the improvements to match the updated storage, but be considerate of limited floorspace, power, and A/C; facilities resources; technical resources; and spending. Changing servers and storage will change the heat and power load. Rework the A/C and power to accommodate the new heat and power load.

15. *Updated SLA.* Again, updating the SLA will help business units appreciate the ways IT spending has been reduced while service levels (where service levels matter) are improved.

Our next roadmap handles applications, managed hosting, and the cloud, as shown in Figure 37.3.

16. *Content management systems to replace shared folders.* Make content easier to find and use. Make stale content easier to identify and retire efficiently (reducing costs of new storage and backup). The project is not complete until you completely remove shared folders and retire or repurpose old hardware. If the shared folders are left in place or if the old hardware is left in place, the savings are not realized.

17. *Managed hosting, phase 1.* This is the first managed hosting effort, so pick a viable project with some substance, but not a critical Tier 1 project. This gives IT practice and familiarity for managed hosting vendor contracts, SLAs, and execution. If there are hidden expenses or shortfalls on the SLA, this project will surface and be resolved early and on a noncritical system.

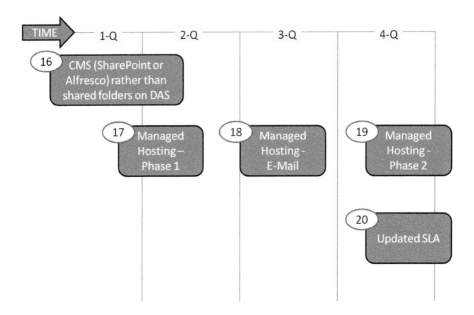

Figure 37.3   Roadmap: Applications, Managed Hosting, Cloud

18.   *Managed hosting e-mail.* E-mail is the most expensive and the easiest thing to move to cloud, with the biggest return on investment. Managed e-mail hosting can be conducted in phases:
transition selected departments/individuals first, then others
later. Be sure to retire old systems (otherwise you're just paying
twice).

19.   *Managed hosting phase 2.* Work on the next application on your
roadmap.

20.   *SLA.* Again, the SLA serves to help business units appreciate how
IT spending has been reduced and service levels (where service
levels matter) have improved.

Figure 37.4 shows the roadmap dealing with Tier 1 dynamic storage.

21.   *Dynamic data migration.* In earlier phases, we set up Tier 1 and
Tier 2 SAN storage. We simply configured the Tier 1 application
on Tier 1 performance storage, and configured Tier 2 applications on Tier 2 capacity storage. With dynamic data migration,
the system includes logic to automatically push stale data to Tier
2. Phase 1 is for one application, to ensure the dynamic storage

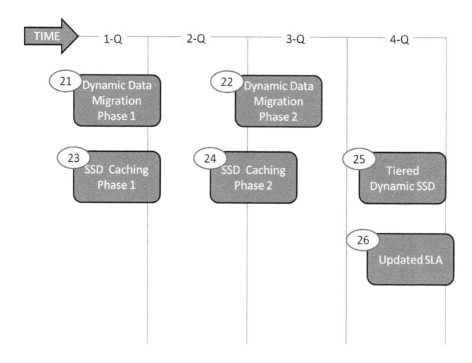

Figure 37.4   Roadmap, Tier 1 Improvements

logic works in conjunction with snapshot, backup, applications, and the like.

22. *Dynamic data migration, phase 2.* Once the process is proven, improve and deploy more.

23. *SSD or SSS Caching.* This serves to further improve performance and replace 15K rpm drives (freeing capacity in the data center).

24. *SSD or SSS caching, phase 2.* Once the process is proven, improve and deploy more.

25. *Tiered dynamic SSD.* As SSDs drop in price and systems software improves to make use of SSDs as a way to affordably improve performance without large numbers of 15K drives, tiered dynamic SSD is a big value, low risk project at the right point in time.

37.1   Managing a Roadmap

Course corrections are a healthy part of any business. Spending changes, business priorities change, customer needs change, markets change, and world economic environments change. Course corrections should be made;

hopefully, lots of minor course corrections, rather than big course corrections or wholesale roadmap restarts.

Roadmaps and progress on existing projects should be reviewed no less than quarterly. The review meeting format is a brief review of the overall roadmap, a review of overall roadmap changes, a project review, a list of risks and escalations (usually presented as a dashboard with green-yellow-red), and a financial review of spending vs savings. The financial portion is required, otherwise human nature will allow everyone to forget or ignore the big picture reasons for Storage improvements.

37.2   Roadmap Execution, Package Phase Definition and Approvals

So, now we have a roadmap! What next? For each project (with a defined scope, schedule, and resources), there are phases: Phase 0 (concept), phase 1 (planning, scoping), phase 2 (implementation)—each phase should undergo a phase exit review for the purpose of confirming that the concept or plan or implementation are on target to deliver business value affordably and without mission creep. For each package, a bit of process must be applied.

Phase approvals (this is just like the tech companies do it) this process for each block on the roadmap (as shown in Table 37.1).

Table 37.1   Product Lifecycle Brief

	Project Lifecycle Described (For Each Project)	Outcome
Phase 0	Project concept is developed and reviewed. What business problems are being solved, what's the business case for spending/earning? Clarify what is in the project and what is specifically excluded (project scope).	The phase 0 exit review with executives establishes a business case with reasonable risk and expense. Establish and review the Plan of Record. In a successful phase 0 exit, execs approve work to plan the project: a technical assessment and establishing a plan of record with committed scope, schedule, resources.

Table 37.1   Product Lifecycle Brief (continued)

	Project Lifecycle Described (For Each Project)	Outcome
		The phase 0 review also serves to kill bad projects and eliminate time, money, and distractions on projects without merit. The phase 0 review can also serve to identify and fund high-merit projects; as ideas frequently come from junior IT people and business units.
Phase 1 -	Technical assessment phase, determining scope, schedule, and resources. Reduce scope, establish quality release criteria, risk assessment, staffing.	The phase 1 exit review with execs reviews business case once again and establishes a plan of record with committed scope, schedule, and resources; risk management plan; staffing and funding plan; a written and reviewed project plan defining what scope will be delivered and when; a deployment plan; and specific quality release criteria. The Plan of Record now includes scope, schedule, and resources (funding and staffing).A successful phase 1 exit review results in moving to phase 2, implementation, with executive commitment for a confirmed scope, schedule, staffing, and funding. One important concept: the project clock starts when resources are available and engaged on the project. If a project is approved and then resources are not available, this creates delays, demotivation, lack of urgency, and credibility problems.

Table 37.1   Product Lifecycle Brief (continued)

	Project Lifecycle Described (For Each Project)	Outcome
Phase 2	Implementation, testing, training, QA	The phase 2 exit review with execs basically confirms the project is ready to deploy, reviews scope (especially defining what is outside of scope). Phase 2 typically focuses on acceptance criteria, pilot results, quality, and risk.
		A successful Phase 2 exit means a "green light" on the deployment.

People complain about process, of course—but the alternative is no process, no prioritization, no strategy, and no execution. Eventually, that approach will lead to a condition of no income and no employment. Yes, there is some expense and overhead, but the process is not a substitute for a brain. It's okay to lighten and simplify the process. Estimates are fine and need not be one hundred percent accurate. Again, the alternative is no planning, no estimates, and no execution. Process, effectively used, improves the workplace by serving to focus execution—to accomplish projects together, rather than just deal with the confetti of disorganized, random requests and break-fix work, day-in and day-out.

Human beings, at the end of the day, need to feel connected to something bigger than themselves as individuals. Humans are motivated by the sense of accomplishing something meaningful and substantial. Humans like clarity, full information, and the big picture. Process (if used sensibly) can help that.

An example of a project lifecycle brief for snapshot and tape reduction is included as Table 37.2.

It's desirable to lighten the process to fit the task; this approach need not be "backhoe in a flowerpot." And it's definitely not a good use of company funds to do more work than is necessary. Processes have a bad name because processes have been poorly run; the processes that are well run get no positive press. The process should be short and simple for little projects; it can be bigger and more detailed for larger projects. The point is that project execution requires resources and risk management. If you are spending significant money on resources, it makes sense to use those

Table 37.2   Example Project Lifecycle Brief

	Example Project Lifecycle: Snapshot and Tape Reduction
Phase 0	Review the business problem/expense of using incremental tape backup. Review the snapshot as an alternative. Briefly review costs and annual savings. Discuss service level improvements (RTO, RPO). Discuss phasing; show which systems are changed and which will remain the same. Review what is outside of project scope. Phase 0 exit: Execs give approval to proceed with technical scoping and project creation.
Phase 1	Plan starts with establishing a baseline for costs in tape, people, and library management. Project plan includes selection of snapshot software and in-house trials.Project plan includes defined scope, schedule, resources, quality criteria, staffing.Project plan reviews data retention and security requirements.Project plan review staffing and resources (people, training, time).Project plan reviews retirement of hardware and tape—tape backups will be done in parallel for some period, then incremental tape backups will be discontinued but tape will be available for recovery. After a predetermined period (several months), the tape and hardware will be redeployed for archiving. Phase 1 exit: Leadership reviews the scope, acceptance criteria, quality, risk, and gives approval to proceed with implementation, as well as for spending and staffing.
Phase 2	Proceed with installation, testing, training, dry-runs, and QA, while still using tape. Phase 2 exit: Leadership reviews the in-house trials, training, risk. Gives approval to proceed with deployment.

resources on specific, high-value projects, and it makes sense that there is a schedule of execution.

Why make a schedule? Schedules never work, right?
- The schedule serves to deliver the beneficial project sooner rather than later.

- A project schedule serves to coordinate multiple interdependent tasks to avoid lots of delays.
- A project schedule serves to avoid projects with inflated price tags. Time is money. "We just need another month," heard seven months in a row, is costing the company limited money. Prolonged projects have a big price tag.

And schedules do work, if properly run.

Chapter 38

Risk Management

Every project has problems.
Risk management boils down to knowing about problems early,
so there is adequate time to deal with the problems without schedule slips.
Poor project execution is invariably rooted in ineffective risk management.

Risk management boils down to simple processes and principles.

Break a big project into lots of little projects or tasks, and for each task, *categorize all the risks*:

- *Acceptable.* The risk is low probability or low impact and is an acceptable risk, but needs monitoring.
- *Reduce or Avoid.* The risk is high probability or high impact; change the plan to avoid or reduce these risks.
- *Backup Plan.* When a high probability or high impact risk cannot be affordably avoided, make a backup plan and a schedule trigger point with adequate time in the schedule to execute the backup plan. Stick to the original plan until the trigger point; at that time, revisit the risk and either stick to the original plan or switch to the backup plan. Do *not* dither.

Organizations and human beings hate uncertainty and they hate risk. The default behavior when encountering uncertainty or risk is to simply stop, stall, wait until uncertainty and risk is removed. In this sense, risk management is highly related to project management (the management of scope, schedule, resources and accomplish a task). Table 38.1 shows an example risk management plan.

Table 38.1   Example: Project Risk Management for Snapshot, Tape Reduction

	Risk	Remedy
Scope	Change from tape-based backup to snapshot-based backup for 16 servers	

Table 38.1   Example: Project Risk Management for Snapshot, Tape Reduction

Risk 1	May encounter problems when attempting to recover lost data	Test first, then pilot program on two servers, then production.
Risk 2	May not be able to meet RPO/RTO expectations	Establish clear RPO/RTO expectations; test first, then pilot program on two servers, then production.
Risk 3	Snapshots will slow down servers or storage	Establish a baseline of backups, then, during pilot, compare snapshot to baseline.
Risk 4	Backup staff not familiar with snapshots; initial snapshots may not work.	Provide training, then practice during test and pilot phases.
Risk 5	Network traffic increases	Establish a baseline of network traffic for backups (the way it's done today), then, during pilot, compare network traffic related to snapshot (the replacement method).
Risk 6	Backup windows increases	Establish a baseline of backups (the window today), then, during pilot, compare snapshot (the window for the replacement method).
Risk 7	Tape library database will not accommodate snapshots	Review the tape management database. Describe revised database use cases and reports. Make improvements and implement them during test and pilot phases.
Risk 8	Maintaining snapshots, lack of clarity as to which servers are doing snapshots and which servers are still doing tape	Review the tape management database. Describe revised use cases. Review process during transition. Make improvements and implement them during test and pilot phases

Reducing risk serves to improve execution, which serves to reduce costs, which serves to create headroom in the budget for additional IT improvements.

Chapter 39

Part III Wrap-Up: Projects Within Reach

- *Improvement 1.* Find the right managed hosting provider for your business.
- *Improvement 2.* Compare managed hosting service level agreements and managed hosting risk management.
- *Improvement 3.* Find the right cloud storage provider.
- *Improvement 4.* Implement cloud-based e-mail.
- *Improvement 5.* Implement cloud-based content management and collaboration.
- *Improvement 6.* Implement a hybrid cloud project.
- *Improvement 7.* Create a storage strategy and execution plan that includes a ZBB, roadmap(s), and supporting phase gate project management/approval process.

39.1   Improvement 1. Find the Right Managed Hosting Provider for Your Business

Create your big-picture of how managed hosting will work for your company. Stage that into manageable stepping-stone projects, and start with a reasonable pilot project that will enable you to complete a managed host vetting and SLA process.

39.2   Improvement 2. Compare Managed Hosting Service Level Agreements and Managed Hosting Risk Management

Your managed hosting evaluation (Improvement 1) puts you in a position of interacting with several managed hosting providers. Capture SLAs and performance contracts from all of them. Compare one to the other. Pay attention to what happens if things go wrong; there should be significant motivation/pain for the managed hosting provider in that case. If there is no substantial penalty, ask why. But think for yourself: *determine what's most important for you* for SLA terms. They need to be simple, understandable, easily/clearly measurable, and actionable. Stick to the important stuff, it's okay to drop the less important stuff.

39.3   Improvement 3. Find the Right Cloud Storage Provider

Cloud is very different than managed hosting (consider it a different tool for a different job). There will be specific needs (e.g., digital content serving to your potential customers) that merit a cloud provider. Other traditional IT needs will merit a managed hosting approach.

39.4   Improvement 4. Implement Cloud-Based E-mail

We spent a bunch of time on storage classification and storage tiering. E-mail users can be classified and tiered too. Classify those who carry sensitive data (e.g., executives, legal, medical, HR, stock trading stuff, trade secret stuff) as your Tier 1. Those who carry less sensitive or nonsensitive data but in high volumes (e.g., operations, sales, and marketing people) are your Tier 2; people who carry low sensitivity and low volumes of data (e.g., labor, assembly, security) are your Tier 3.

Migrate Tier 3 first, then Tier 2. It is likely that you'll never migrate your Tier 1.

39.5   Improvement 5. Implement Cloud-Based Content Management and Collaboration

Tiering again; there are certain high-value, high-risk collaborations. Others are lower risk; migrate those first. The others can be migrated later.

39.6   Improvement 6. Implement a Hybrid Cloud Project

Work with your managed hosting or cloud provider to identify hybrid capabilities and organize a pilot project. Be sure to test the backup and recovery. Be sure to test removing the hybrid logic as insurance for if/when there is a problem and the system needs to be debugged.

39.7   Improvement 7. Create a Storage Strategy and Execution Plan that Includes a ZBB, Roadmap(s), and Supporting Phase Gate Project Management/Approval Process

Process is not easy. Even organizations who frequently use project management and phase gate processes struggle with it. It's a learning situation, and people don't instantly get it. The trick is to communicate "why" we use the process, the benefits of using the process, and the disadvantages of not using process. Catch people doing things right. Be patient and encouraging with the people who don't get it right away.

Your executives will appreciate the ZBB discipline and the roadmap, in which one phase leads to another.

Part III Conclusion

Well, that's a wrap.

My closing advice: Look for the battles that will address the most money wasted by your company, with the least amount of risk. If you take care of some portion of these concepts; it's my strongly held belief that you will save your company large coin, potentially millions, while delivering equal or better service, reliability, and protection.

Hope it was a worthwhile and enjoyable read.

I'd be delighted to get your feedback: hubbert@hubbertsmith.com

Appendix A

Storage Protocol Basics

Storage protocols, such as iSCSI, serial attached SCSI (SAS), serial advanced technology attachment (SATA), and Fibre Channel (FC), define how storage communicates to the outside world.

Since I have been involved with storage, the data rates have gone from 40 Mb/s (yes, megaBITs) to 6 Gb/s. I never cease to be amazed that the industry (often direct competitors) can collaborate to build systems that can reliably deliver *6 billion bits per second* from point A to point B. And soon enough, industry standards that are currently on the drawing board, will grow to *40 billion* bits per second.

Storage protocols have the same basic elements.
- *Physical layer* (the wire, the connectors, the electrical signal)
- *PHY and Link layer* (primitives to establish digital communications once and electrical connection is established, as well as handle errors)
- *Transport* (addressing and trunking)
- *Application* (payload)

The *physical layer* defines connections on HDDs, or cables, or backplanes, or storage switches, or servers from one manufacturer that will connect to stuff from a different manufacturer. There are a variety of connectors, and these need to fit reliably. One of the critical difficulties for the adoption of SATA (it seemed trivial at the time) was a specification with inadequate definition of connector tolerances, which resulted in loose connectors, which furthermore resulted in a bunch of bad press over a situation that was easily remedied with a specification errata note to fix the industry interoperability issue.

Cables are specified by as part of the physical layer. Cables need to be durable and shielded. Cables also need to be inexpensive to buy and easy to manufacture. Serial cables consist of two pairs of wires: one pair for transmit and another pair for receive. The challenge presented by the higher frequencies creates a risk of intrapair skew—like two runners on a track, the runner on the shorter inside lane gets there first. Cable specifications serve to keep conductor lengths the same so the electrical signal on one wire gets to the destination at exactly the same time its companion electrical signal arrives at the destination. The higher the frequency, the tighter the specification for matching conductor lengths.

Electrical characteristics for the data pairs define maximum and minimum voltages, cable lengths, backplane lengths and similar. The electrical standard specifies a thing called an "eye diagram" to test the voltage and frequency on a signal pair to ensure the electrical signal is clean enough to reliably transmit data; the voltage on these pairs of wires switches at a rate of 6 billion times per second. Related to this, the electrical characteristics for the power side establish power delivery, handle LED behavior, and handle hot-plug and hot-unplug events.

Once the physical connection is made from point A to point B, the *PHY and link layer* will establish the digital communications connection. The first step is out-of-band negotiation; each end of the wire connects to a silicon PHY. The PHYs on both ends of the wire will handshake, acknowledge, and then speed-negotiate to determine the fastest data rate. If one is a new 6 Gb/s device and the other is an older 3 Gb/s device, they will handshake and negotiate down to the 3 Gb/s speed and begin to trade digital information. The PHY and link layer handles digital signaling like hot-plug and hot-unplug events. The PHY and link also do primitive error handling with cyclic redundancy check (CRC), similar to a checksum. A calculation is performed for each frame information structure (FIS) to ensure the data received matches the data sent.

Once the physical connection, the electrical connection and the digital connection is made, the *transport layer* takes over to create, deliver and confirm delivery of payloads: frame information structures (FISs). The transport layer handles addressing. Storage protocols (Figure A.1) often connect multiple devices on a single wire; they include a global address so the data sent down the wire goes to the right destination. Think of each FIS as a packet with a start of frame, an end of frame, and a payload. The payload can be either data or command; here are the list of SATA FIS types (SAS and FC are similar but not identical):

- Register host to device—a handshake
- Register device to host—a handshake

- Data—a data payload
- DMA activate—direct memory access, send data to a specific address in system memory
- PIO setup—legacy PATA command for queuing and similar
- Set device bits—device setup, turn off and on various drive settings
- DMA setup—direct memory access, send data to a specific address in system memory
- BIST—built-in self-test

Table A.1   Example Storage Protocol Frame Structure

Start of Frame	Frame type	Destination & Source Address	PortID	CRC	Payload: Data Frame or Command Frame	End of frame

This is remarkably similar to the fundamental workings of the ethernet protocol. Storage protocols (iSCSI, SAS, SATA, FC) each have their strengths and weaknesses. The differences mostly lie in the numbers of addressable devices, SAN switching capabilities, and cabling options. The differences also lie in the price tag.

Summary on storage protocols: these are both simple and incredibly robust and complex in the same moment. The real merit in a storage protocol lies in its ability to handle errors. What happens when connections are abruptly created or dropped? What happens when delays occur or acknowledgements are not received? Error handling is where all the magic happens. Just be aware that they have different price tags and different capabilities; use the right tool for the job.

Appendix B

Project Management

I've added this Project Management appendix in the interest of improving your successes; after all, the usefulness of this book is only as good as your ability to execute and put it to work.

Every project boils down to key components: Scope, Schedule, Resources, and Risk.

First, you must set objectives and review them. Write down the project objectives (this can include desired deliverables or outcome, budget, schedule), and review these with your team. Ask for feedback from your team, and improve your plan based on their suggestions. Ask for an executive sponsor, someone who will make sure there is budget for the project.

Next, you must set the scope. Ask your team to consider the objectives, do some thinking and investigation, and then meet again for a Project Map Day. The team members (or functional leads) will need to come prepared with a list of tasks, each with predecessors, successors, duration, and resources (estimated staff-days, skills). Each task can be recorded on a form like the one shown in Table B.1. On map days, photocopy a bunch of these, have your functional leads fill them out in as much detail as possible and stick them up on the wall in sequence.

The next step is to establish the schedule and identify necessary resources.

Basically, we are breaking a big, hairy, complex problem into an smaller, simpler, easier-to-understand list of tasks. The granularity level should reflect this: each task should require no more than five days, and no less than two days.

The most successful map days I've seen involve getting into a big room and doing the review and discussion after the wall is populated. The value is the discussion. Most people don't like confrontation, so you can expect people to avoid asking for something from other people (it's a form of confrontation). The collaborative act of putting up the entire project serves to avoid

Table B.1   Map Day Template

Task #, name		
Predecessors		
Successors		
Duration		
Owner, Resources, Skills		
Comment/Risk		

the whole confrontation thing; if people know something's coming, there is less perceived confrontation involved in asking about something they already know about and have agreed to.

Once you have assembled all these tasks, you or the project manager can organize them into a project timeline. Take a look at the things that can be done in parallel. Pay particular attention to the tasks that must be done in sequence (one task completed before the next task can start). There are often creative ways to tighten the timeline. This will deliver some semblance of schedule and resources.

Very few people are familiar or comfortable working in a schedule-driven project environment, particularly one in which they have had no input. The best way to overcome this resistance is to involve the participants in the map day, so that they have a hand in establishing adequate time and resources to do their work.

Perhaps the biggest risk to any project is the reality that urgent things get in the way. The key to successful project management in an IT organization is taking steps to keep resources on task and keep them from leaking onto other urgent (but perhaps less important) stuff. Go to the managers of the people involved; make the case that these folks need to be allocated to the task, and secure the managers' commitment that the resources will not evaporate on your project. Ask for the commitment specifically—if the managers do make a firm commitment of resources, make sure those resources are used well. If the managers do not make a firm commitment to resource, it is best if you go up the management chain and state that the project will not materialize without resources.

Keeping on task takes a bit of focus, but basically, "that which gets measured, gets done." The easy way to ensure that is to make a list of the map

Table B.2 Task and Schedule Tracking, Simple Template

Actual Date	Plan Date	Task	Owner	Note
c-2009-03-15	2009-03-15	1		
c-2009-03-25	2009-03-15	2		
2009-04-15	2009-04-15	3		
2009-04-18	2009-04-15	4		
2009-04-21	2009-04-15	5		
Task 1 completed on schedule Task 2 completed, but 10 days late Task 3 appears to be running on schedule Task 4 appears to be running 3 days late Task 5 appears to be running 6 days late				

day output and track tasks to completion. Just call a meeting, walk down the list, and ask each owner for status.

A project task tracking template is shown in Table B.2. The *c* means complete.

Good project management boils down to finding out about problems in time to take action and fix them.

The point is to track progress so that you can give visibility. Those who are performing are getting positive visibility, those who are falling short are getting negative visibility. When this happens, it's important to consistently acknowledge "the *xyz* task is in need of help." The subtle message here is that it's about the task, not the person; it's about getting help to execute to success, rather than hanging someone out to dry.

To run a project meeting, meet once a week to walk through the project list, focusing on upcoming items. This walkthrough will generally produce some new things that need to get done. On projects I have managed, each week the project manager (me) produced a list of actions with an owner and a date (or date for a date). I got in the habit of using my laptop to take notes during the meeting. I ended the meeting five minutes early. And in that last five minutes, I'd scrub my notes and e-mail the agenda and the action list for next week's project meeting. The participants had the entire week, every possible moment, to work their issues. Then, at the next meeting, I'd crack open that e-mail and start down that list. Pretty quickly, participants got the hang of it and came prepared to address the actions that had been assigned to them. The tone we set: Set people up for success by giving them adequate time to get their work done, get them help if needed, manage risk. People pick up on that and respond.

Appendix C

People, Process, Technology

There are many, many books written on this topic, and I will not attempt to repeat them here. But without a people-process-technology approach, execution and delivery of the improvements in this book will not happen.

The fundamental principles that work for me include the following.

C.1 Push Decisions into the Hands of Those Most Capable

A big component of being a good manager is the practice of breaking a big problem (such as how to improve on the delivery of storage SLAs and spend less money) into smaller, more manageable problems. Involving people familiar with the difficulties and challenges of day-to-day frontline issues will improve the quality of the output of breaking a big problem into lots of manageable, executable problems. This is the principle of map day: involving those in-the-know on the project breakdown. The same principle applies whether the project is something large or something small and day-to-day; it's important to frame the problem but avoid dictating the solution. People study engineering and technology because they want to solve problems and want to build things. This gives them workplace satisfaction. It's been my experience that when I simply frame the problem, rather than dictate the solution, technology people will provide a solution that can do more than solve the immediate problem. As a manager, you must recognize limits: Each individual has different capabilities, so hand each person problems that are within their means to solve. Tell them clearly, "Your responsibility is to solve this, don't wait on others to tell you what to do, track progress on your status report, ask for help if you get hung up."

C.2 Develop a Culture of Peer Reviews

Even small tasks should be peer reviewed; in fact, it's best to establish peer review culture by starting with small stuff. Peer reviews drive the right behavior. Establishing a meeting for a peer review creates a deadline for completion. Peer reviews allow others to provide input on how to improve the solution. Peer reviews create confidence and two-way respect—the senior people generate more respect for junior people, and vice versa. At the end of the day, you want to push your problems to the least expensive, most capable human resources in the organization. Peer reviews create a culture of written, well-communicated best practices and continuous improvement. Peer reviews also create bench-strength, where more than one individual can deal with a given situation; this reduces risk when people take vacations, are promoted, or are assigned to another task. I know of many people (including me) who left a job because the company refused to promote a competent person, even though a slot was open, because they could not backfill the vacated position. Peer reviews reduce that problem to something more manageable.

C.3 Give Credit Where Credit is Due

Allow subordinates to report good news up the management chain. When subordinates report good news, they get recognition (reward), and they will be encouraged to do more. If you report good news, then it's easy for them to assume you are taking credit for their work, they get no recognition, and the predictable behavior is more apathy, more passive resistance, less self-starting, and more "wait on the boss to tell us what to do" behavior.

C.4 Create an Environment Where it's Okay to Ask for Help

Time is money. Schedule is important. Ask for help. That message should be embraced by everyone in any business, especially in IT.

Technical individual contributors, sooner or later, will get over their heads with a task that is more challenging than anticipated. There are three possible outcomes:

1. The individual completes the task.
2. The individual asks for help and completes the task

3.   The individual stalls out and takes too long to complete the task, or never completes it, or completes something substandard.

As we enter the workforce, this is a tough change to digest and embrace: The typical technical education teaches us to work alone, complete our assignments alone, prepare for, and complete exams alone. The test schedule was the deadline.

As we enter the workforce as individual contributors, the work environment is no longer event driven (with tests). It's a continuous treadmill of assignments and problems. This often leads to a situation in which an individual contributor can fall behind and resort to a mental approach of "This will take as long as it takes for me to get this done, and the schedule is unimportant." The preferred approach, of course, is "The schedule is important," and if the task is difficult, ask for help.

But simply saying "Go faster, the schedule must be met!" is not a workable remedy, because inevitably we run into tough problems that are not easily solved.

The workable remedy is, "Go fast, the schedule is important, but if you run into problems, ask for help."

Completing tasks on schedule without help is ideal—the best possible result. Completing tasks on schedule with help is satisfactory. Asking for help is encouraged, that way we learn from each other. But completing tasks late, without asking for help, is unsatisfactory.

Ask for help. It's okay.

In fact, most people dislike any form of project management for this reason. A schedule is established, and the perception is that if the task isn't completed on schedule, that constitutes failure. They feel they are being set up for failure. That's just emotionally exhausting. But the reason we use project management and have schedules is so we can identify when tasks are taking too long and then do something about it (by providing the needed help).

Catch your people doing something right—when someone asks for help, commend them for it. When someone flounders, gets distracted, or otherwise does not execute, *give* them help, and say, "Next time, it's your responsibility to ask for help, don't blow it." By creating this simple "ask for help" environment, you are creating a healthy, less-stressful work environment with lower turnover. Additionally, you are transferring knowledge and know-how from your senior folks to your junior folks and creating an IT organization with bench-strength.

C.5   Create Status Reports with a Project Management Slant

Status reports should be issued weekly, without exception, and they should be short and simple. The report should consist of a list of work items (consistent week to week)—not huge tasks, but not minute tasks either. Weekly status reports should consistently list open tasks with their percentage complete (0%, 25%, 50%, 75%, or done). When a task is complete, some written closure is required—an entry into a systems log, an entry into a knowledge base, a root cause analysis–closed look corrective action (RCA-CLCA), or a peer review.

C.6   Encourage Communication and Require Transparency

In every organization, decisions and course corrections happen: reporting relationships are reorganized, people come and go, budgets are adjusted, the company earnings and spending fluctuate. Problems occur in the absence of course corrections, which usually leads to a big course correction; massive course corrections usually indicate poor decision-making in the past. Lots of little, minor course corrections are healthy; these are the hallmark of a good company. However, a little course correction, viewed from the lower levels of a company, can appear massive. It's your choice how to handle communications, decisions, course corrections, and communications. You can be transparent; or you can avoid communication and let your people be in the dark until someone tells them, or they run with speculation, rumor, and secondhand information. In the absence of communication, people simply stop.

Establishing transparency is usually not easy; sometimes it's like seeing the sausage being made—it makes you want to become a vegetarian. But the alternative (darkness, silence) is less desirable. If there is a reduction in force, just say so; they'll find out eventually. But also use the opportunity to communicate: tell them there was a course correction, such as a reduction in force or a budget cut, but don't stop there. Keep going and explain why it happened and why it was necessary. If your group is impacted, then tell them what you'll do about it. If your group is not impacted, then close the issue with comments along the lines of "it was driven by business situations, but we are not impacted; let's put it behind us and get back to work." If someone has been let go, that can create assume-the-negative "I'm next" thinking, but it is also a sign that the company is willing to make some tough decisions in the interest of running an effective business. It's always a good practice to offer a one-on-one discussion if anyone has questions or concerns. The bottom line is that people will find out about bad news sooner or later. Use it as an opportunity to communicate the reason and the response.

C.7   Insist on Execution; Find and Resolve Dysfunctionality

Based on its author's firsthand experience, the *Dilbert* comic strip is firmly rooted in reality. Dysfunctionality refers to social function (as in dysfunctional family), describing situations with significant communication problems in which the expectations of one person or group do not match reality and communication problems disallow resolution. Whenever execution problems are evident, it's likely there are goal misalignments, and execution becomes stalled. In these situations there are invariably two parties and two sides of the story. Identify and reward execution.

> *From retired General Colin Powell's Leadership Primer*
> *http://www.chally.com/enews/powell.html*

> **Being responsible sometimes means pissing people off.**
> *Good leadership involves responsibility to the welfare of the group, which means that some people will get angry at your actions and decisions. It's inevitable if you're honorable. Trying to get everyone to like you is a sign of mediocrity: You'll avoid the tough decisions, you'll avoid confronting the people who need to be confronted, and you'll avoid offering differential rewards based on differential performance because some people might get upset. Ironically, by procrastinating on the difficult choices, by trying not to get anyone mad, and by treating everyone equally "nicely" regardless of their contributions, you'll simply ensure that the only people you'll wind up angering are the most creative and productive people in the organization.*

Address problems directly, through normal channels. But, if attempts to directly address problems through normal channels fail, go right to the top.

Execution matters. Sort out the individuals who are trying to execute from the individuals who are not. Help the people trying to execute.

Appendix D

Root Cause, Corrective Action Process

Here's an example of applied root cause analysis–closed look corrective action (RCA-CLCA): My very first tech job was as a computer analyst working on computer-aided design (CAD) systems. During the day, the CAD users would do their thing; the workload was mostly random. During lunch-hour, the systems folks ran incremental backups. The systems folks started to run the backups earlier and earlier. CAD users complained that the system was really unresponsive immediately before lunch, and they were having problems getting their work done. In this case, the system was burdened by both random workloads (the CAD users) as well as a sequential workload (the backup). The business unit manager created a great ruckus about how the system was "always on its knees." He thought the cure was to replace that CAD system with a different CAD system from a different vendor, buy new hardware, move the entire CAD file library to a different CAD file structure, and retrain all the end users. I thought it was a better use of the company's time and money to identify the root cause rather than just replace the system with a different CAD system, with all the associated expense of new hardware, user training, data transition. Good times.

This problem relates to process. The immature approach to the problem was "buy a new computer," but the root cause was backup. The cure to the CAD problem was not new hardware, it was a process thing. We could have spent all the time and money on a new system and still had the same backup-related performance problem.

- *Root cause*: There were two workloads.
- *Corrective action*: Relieve the system of two workloads so it can perform the main mission during working hours. The alternative, replace the CAD system, would have cost millions of dollars in hardware, software, implementation, manpower, training, and generally lost time due to a less familiar system.

It's not always about technology. Many times, I'd argue, most times, problems are rooted in people and process.

To improve execution problem solving and to create an environment of continuous improvement, there is a simple but highly effective quality approach: Root Cause Analysis—Closed Loop Corrective Action.

The steps are simple. When a problem is encountered, first capture the root cause; then correct it. Store this information on searchable media (an IT support Web site, a support database, or similar), to reduce the chance of having to reinvent the wheel should the problem crop up again.

This sounds obvious, yet it's almost too obvious—so, surprisingly, few IT shops have this implemented. The alternative is a "no rules" Calvinball (from the cartoon) approach, which creates an environment of constant emergencies and fire-drills. In this environment, individual "diving catch" behavior is rewarded, not teamwork. Without RCA-CLCA, organizations stall, they do not grow or improve, they do not have continuous improvement, they repeatedly encounter the same problems and repeatedly fix them. They are in constant fire-drill mode.

To implement RCA-CLCA culture, simply tell the staff RCA-CLCA is required, and review and measure it. How many problems total? How many problems generated new RCA-CLCAs? How many problems were covered by existing RCA-CLCA? Acknowledge the people consistently contributing to RCA-CLCAs. Consistently ask, "What did the RCA-CLCA system have on this problem?" or state, "I assume this is now in the RCA-CLCA system." And periodically ask for a pareto chart of commonly encountered issues in the trouble ticket database, cross-check these issues with entries in the RCA-CLCA system, and cross-check them with humans involved as evidence that those individuals either are or are not contributing to and using the RCA-CLCA system. Ask for RCA-CLCA on status reports. Acknowledge and reward good behavior, acknowledge and correct poor behavior.

That which gets measured, gets done.

Appendix E

Iometer: Performance Testing in the Lab

The objective of this DIY Performance Testing Appendix is to give you the tools to improve your foundational understanding of disk drive and storage array performance, as well as to give you the tools that will enable you to affordably benchmark just the important stuff, without great huge hardware labs or great huge investments in learning curve or time to test.

All in the interest of the right tool for the job: Iometer gives useful insights into how and why products perform well with some workloads and poorly with others. These insights help us economically apply the right tools for the job. Really fast (and proportionally expensive) storage hardware should be used for high-transaction storage, and economical capacity-optimized storage hardware with good-enough performance should be used for data with low transactions.

The strength of Iometer is that it is simple and easy to understand. The problem with Iometer is that it is a lab tool, not a tool to measure performance of a production system. Iometer will mount a volume and put data across that volume prior to measuring performance, which makes Iometer unfeasible for production monitoring. Thankfully, there are other storage profiler tools available for that task.

E.1 Which Benchmark?

"Why Fileserver?" Why not other measures, or many other measures?

We selected the Iometer file server benchmark for phase 1 for three reasons:

1. Simpler tools tend to be PC-oriented; the Iometer Fileserver profile finds that middle ground with a both a simple benchmark and a multiuser enterprise benchmark.

2. The Iometer fileserver benchmark does an adequate job of covering (see above) file serving, data protection and e-mail workloads.

3. Using Iometer's file server benchmark gives us a convenient and verifiable way to compare a variety of systems and devices ourselves and with the StorageReview.com database.

StorageReview.com is an independent third-party Web site focused on disk drives. StorageReview.com has an extensive database of performance test results for many different makes and models of hard disk drives, which can be added to your own analysis for comparison.

We can compare to other 7200 rpm drives and win; we can also win with performance/power. And we can compete against the adjacent 10,000 rpm market with "adequate performance, close-enough performance" positioning.

E.2   The Iometer Fileserver Benchmark

StorageReview.com has standardized on the Access Patterns shown in Table E.1. Table E.2 demonstrates how to set up and run a file server performance test.

Table E.1   Fileserver I/O profile, Iometer

Access Patterns			
% of Access Specification	**Transfer Size Request**	**% Reads**	**% Random**
File Server Access Pattern (as defined by Intel)			
10%	0.5 KB	80%	100%
5%	1 KB	80%	100%
5%	2 KB	80%	100%
60%	4 KB	80%	100%
2%	8 KB	80%	100%
4%	16 KB	80%	100%
4%	32 KB	80%	100%
10%	64 KB	80%	100%
Workstation Access Pattern (as defined by StorageReview.com)			
100%	8 KB	80%	80%

Table E.1   Fileserver I/O profile, Iometer

Database Access Pattern (as defined by Intel/StorageReview.com)			
100%	8 KB	67%	100%

Table E.2   File Server Performance Test, Map Day Template

1	Download Iometer (http://www.iometer.org/doc/downloads.html); use the 2006.7.27 version	
2	Connect a Drive Under Test (DUT) to the system.	
3	Format the Disk: Control Panel Administrative Tools Computer Management Storage Disk Management Right-click on DUT, perform quick format	
4	Open Iometer	
5	The DUT should appear on the Iometer Disk Targets tab; select the DUT (see Figure E.1)	Use the "Disk Targets" tab
6	Delete unnecessary Iometer workers (see Figure E.2)	Use the "Disk Targets" tab
7	Load the FILESERVER workload script (see Figures E.3 and E.4)	Use the file folder icon to open the Iometer script . The FILESERVER script is attached in this file
8	Select the FILESERVER workload (see Figure E.5)	Use the "access specifications tab"
9	Select the number of outstanding I/Os to 1 (same as queue depth) (see Figure E.7)	Use the "Disk Targets" tab
10	Start the test: You will be prompted to choose a file where the results will be stored; additional testing results will be appended to that same file (see Figure E.6)	Use the green flag icon
11	View results: You may need to change the "update frequency settings to 1 second" (see Figure E.6)	Use the "View Results" tab

Table E.2   File Server Performance Test, Map Day Template

12	Stop the test: You have completed the test for queue depth of 1.	Use the stop-sign icon
13	Proceed to the next test	
14	You will need to rerun the tests for queue depths of 2, 4, 8, 16, 32, 64, 128 (rerun steps 8 through 11 for each queue depth) (see Figures E.7 and E.8)	
15	Chart the results (see Figure E.9)	

E.3   Diagrams

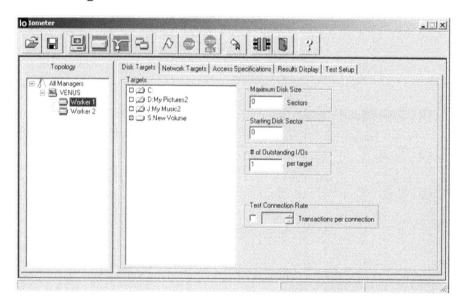

Figure E.1   Selecting the Device Under Test (DUT)

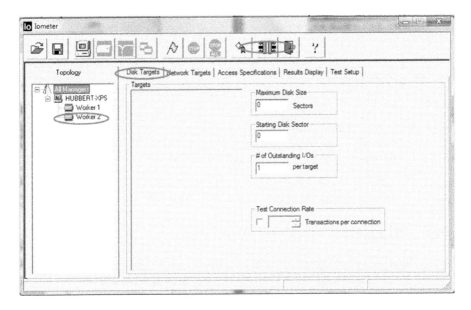

Figure E.2   Delete Unnecessary Workers

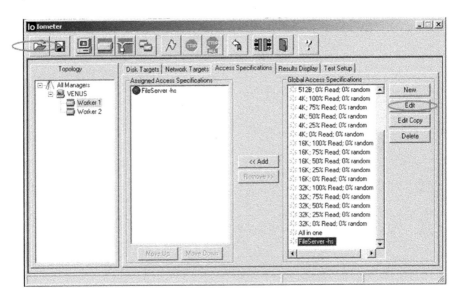

Figure E.3   Load Iometer Script, and Select Workload

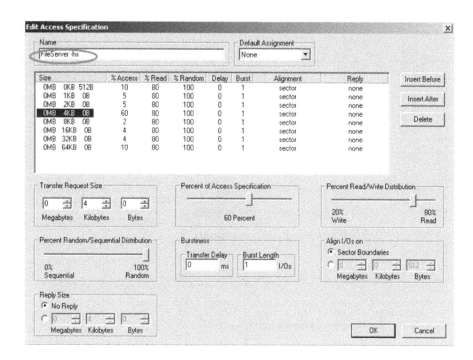

Figure E.4   Review Fileserver Workload Script

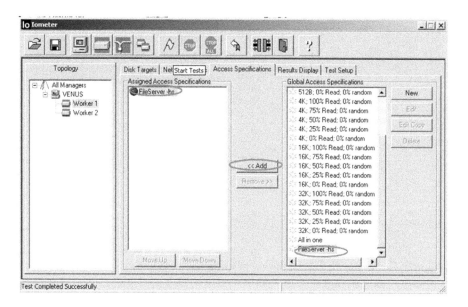

Figure E.5   Prepare to Run Test Using FileServer Script

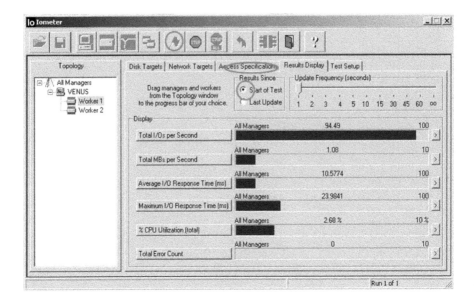

Figure E.6   Running Test, Displaying Results

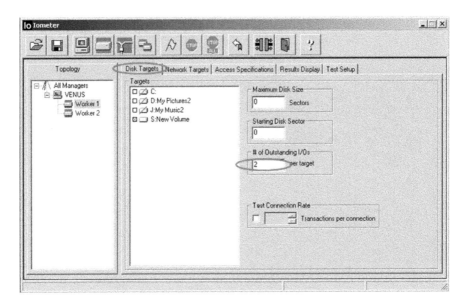

Figure E.7   Set the # of Outstanding I/Os (Queue Depth) to 2

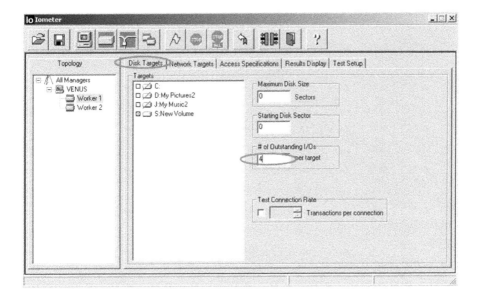

Figure E.8   Set the # of Outstanding I/Os (Queue Depth) to 4

E.4   Reporting and Interpreting the Results

The objective is to show how close or how far away the performance is for different drives. Because bits are more tightly packed together in high-capacity drives, they can approach the performance of older 10K drives with lower bit densities.

Disk drive queuing is conceptually similar to the elevator algorithm. The I/Os arrive in a random order (like elevator passengers pushing buttons for different floors). The queuing algorithm on the disk drive is smart enough to organize the I/Os so they'll be processed in an efficient order (like the elevator going from floor 2, to floor 4, then floor 6, then floor 8. rather than in the order the buttons were pushed). Queuing is not important in single-user PC workloads or sequential workloads, such as backup, but it is very important in random workloads. The performance curve flattens out in higher queue depths, because of limits in the protocol SATA, SAS, or FC protocol.

E.5   Conclusion

If we present data that is too complex for normal folks to understand, it will only serve to create confusion and cause inaction. The performance marketing messages need to be extremely simple to understand and should easily

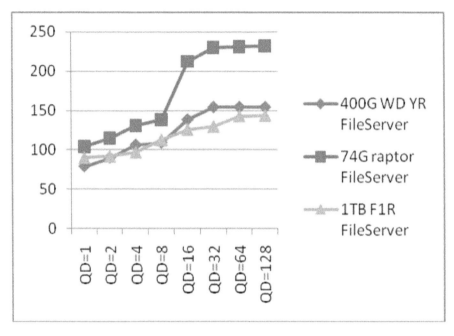

Figure E.9   Plotting the Performance Results at Queue Depths of 1, 2, 4, 8, 32, 64, and 128

demonstrate how one product is better and different than other products in measures that are meaningful to you.

Enterprise performance measurement today consists of lots of complex models, which are useful for engineers attempting to improve their systems. But these models are not useful for customers (especially distribution channel customers) attempting to make informed decisions regarding performance.

It's a good idea to consistently run the Iometer performance test for all old and new storage devices. This consistent benchmarking will help you develop a working practical knowledge about what device is needed for what workload in your shop. Also, practice looking closely at other information provided by Iometer, such as MB/s, average response time, and maximum response time in the interest of understanding and improving the balance of delivery of service with cost to your organization.

There is a tool called IPEAK and there is an audited system level storage performance analysis suite from the Storage Performance Council (links included in References).

E.6   References

- www.storagereview.com
- http://www.iometer.org/
- http://www.storageperformance.org/home

Glossary

Access control lists—Operating system–level security that governs read-write-execute-delete privileges of any file, folder, or program by any individual account or account group.

Advanced replacement—A service purchased with, or included with, hardware. If a hardware component fails, the hardware supplier will ship a replacement part in advance of receiving the failed part from the customer. Without advanced replacement, the failed part is shipped and received, then the replacement part is shipped, often resulting in several weeks of hardware-out-of-service.

Annual Failure Rate (AFR)—A reliability metric published by disk drive manufacturers. For an installed statistically valid sample of disk drives, the number of drives which will fail in 365-day timeframe.

Async replication—When the host writes to primary storage, the write is complete. The replication occurs later, either as a single I/O or as multiple I/Os that can be delivered in groups to the replication target storage at a later time. Synchronous replication requires the host to receive confirmation of write complete from both primary storage and target replicated storage.

Automated tiering—Software logic that will relocate data based on aging and frequency of reads and writes. Automated tiering also leaves pointers in the data's old location that point to the new file location so the data can be found in its new location.

Block mode data access—A client computer or server runs a database and accesses storage blocks on another computer or shared storage array. The application (database or similar) organizes the blocks into useful data. In block mode, the file system (or the database structure equivalent) resides on the server. In file mode data access, the file system resides on the storage.

Business Continuity/Disaster Recovery (BC/DR)—General term for tools such as replication and failover, which minimize interruptions to data access when disasters such as fire, flood, or act of war occur, as well as when facilities-related problems such as electrical outage or network interruption occur.

Cache hit—Data is stored on disk drives; additionally, for data in frequent demand, copies of frequently read data are also stored in faster solid state storage (DRAM or Flash) such as disk drive cache, storage controller cache, or server memory. A cache hit occurs when a copy of the desired data is found loaded in fast media rather than needing to be retrieved from the HDD.

Capacity optimized enterprise hard drives—Disk drives offering the highest available capacity (at the time of this writing, 2 TB 7200 rpm with SAS or SATA interface), typically spinning at a lower RPM rate and demonstrating lower performance than performance-optimized hard drives.

Common Internet file system (CIFS)—Functionally equivalent to NFS, but Microsoft-specific. CIFS provides shared file access and printer access via Server Message Block (SMB) to servers and clients running Microsoft Windows and participating in the Microsoft Windows Network. The server directly connected to the storage runs the file system. If that server is inoperable, the data is unavailable until the server is back in service.

Cloud provider—Business entity providing complete virtualized infrastructure and services, such as Web hosting, content delivery, storage, applications (e.g., Salesforce.com).

Co-location (CoLo)—Refers to facilities capacity: redundant high-speed network drops, floorspace, air conditioning with backup, and power with redundant source. The thing being bought is floor space, redundant power, redundant air conditioning, network access, and physical security.

Content management systems (CMS)—Enable collaboration between multiple users, providing a simple means of posting files and other data to an information-sharing structure. CMS can be general purpose (Microsoft SharePoint, Linux Alfresco) or special purpose for mechanical design, film editing, software development, and the like. Most CMSs have the advantage of being block based (not file based), so they can be accessed by multiple simultaneous computers. CMS systems track aging data information (when last edited, when last read, regulatory tags, etc), making aging data significantly more manageable on CMS than on shared files.

DRAM—Dynamic random access memory, like the memory in your PC or server.

Data constipation—Situation occurring when the incoming rate of new data is not matched or exceeded by the rate at which data is archived. As a result, data accumulates and fails to exit the system (constipation). The result is that systems gather more and more disk drives, backups get bigger and take longer, and performance erodes.

Direct attached storage (DAS)—Servers connected to storage via the server's SAS or SATA ports, a Host Bus Adapter, or a RAID adapter in the server. DAS systems have server-based file systems; typically, only one server can access the data. There are methods to make a server act like a NAS and share data with other servers or clients. The alternative to DAS is NAS or SAN attached storage.

Desktop virtualization—Concept in which the virtual desktop runs as a virtual machine on a server, rather than as a physical PC or laptop. The advantage is that security is significantly improved and the machines are significantly easier to manage and maintain.

Dynamic data center—A managed hosting capability to add or remove compute or storage resources very quickly; usually, in a matter of minutes or hours after a customer request for server or storage resources, the resources are provisioned and ready for use.

Dynamic storage tiering—When data ages, the dynamic storage tiering systems software, which has Tier 1 storage capacity and Tier 2 storage capacity, will determine if data is frequently accessed. If so, it will keep that data on Tier 1 storage. If the dynamic storage tiering software determines that the data is infrequently accessed, it will keep that data on Tier 2 storage.

Dynamic storage tiering and hybrid-cloud—Keeps active data locally on premises, uses tiering logic to move infrequently accessed data to a more affordable managed hosting site.

Failover with replication—Also referred to as "shared nothing" failover, this involves a replicated copy of the data. When a server fails, another server senses the failure, redirects user IP traffic, and accesses the replicated copy of the data to offer continuous or near-continuous service in the case of a failure.

Failover with storage-array based replication—Also referred to as "shared nothing" failover, this involves using the storage to provide replication service, rather than server-based replication. When a server fails, another server senses the failure, redirects user IP traffic, and accesses the replicated copy of the data to offer continuous or near-continuous service in the case of a failure.

Failover without replication—Also referred to as "shared everything" failover, this involves several servers accessing a common copy of the data. When a server fails, another server senses the failure, redirects user IP traffic, and accesses the storage volume to offer continuous or near-continuous service in the case of a failure.

File migration—As data ages, files (and other data) are moved from performance-optimized storage to capacity-optimized storage. File migration is also employed in use cases for data-mining, branch-office, and central-office operations.

File mode data access—A client computer or server uses a file system protocol (NFS, CIFS, etc.) to access a file system on a NAS storage array or NAS server. In file mode access, the file system (or the database structure equivalent) resides on a NAS storage array or NAS server. (In block mode, the database server organizes the blocks into meaningful information.)

Flash—A type of computer storage in an integrated circuit (a chip) that can be electronically written and erased. Flash is nonvolatile, meaning electrical power can be withdrawn (for example, in an unexpected power outage) and the flash storage will still retain the data when the power is restored.

Frame information structure (FIS)—Describes a chunk of data handled by a storage or network protocol. A FIS has a *start-of-frame*, including addressing information; a *payload*, which is either a command or a chunk of data; and an *end-of-frame*.

GB/$—A key ratio for comparing cost and capacity of a disk drive or storage system (bigger is better). Using key ratios clarifies capacity-price-performance decisions, which can be clouded by different drives at different capacities and prices

GB/watt—A key ratio comparing power and capacity for a disk drive or storage system (bigger is better). Using key ratios clarifies capacity-power-performance decisions, which can be clouded by different drives and different capacities.

Hard disk drive (HDD)—The basic building block of enterprise storage. An HDD consists of a motor, one or more platters (to store the data), heads (to read and write data off the platters), and an arm or armature and coil to move the head to the right position (track) on the platter. HDD electronics include a power supply chip and a combination chip including a core processor, buffer, and PHY; it is connected to the computer with a connector for power and one or two data channels.

Hierarchical storage management (HSM)—Automatically moves data between performance-optimized and capacity-optimized storage.

Information lifecycle management (ILM)—Applies policies to manage information through its lifecycle. Applies to database data, engineering data, video data, and the like.

Input/output operations per second (IOPS)—A general term for a read or write operation. The most common size of an IOP is 4 KB, but an IOP can be very small (512 bytes) or very large (64 MB).

Iometer—A performance tool to measure performance (including IOPS) in the lab. It is free and open source. Iometer can simulate a variety of different storage loads (read-write, randon-sequential, mix of block sizes at varying queue depths from multiple simulated users). It is only acceptable in the lab because it completely fills the drive or RAID volume with Iometer test data.

IOP/$—A key ratio comparing cost and performance for a disk drive or storage system (bigger is better). Using key ratios clarifies capacity-price-performance decisions, which can be clouded by different drives at different performance and prices.

IOP/watt—A key ratio comparing power and performance for a disk drive or storage system (bigger is better). Using key ratios clarify capacity-power-performance decisions, which can be clouded by different drives at different performance and prices.

Latency—Describes the waits or delays as data is moved across various busses or networks from one location to another.

Local replication storage—Replication is the process of copying data. Every time a write command is received, the same data is written to another storage system (sometimes several storage systems), usually within the same computer room. Any copies over a wide area network (WAN) are consider remote replication (not local replication).

Managed hosting—Dedicated or shared hardware running some software, such as e-mail or financial software, specifically used to conduct company business. The thing being bought is a service level agreement (SLA) for application delivery, usually including uptime, capacity, bandwidth, data protection, and some sort of backup/recovery. Managed hosting can be shared hardware, but is typically dedicated servers and storage allocated to a specific company.

Manual storage tiering—When data ages, the systems administrator will manually move data or use scripts to move data from Tier 1 to Tier 2 as data ages. Works well for structured data.

Mean time between failures (MTBF)—A statistical analysis based on the reliability demonstration test (or similar) results. For HDDs, typically 1.2 million hours between failure. Sometimes this is reported as mean time to failure (MTTF), because drives fail and they do not get fixed. Systems and electronics MTBFs are typically in the 100,000 hour range.

Metadata—Data about data. Usually refers to file system or similar, where the lists of blocks on disk drives are addressed to present a file, or database or similar data structure to the host computer.

Multi-layer cell flash (MLC)—MLC is a type of flash memory typically found on USB memory sticks or camera memory cards. Now increasingly found in laptop-class SSDs. Has the advantage of low cost, has the disadvantages of low write cycles and low performance as compared to single-layer cell (SLC) flash.

Multipath IO—A fault-tolerant technique configuring more than one path between the server and the storage. Can also refer to multiple fault-tolerant paths involving controllers, cables, switches, expansion storage shelves, and similar. Includes the logic to sense a failure and re-establish a new path.

Microsecond—one millionth of a second (10^{-6}), abbreviated μs

Millisecond—one thousandth of a second (10^{-3}), abbreviated ms

Network attached storage (NAS)—An NAS array includes disk drives organized into RAID groups and a controller that reads and writes to the RAID groups. The key attribute of a NAS system is that the file system runs on the NAS head. This allows multiple servers to access the same storage simultaneously (but not write the same file simultaneously).

Network backup—A system involving complete backups or incremental backups processed by one or more servers. In contrast with backups processed by the storage array.

Network file system (NFS) protocol—A protocol that allows client computers to access files over a network on an NFS host computer.

Nontraditional applications—Applications that store and manipulate digital media, such as broadcast content editing, broadcast content delivery, video surveillance, call center, or Web-delivered content like video advertising clips. In contrast to traditional IT applications such as databases or e-mail.

OpX—Operational excellence. The cost of people and the work they accomplish.

Overprovisioning—Occurs when multiple applications each have storage and each have unused storage allocated for future growth. Individually, each application's additional future capacity is acceptable, but when multiple applications' future allocation is combined, it is overprovisioned.

Performance-optimized enterprise hard drives—Hard disk drives, usually at 15,000 rpm or 10,000 rpm, demonstrating fast seek (typically 3–5 ms).

Point-in-time snapshot—Involves establishing a baseline (complete image), then as time passes and the data changes, new snapshots capture only the changed blocks. Snapshots can be used to recover data that is accidentally deleted, or effected by virus, or effected by some data corruption. Snapshot technologies can be creatively applied to produce a "live copy" of data that can be read and manipulated without creating an entire duplicate and without impacting the main production data; this is useful for debugging or data mining situations.

Public cloud—A shared resource, such as search engines, ad-sponsored mail, and ad-sponsored applications. Examples include Gmail, Facebook, YouTube, Yahoo, eBay, Digg, Amazon, Priceline, and so on. The things being bought (or bartered for seeing advertising) include e-mail, search, personalized news, a social media account, entertaining content, and searchable shopping/deals/coupons, among others.

RAID edition or NL-near line—Analogous to capacity-optimized HDD.

Reliability Demonstration Test (RDT)—An exercise to determine whether a new preproduction HDD demonstrates adequate quality to move into production. Typically involves 1200 disk drives in test chambers running at elevated temperature and elevated I/O load; invariably, drives fail, root causes are found, and corrections are made.

Remote replication—The process of copying data. Every time a write command is received, the same data is written to another storage system (sometimes several storage systems), remote replication copies data over a wide area network to storage a substantial distance away.

Seek—For hard disk drives, the speed of head-actuator movement from one track to another track. For capacity-optimized drives, seek is typically around 11 ms; for performance-optimized drives seek is typically 3–5 ms.

Single layer cell (SLC) flash—is a type of enterprise storage-grade flash memory which is faster and more durable than SLC flash, laptop-grade flash memory. SLC is also more expensive than MLC flash.

Storage consolidation—Organizing enterprise data on a single or a few large storage arrays; as opposed to storing data scattered on multiple servers or smaller storage arrays.

Server area network (SAN) attached storage—Fibre Channel or iSCSI or SAS can create a storage area network in which multiple servers can access a common set of logical unit numbers (LUNs) in block mode.

Solid state device (SSD)—A device that stores data and functionally is equivalent to a hard disk drive, but the storage uses either MLC or SLC solid state memory. As a result, SSDs are usually more expensive than HDDS. SSDs have a SAS or SATA host interface and storage protocol similar to a hard disk drive and the physical form factor of a disk drive, allowing the SSD to be a direct replacement for an HDD.

Solid state storage (SSS)—A device that stores data and appears to the computer operating system as a hard disk drive, but uses either MLC or SLC solid state memory. As a result, SSSs are usually more expensive than HDDs, but are also significantly faster and significantly lower power than SSDs. SSSs are different than SSDs. SSSs have PCI or related high-speed interface instead of a HDD-style interface; SSSs fit in a PCI card or separate box formfactor, not an HDD formfactor. SSSs have the advantage of not being burdened with antiquated protocols designed for hard disk drives and tape.

Static storage tiering—Organization model in which specific applications are assigned to specific tiers and the data generated stays on that tier until archived. For example: Transaction databases (and similar) are run on Tier 1; e-mail (and similar) are run on Tier 2. When data ages, archive it to clear space for incoming data. Different from dynamic storage tiering, which will involve moving data from tier to tier as it ages.

SSD or SSS storage caching—Systems storage software will use SSD or SSS as a cache and copy frequently accessed data to the SSD or SSS, typically in the server, not in the storage array. Caching uses SSD or SSS to hold a copy for fast access. Tiering involves moving the data.

T-10-DIF—T10 is an industry standards group (www.t10.org) that creates interoperability industry standards. T10-DIF (also known as T10-PI) is a system of adding additional data to communications between servers and storage, whereby on the server additional check-sum data is appended to every IO, and that is carried all the way to be written on the disk drive. The check-sum is used to confirm that the data written to the drive matches the data originating from server (and vice versa for a read operation).

TIA-942 11—A classification system for data centers.

Thin provisioning—For large scale storage systems; allocates disk space with a pool of unused storage for future use. Pooling the additional storage reduces overprovisioning. Thin provisioning actually allocates a limited amount of real storage and communicates a bigger number to the server; when the initial allocation is used up, additional storage is allocated from the pool.

Throughput—Describes the data transfer rate, typically measured in MB/s.

Tier 1 storage—Designed for performance-sensitive, outage-sensitive data, such as point-of-sale transactions, reservations, banking, e-commerce sites, and the like. Performance and uptime are primary concerns, backup/snapshots are frequent, cost is a secondary concern.

Tier 2 storage—Designed for good-enough-performance: good-enough-uptime for uses such as e-mail, SharePoint and other content management systems, informational Web sites, and similar. This tier is designed to absorb the majority of the data growth.

Tier 3 storage—Designed for data that is about to be archived but will be accessed infrequently. A virtual tape library (VTL) is the usual tool for a Tier 3 storage system allowing users to access aging data without retrieving from tape archival.

Web hosting—A service that runs company Web sites, including both external company sites and internal company portals for employees, customers, partners, and suppliers. Typically HTTP, HTTPS, and e-commerce. The things being bought are the Web site(s), e-mail, and other services, limited on bandwidth and storage space. Typically the economies of scale revolve around a specific software stack and specific operating system, such as LAMP (Fedora Linux, Apache Webserver, MySQL database, PHP for scripting and Web development).

Zero Based Budgeting (ZBB)—Grouping all spending into spending packages, and rank-ordering those packages based on cost and value. The rank-order list is compared to the available money; you go down the list and draw the line where the money runs out. Lower priority packages that did not merit spending in this budgetary cycle are refered to as "below the line" and not funded (at least not in this time period). Generally, ZBB refers to a planning method and decision methods where the entire budget is reviewed (not just the budget increases). ZBB process allocates resources for spending packages with high value, high benefit, and high return on investment, and pushes lower value spending packages below the line.

Index

For Product Safety Concerns and Information please contact our EU
representative GPSR@taylorandfrancis.com
Taylor & Francis Verlag GmbH, Kaufingerstraße 24, 80331 München, Germany

www.ingramcontent.com/pod-product-compliance
Ingram Content Group UK Ltd.
Pitfield, Milton Keynes, MK11 3LW, UK
UKHW021622240425
457818UK00018B/698